A Cinema of Poetry

A CINEMA OF POETRY

Aesthetics of the Italian Art Film

JOSEPH LUZZI

JOHNS HOPKINS UNIVERSITY PRESS   BALTIMORE

Johns Hopkins Paperback Edition, 2016
2 4 6 8 9 7 5 3 1

Johns Hopkins University Press
2715 North Charles Street
Baltimore, Maryland 21218-4363
www.press.jhu.edu

The Library of Congress has catalogued the hardcover edition of this book as follows:

Luzzi, Joseph.
A cinema of poetry : aesthetics of the Italian art film / Joseph Luzzi.
pages cm
Includes bibliographical references and index.
ISBN-13: 978-1-4214-1166-8 (hardcover : alk. paper)
ISBN-13: 978-1-4214-1296-2 (electronic)
ISBN-10: 1-4214-1166-0 (hardcover : alk. paper)
ISBN-10: 1-4214-1296-9 (electronic)
1. Motion pictures—Italy—Aesthetics.
2. Motion pictures—Italy—History. I. Title.
PN1993.5.I88L89 2014
791.430945—dc23   2013033053

A catalog record for this book is available from the British Library.

ISBN-13: 978-1-4214-1984-8
ISBN-10: 1-4214-1984-X

*Special discounts are available for bulk purchases of this book. For more information,
please contact Special Sales at 410-516-6936 or specialsales@press.jhu.edu.*

Johns Hopkins University Press uses environmentally friendly
book materials, including recycled text paper that is composed of
at least 30 percent post-consumer waste, whenever possible.

For Yolanda Luzzi

Imagine what the cinema of poets could be.—Jean Cocteau

CONTENTS

This book follows a generally chronological structure. The two chapters in part 1, "Neorealist Rhetoric and National Identity," show how certain films grouped under the term *neorealism* established cinematic discourses that illuminate our understanding of concerns in the history of art while reflecting on the question of Italy. Chapter 1 studies a key term in the neorealist lexicon—the word chosen by Rossellini as its defining quality, *coralità* (chorality)—in connection with the political aims of neorealist filmmakers and, more broadly, the historical connotations of the chorus going back to Greek tragic theater and its influential theorist Friedrich Nietzsche in *Die Geburt der Tragödie* (*The Birth of Tragedy* [1871]). I focus on the links between neorealist *coralità* and the question of *italianità*, to show how filmmakers drew on religious (Rossellini) and political (Visconti) traditions to create visual discourses of chorality that bear analytical witness to the rebuilding of national identity after decades of world and civil war. Chapter 2 examines the relation between symbol and allegory, a rhetorical crux that stretches back to Homer and informs two critical moments in the formation of Italian national identity: literary romanticism and cinematic neorealism. I first explain why, in contrast to the triumph of the symbol in romantic Europe, Italian authors favored allegorical forms because of their potential for moral and political instruction. The argument then proposes that the terms of this ancient aesthetic crux reappeared, after the vigorous mediation by Verga, in the transition from the allegorical neorealist Italian cinema of the 1940s to the symbolic auteur films of the 1950s and 1960s, as each group sought to represent national identity onscreen.

Organized around the themes in Pasolini's landmark essay on cinematic *poesis*, part 2, "Cinemas of Poetry," continues the rhetorically inflected discussion of part 1 by looking at how film and poetry interact. Chapter 3 analyzes *Voyage to Italy* in light of the historical link between film and nonnarrative, lyric poetry. I aim to show how Rossellini's film establishes a unique position in the international debates in the early 1950s about film's relationship to literary art forms by continually citing a make-believe poem and incorporating its forms and themes, using this dialogue between the visual and literary image to critique a category in aesthetic and cultural history (romanticism), and generating relations between visual and verbal signs to create a "cinema of poetry" that anticipates many of Pasolini's theories on the supposedly pregrammatical, irrational forms of knowledge produced by film. The argument also considers three challenges that have conditioned the connection between film and lyric poetry: the perceived threats of verbal discourse, ocular vision, and causal narrative to cinematic representation. Chapter 4 provides an overview of the most salient points of Pasolini's essay "Il 'cinema di poesia,'" to show how the notion of *poesis* articulated in it, and embodied in his eponymous film adaptation of Giovanni Boccaccio's *Decameron* (1971), illuminates concepts linking film to the other arts, including the free indirect style in its verbal and visual forms, as well as Benjamin's figure of the storyteller. I also seek to connect what I call Pasolini's "visual philology" and reflections on cultural production by the Neapolitan philosopher of history Vico.

Part 3, "Aesthetic *Corsi* and *Ricorsi*," picks up on a Vichian trope for understanding what Vico calls the *vita comune delle nazioni* (common life of nations), where earlier cycles of cultural expression *(corsi)* continue to reappear but with diminishing force as their original vigor is blunted by intellectual thought and abstract reasoning *(ricorsi)*. In this spirit I explore how certain concepts in the history of Italian cinema resurface like a hydra's head, often in ways indistinguishable from one generation to the next. Chapter 5 examines a problem in the Italian film debates of the 1940s and 1950s, the perceived threat of realist representation to the expressive capacities of the cinematic medium, in the films of Antonioni. I aim to show how Antonioni's retreat from the referential claims of the image—which are often associated with death in *Blow-Up* (1966) and the trilogy *L'avventura* (1960), *La notte* (*Night* [1961]), and *L'eclisse* (*Eclipse* [1962])—reflects his desire to separate the "fact" from the "image," a relationship he theorizes in a little-known essay from 1963. In chapter 6 I argue that another recurring aesthetic form—the chiasmus—became the symbol par excellence for the shifting nature of Italian political life during two key moments of political transition: the Risorgimento and Fascism. In the literary and film versions of *Il Gattopardo (The Leopard)*—by, respectively, Giuseppe Tomasi di Lampedusa (1959) and Visconti (1963)—the chiasmus represents the *trasformismo* (transformationism) that witnessed the shifting of power from one unprincipled ruling class to another in pre- and post-Risorgimento Italy. In a related manner, and in one of the many films on Fascism to appear some three decades after Benito Mussolini's fall, Bertolucci's *Il conformista* (*The Conformist* [1970]) employs the chiasmus to expose the double speak of Fascist political discourse and the Freudian nature of the film's erotic substitutions—a process of doubling and inversion that also permeates the film's literary source, Alberto Moravia's novel of the same name (1951). Chapter 7 analyzes two later films by Fellini, *Casanova* (1976) and *La voce della luna* (*The Voice of the Moon* [1990]), to show how a technique associated with film, montage, finds a literary mode of expression and how the literary figure of apostrophe takes on cinematic form. The epilogue focuses on the afterlife of the neorealist and auteur Italian art-film tradition and the cinematic poetics it inspired in a core of films from the new millennium: Emanuele Crialese's *Respiro* (2002), Frammartino's *Le quattro volte,* and Marco Tullio Giordana's *La meglio gioventù* (*The Best of Youth* [2003]).

Unless otherwise indicated, translations are my own. Foreign titles are given alongside their English translation and year of publication (books) or release (films) the first time they appear in the book. Since some Italian films are better known by their original title than by their English rendering, they appear without translation (e.g., *La terra trema* and *La strada*).

This book was born in the classroom. I began teaching film at Columbia University in 2001, and my first screening was Roberto Rossellini's *Rome, Open City.* Though my research until then had focused on literature, this encounter would change the course of my career. The moral force of Rossellini's vision, his unembarrassed portrayal of heroism when the soul of his nation was at risk, revealed the power of cinema to remake people's lives. On the train back to New Haven from New York that winter night, I carried inside images from Rossellini's film that I had yet to find words for. Since then, the privilege of teaching cinema, first at the University of Pennsylvania and then (and especially) at Bard College, has helped me find those missing words. My writing on film owes its life to years of conversation with my students. To all of you, my warmest thanks.

Portions of the book appeared in the journals *Adaptation, Modern Language Notes,* and *Modern Language Quarterly,* as well as the audio course *The Blessed Lens: A History of Italian Film.* I owe a special debt of gratitude to my friends at the National Humanities Center, where I spent a blissful year writing this book thanks to a fellowship from the National Endowment for the Humanities.

It is a great pleasure to thank my team at Johns Hopkins University Press for their outstanding work, especially Matt McAdam, Melissa Solarz, and Kim Johnson. I also extend my gratitude to my copyeditor, Joe Abbott, indexer, Alexa Selph, and Jacopo Gorini for their superb assistance with the manuscript. Finally—and most of all—I thank my wife, Helena, and daughter, Isabel, for their unending love and support.

A Cinema of Poetry is dedicated to my mother, who has never said a word to me about Italian film but who has, with the deepest care and generosity, taught me more than anyone else has.

A Cinema of Poetry

Introduction: Toward a Poetics of the Italian Art Film

The first thing I notice about a film is its light. There's something about the light of Rossellini's *Voyage to Italy* that announces Antonioni's *L'avventura*.

—Bernardo Bertolucci

On 19 August 1916 Giovanni Verga wrote to his screenwriter that he was taking matters into his own hands: "Ho creduto meglio di stendere io stesso la trama delle scene . . . onde evitare uno dei soliti pasticci chilometrici che fanno assomigliare la cinematografia al romanzo di appendici per analfabeti" ("I thought it would be better if I myself wrote the plot for the film scenes [based on my play] . . . to avoid the usual reels of mess that make cinema seem like a serial novel for the illiterate") (Raya 91). Verga's words reveal the intense cinematic involvement of arguably Italy's most important living author, whose work became a major point of reference for filmmakers during the Fascist and neorealist eras. They also show the cross-fertilization of the nascent film medium with other art forms and point to the aesthetic issues that would drive film's relations with the sister arts: the legibility of the cinematic image as opposed to the more restricted realm of literary language, the potentially corrosive effect of cinema's commercialism on artistic concerns, and the mix of uneasiness and excitement that artists like Verga felt about the new celluloid medium.

In the spirit of Verga's letter I consider how films made in the age of neorealism and its auteur aftermath shaped the history of aesthetics and abiding issues in cinema's relations with other art forms, especially literature. In what ways do filmmakers think through long-standing aesthetic questions? What are the principles, or "poetics," of cinema that connect it to the practices of its artistic counterparts? What qualities of film—its link with technological processes, capacity for mass distribution, synthetic virtues (or vices) as the so-called total art—have reshaped centuries-long aesthetic debates? And why did a critical mass of these sophisticated and critically acclaimed films appear during Italy's neorealist and auteur periods? This book answers these questions by examining them in a group of works that have long been acknowledged for their artistic and sociopolitical influence. My argument centers on the following three elements in the richly intermedial and formally complex nature of what I will call the nation's "art-film" period.

1. Italian cinemas of poetry. The qualities of Italian literary history—its strong traditions in lyric poetry, its role in establishing a unifying Italian language, and the great political influence of some of its poets—made Italian cinema dependent on poetry's institutions and cultural prestige as early as Giovanni Pastrone's historical blockbuster *Cabiria* (1914), which featured intertitles by the self-proclaimed *poeta vate* (poet-prophet) Gabriele D'Annunzio. I will argue on behalf of the ongoing impact of poetic modes of expression in Italian cinema and show how the emergence of a "poetic cinema" was central to the development of Italian film as it moved out of neorealism and into the more stylized auteur period. To that end my book focuses on the implications of arguably the most famous essay by an Italian filmmaker, Pier Paolo Pasolini's "Il 'cinema di poesia'" ("The 'Cinema of Poetry'" [1965]), which borrows semiotic theories from literary criticism to link cinematic and poetic expression. Overall, I seek to challenge the commonplace—advanced in the writings of Walter Benjamin and Siegfried Kracauer, among others—that film is bound to the novel above all other literary genres because each shares qualities capable of representing the elusive term *reality.* I contend instead that Italian directors have often looked to poetry to capture nonmimetic and nonnarrative forms of so-called reality that unveil the unconscious of their characters and the discontinuities of history—what Pasolini called "the world of memory and dreams."

2. "Italianità" and the aesthetics of film. Although the term *national cinema* is highly controversial, especially when linked to the embattled drive for Italian political identity, this unstable issue of *italianità* led filmmakers with competing aesthetic agendas onto common paths of cinematic expression.[1] As early as the influential articles by Giuseppe Prezzolini in *La voce* (1912–13), the film medium provided an irresistible forum for considering the issue of national identity. The intersection between the politicized component of rhetorical imagery and its aesthetic qualities coalesces in a defining quality of Italian cinematic history: *the predominance of an intermedial and interdisciplinary poetics,* in which certain films contributed to transnational aesthetic debates while meditating on the question of what it means to be Italian. My book explores how key historical moments—for example, the reconstruction after World War II, as well as the representation of the Italian Risorgimento and Fascism in the 1960s and 1970s—elicited cinematic responses that engaged major notions in the arts to make political and ideological points about Italian identity.

3. *Polemics and schools.* Beginning with the debates about the putative school (or lack thereof) of neorealism, Italian filmmakers faced the daunting question of labels, especially in the highly partisan atmosphere of the postwar. The need to define their positions pushed many Italian directors to speculate on their métier, which in turn motivated them to locate their aesthetic vision in the history and categories of aesthetic theory and practice. For example, Michelangelo Antonioni defined his version of realism against that of neorealism by establishing a tension between traditional (that is, mimetic) realism and the term's more abstract, Platonic associations—a tension that Antonioni described in terms of a distinction between the "fact" and the "image." Moreover, other directors who learned their cinematic craft under neorealism, especially Fellini and Pasolini, built their careers more in reaction to the tenets of this movement than to any other aesthetic or cultural factor. All told, the intensely collaborative—and at times confrontational— cinematic world of the Italian postwar decades led filmmakers to position their work in relation to one another as they explored intermedial practices, especially the cinematic adaptation of literary sources.

Along with these three elements, two key terms in my title suggest the larger aims of the book: *cinema of poetry* and *art film.* Going back to philosophers including Giambattista Vico and Benedetto Croce—and culminating in the cinematic theories of Pasolini—Italian thinkers have used the term *poesia* not only in the usual sense of "written poetry" but in the etymological sense of the Greek *poiesis* and Latin *poesis,* "creative making," in all its forms. The aesthetics of Italian cinema, I will argue, is beholden to this distinctly Italian, cross-disciplinary, and intermedial understanding of poetry. In the neorealist debates in Italy of the 1940s, the word *poesia* assumed an elastic web of signification inflected by one of the most influential theorists in the nation's philosophical tradition: Croce. In their seminal defense of adaptation, "Verità e poesia: Verga e il cinema italiano" ("Truth and Poetry: Verga and the Italian Cinema" [1941]), Mario Alicata and Giuseppe De Santis disregarded the possibility of a "pure" cinema divorced from predecessor art forms and claimed instead that the emergence of film should be understood in the context of existing literary and artistic tastes. Alberto Asor Rosa locates the inspiration for Alicata and De Santis's promotion of a "literary" neorealism in Croce, whose shadow lingers over two of their claims: first, a work's *poesia* is the result of "una ispirazione creatrice superiore a ogni pratica distinzione di generi" ("a creative inspiration superior to any practical distinction in genre"); second, any distinction among lyric, narrative, picturesque, or other forms of cinema is invalid because "in tutti questi casi bisognerà solamente parlare di opera d'arte realizzata o di opera d'arte non realizzata, vale a dire più semplicemente di poesia e non poesia" ("in all these cases, it is necessary to speak only of successfully or unsuccessfully realized works of art—which is to say, of poetry and nonpoetry").[2]

By voicing Croce's controversial definition of the "poetic" as the successful synthesis of artistic intuition into formal expression, Alicata and De Santis use the term *poesia* as a transcendental category to denote the successful work of art. Their generic sense of poetry as heightened artistic expression and self-contained lyrical perfection, a Crocean saw of profound impact in the history of Italian aesthetics, also informs the unexpected use of the term by Cesare Zavattini, the militant Marxist screenwriter averse to aesthetic expression not grounded in socioeconomic realty. Zavattini's essay "Poesia, solo affare del cinema italiano" ("Poetry, the only obligation of Italian cinema" [1945]) invokes the powerful signifier *poesia* to suggest cinema's need for unbridled imagination: "bisogna spalancare le porte alla fantasia" ("we must burst open the doors to fantasy"). Most important of all, Pasolini's essay on the cinema of poetry—a recurrent subject of my book—offers a theoretical model for grasping the interplay between poetic and cinematic aesthetics, while establishing the centrality of the term *poesia* for a range of filmmakers including Antonioni and Bertolucci. Thus, beginning with the debates about adaptation in the 1940s and extending into the auteur period of the 1960s, the word *poetry* functioned as a malleable signifier that recalls Friedrich Nietzsche's autopsy of the term *romanticism* as the empty vessel filled with whatever its theorists wished (or needed) to supply. We will see how the legacies of this "poetic cinema," broadly defined, have continued to produce a rich vein of filmmaking, as recently as Michelangelo Frammartino's *Le quattro volte* (2010), which returns us to the tenets of Pasolini's essay while creating its own view of what constitutes the *cinema di poesia*.

The recent edited volume *Global Art Cinema* (2010), by Rosalind Galt and Karl Schoonover, shows that the term *art cinema* is difficult to define in any context, let alone the Italian one. Yet it continues to be used fruitfully—if controversially—throughout the cinematic world.[3] Attempts to define the art film have been many, including David Bordwell's emphasis on it as a "mode";

Steve Neale's thesis that it is an "institution"; and Barbara Wilinsky's claim that it denotes practices of exhibiting films in the emerging "art-house" cinema.[4] Galt and Schoonover define the art film as the aesthetically complex work that transcends its local public and enters the global marketplace. Such films, they argue, inhabit an "impure institutional space: neither experimental nor mainstream," as they move "uneasily between the commercial world and its artisanal others"; articulate "an ambivalent relationship to location," as well as "a complexly ambivalent relationship to the critical and industrial categories that sustain film history, such as stardom and authorship"; "trouble notions of genre"; and constitute "an impure spectator," who is often led to contradictory responses (Introduction 7–9).

Although this definition succeeds in identifying a certain strand of international art cinema, it fails to describe the Italian version. For example, a film invoked by Galt and Schoonover, Rossellini's *Roma, città aperta* (*Rome, Open City* [1945]), cannot be said to display an "ambivalent" relation to location or lead spectators to "contradictory responses": the film presents itself as an on-location depiction of the Roman Resistance with its local dialect and customs, in a straightforward battle of good versus evil that pits Italian heroes against Nazi villains. Other examples of acknowledged cinematic excellence in Italy also refute Galt and Schoonover's definition: Visconti's *La terra trema* (1948) did not seek to "trouble" the neorealist genre with which it aligned itself, and his highbrow *Senso* (1954) made no pretense of infiltrating the "commercial world." Moreover, no film by Pasolini or Antonioni displays "ambivalence" toward the notion of authorship, and many works by Fellini embraced the category of "stardom" that Galt and Schoonover regard with suspicion. The shortcomings of their definition suggest that, like politics itself, the essence of the Italian art film lies in the local, not the global.

The term *art film* has not only a local but a technical resonance in Italy, whose government created the category of *film d'essai* or *film d'autore* to contribute "alla diffusione della cultura cinematografica ed alla conoscenza di correnti e tecniche sperimentali" ("to the diffusion of cinematic culture and to the understanding of experimental currents and techniques") (Decreto Legislativo 22 gennaio 2004, n. 28).[5] But no legal definition alone could account for the term's manifold resonances. In Italy, art film has generally been associated with the cinema from post–World War II neorealism to the auteur period of the 1950s and 1960s, when producers including Dino De Laurentiis, Carlo Ponti, and Franco Cristaldi offered international audiences films with what Geoffrey Nowell-Smith calls "a general if indefinable air of 'quality' about them" (*Making Waves* 152–53). The ongoing presence of these films in scholarship, journalism, festivals, and curricula attests to the cultural value they have accrued. Moreover, they continue to inspire filmmakers to revisit their aesthetic issues and concerns in an ongoing negotiation with their cinematic legacies. Speaking not just about the Italian tradition but "art cinema" in general, Dudley Andrew emphasizes the sense of aesthetic discovery in such films: "The art cinema promises something that no other group of films can: to question, change, or disregard standard film making, in seeking to convey the utterly new or the formerly hidden" (*Aura* 5–6).

Building on Nowell-Smith's periodization and Andrew's sense of aesthetic discovery, I use the term *art film* to designate a group of interconnected Italian films from the 1940s to the 1970s that contain the following qualities. First, the Italian art film links directors who both directly and indirectly engaged with one another's work and ideas as they explored common aesthetic concerns. Second, it raises questions about cinema's relation to other arts, especially literature and the cinematic adaptation of literary sources, as adaptation assumed a distinctly "Italian" dimension because of the specific characteristics of the nation's literary history. Third, the Italian art film often demonstrates its debt to the neorealist era, which established a cinematic framework—figuratively speaking, an informal "film school"—that nurtured the aesthetics and conditioned the ideologies of directors who either aligned themselves with this pioneering movement or set their work in opposition to it. Last, my version of the Italian art film sets aesthetic concerns in dialogue with social and political ones, so that the model of the "engaged" filmmaker— a particular legacy of neorealism—became a touchstone for directors who, as the neorealist refrain went, sought to *rifare l'Italia* ("remake Italy").[6]

My model is by no means meant to be prescriptive or categorical. The directors I refer to did not labor under the lofty abstraction "art cinema," which is a value judgment made in retrospect. And of course, other films worthy of the designation *art film* have appeared in Italy in other periods, movements, and contexts than the narrow ones I propose. But by referring to the art cinema produced in a specific period of Italian cinematic history—roughly, from the immediate postwar to the heyday of auteur film—I establish the parameters of what I believe is a well-articulated phenomenon whose cultural legacies continue to impact Italy's sense of cinema and its sense of self.

Angelo Restivo offers a useful model for construing the art film by drawing our attention to the place of neorealism in the Italian filmic imagination and its link to questions of national identity. "The Italian art film of the sixties differentiates itself from the 'low art' of the period insofar as it self-consciously addresses itself to a national cinematic tradition: the tradition of neorealism, so crucial to the process of national reconstruction after the war" (9). I agree with Restivo's emphasis on the role that neorealism has played in determining the aesthetic hierarchies of Italy's cinematic tradition, but I would take his argument a step further and add that this very pervasiveness raises two methodological challenges: first, the problems of taxonomy and definition posed by a term as contentious and hotly debated as *neorealism;* second, the burdens of interpretation created by the canonicity of these same neorealist films, the subject of ongoing scholarship and critical inquiry whose sheer quantity would appear to make it difficult to say anything new about them.

To begin with the problem of definition, we dispensed long ago with simplified notions of neorealism as a monolithic movement or school characterized by documentary-style techniques, nonprofessional actors, long takes under natural lighting, and improvisational story lines that rejected script, set, and other vestiges from supposedly more artificial predecessors, ranging from the historical melodramas of Pastrone and Filoteo Alberini to the propaganda of the Fascist screen and the mannered Calligraphic and White Telephone eras. Even those films designated "neorealist" often broke with the dogma and clichés ascribed to the putative movement: for example, Vittorio De Sica's *Sciuscià* (*Shoeshine* [1946]) and *Ladri di biciclette* (*Bicycle Thieves* [1948]) made extensive use of montage and mise-en-scène, even though De Sica's cowriter, Zavattini, famously called for "story-less" films. And no less than the movement's supposed founder, Rossellini, employed stars on the order of Anna Magnani and Aldo Fabrizi in *Rome, Open City* in addition to his cast of nonprofessionals.[7] As Stefano Parigi points out, the word *neorealism,* like so many terms from the history of art, arrived a posteriori: a critical designation born in 1948, it began to circulate "quando quelli che a tutt'oggi si considerano i 'capolavori' del dopoguerra sono già stati realizzati" ("when those films that nowadays are considered the 'masterpieces' of the postwar had already been shot") (92).[8]

Thus, the fluid signifier *neorealism* was and remains highly controversial, as evidenced in the following words from Lino Miccichè, one of the movement's most authoritative voices: "Is it really possible that, half a century after the phenomenon [of neorealism], we cannot aspire to having not just a survey of diverse and programmatically partial opinions on authors, film, and problems, but . . . a compact, unifying monograph that . . . can analyse and historically reconstruct the overall phenomenon, which was certainly complex, but just as well certainly unified even in its compound richness?" ("Sul neorealismo" xxi; qtd. in Wagstaff, *Italian Neorealist Cinema* 39). Many would take issue with Miccichè's description of the movement as "certainly unified": as early as 1949, Nicola Chiaromonte doubted the term's validity (628), and dissenting views persist, ranging from Mira Liehm's Marxist critique to Peter E. Bondanella's claim that the movement lacked aesthetic unity (Liehm 92–94; Bondanella, *Italian Cinema* 32–34). Other scholarly positions, including the schematic defense by George Sadoul and the famous celebration by André Bazin of neorealism as a moral position, fought to preserve the idea of an integral movement—a certain tendency of postwar French criticism, as Alessia Ricciardi has shown.[9] A prevailing opinion holds that despite the movement's inconsistencies, a unifying sense of ethical *impegno* (engagement) obtained in the cinema of the Italian postwar.[10] Such a defense, however, has received its share of attack, most recently in a polemical article by Alan O'Leary and Catherine O'Rawe.[11] In more measured fashion Francesco Casetti posits a hybrid notion of neorealism that reflects the varied theories and practices of its practitioners, ranging from Zavattini's pursuit of immediacy through a "poetics of shadowing" to Guido Aristarco's call for mirroring of reality through a "poetics of reconstruction."[12]

It is not my intention to pronounce on what Christopher Wagstaff describes as the "institution" of neorealism, as distinguished from the films grouped within it.[13] I am more concerned with the principles and poetics of the films considered to be neorealist than with debates about movements, schools, and other post hoc classifications. For example, when I argue that Antonioni looked back to the cinematic forms of Rossellini, the question of whether the films are "neorealist" or "auteur" is extraneous to my larger inquiry into the relations between their actual films. There are certainly instances, however, when a term or concept from cinematic history impacts the decisions of a filmmaker—for example, the idea of "reality" and "realism" for Pasolini and Antonioni. Despite these rare occurrences, I share David Forgacs's view that the use of the term *neorealism* tells us more about the critical conversations surrounding films than about the films themselves.[14] As such, I will use the term *neorealism* as a general tag for the core of films made in the late 1940s and early 1950s that have come to be associated with the documentary-style techniques and strong element of sociopolitical commentary that for many heralded a "new realism" in Italian cinema, however varied its expression and agendas. Thus, the ultimate validity of the label "neorealism" remains peripheral to my analysis of the forms and ideas of filmmakers who, as a rule, placed aesthetic and sociopolitical objectives above questions of classification.

To return to the problem of neorealism's canonicity, it is of course indisputable that neorealist films have received a library of critical responses that would seem to work against the possibility of offering a fresh perspective on them. Yet much remains to be said. In the first place, like the debates over neorealism, responses to the individual works of Rossellini, Visconti, De Santis, De Sica, et al. (and the auteur directors they inspired) reveal a great deal about the critics and cultures commenting on them. For example, Bazin's emphasis on the moral scope of neorealism drew on his telling comparison between the Italian and French Resistance, and Guido Aristarco's critique of Rossellini's alleged betrayal of neorealism reflected the impact of Marxist and leftist principles in postwar Italian culture. Further justification for returning to the classics of neorealism comes from the many Italian directors, from the postwar to the present, who have continued to draw inspiration from them. To make a film based on a preexistent source is to read it deeply and creatively as one updates it to respond to present needs. That certain neorealist works remain such a fecund source for adaptation suggests their ongoing capacity to fuel the most powerful interpretations possible: new works of art.

To echo Shelley's definition of the classic in *A Defence of Poetry* (1821), the major films of the neorealist era and their auteur offshoots are ones that renew themselves for each generation that encounters them; they are like "the first acorn, which contained all oaks potentially." Despite all the ink devoted to these films, we lack a study that locates the aesthetic principles of neorealist and auteur works in the broader context of the sister arts and the larger aesthetic questions they raise. Examining this art-film tradition in relation to literary poetics and other noncinematic elements, I show how some of Italy's most important filmmakers grappled with the relation between symbol and allegory, the nature of the chorus, the literary prehistory of montage, and other crucial aesthetic issues. Finally, I offer individual readings of films that I hope can be ends in themselves, independent of the theoretical claims they make or the scholarly knowledge they might impart. For it is in the mysteries of these films and their interpretive challenges where we find the greatest justification for the label "art film." As Dudley Andrew writes, at their best, cinematic art and interpretation reinforce each other: "Whatever we concentrate on through our choice and our discourse is the value of a film. . . . Only when we expose a film and its workings to our sight and talk, only when it is handed down, does it become more than a document and enter the meaning-life we lead in culture" (*Aura* 198).

Like neorealism, another key term of my study has an embattled history: *auteur*. As John Caughie notes, the word *auteur* from French film criticism identified either the "author who wrote the script" or, more generally, the "artist who created the film"; it was only with the ascendancy of the directors associated with the influential journal *Cahiers du cinéma* that the term came to signify "the artist whose personality was 'written' in the film" (9). Following such seminal definitions as François Truffaut's in "Une certaine tendance du cinéma français" ("A Certain Tendency of the French Cinema" [1954]), I will use the designation *auteur* to describe those films that reflect a director's personal creative vision and resist the imposition of commercial demands, studio interference, cultural norms regarding taste and genre, and other external restraints.[15] To put a finer point on it, I will distinguish between what Caughie calls the *auteur* versus the *metteur en scène*, with the former "consistently expressing his own unique obsessions" and the latter "a competent, even highly competent film-maker, but lacking the consistency which betrayed the profound involvement of a personality" (9–10).[16] Because the term *auteurism* is imported from French film criticism, it has not been as hotly debated in Italian circles as has *neorealismo*. I will therefore apply it more as a general rubric than a specific label to describe the auteurist group of directors who came of aesthetic age during neorealism but then went on to make their greatest films after its heyday (especially Fellini, Antonioni, and Pasolini).

As will be clear in my discussion of *Voyage to Italy*, this French-inspired notion of auteur film would be greatly influenced by the shift in Rossellini's practices after his neorealist trilogy in the late 1940s and into the more subjective and psychological films that he made with Ingrid Bergman in the 1950s.[17] My intent is neither to offer an exhaustive treatment of the auteur period nor to establish its exact parameters in Italy. Rather, in keeping with my goal of tracing the life of aesthetic issues as they migrate from one medium and period to another, I aim to show how directors who were considered auteurist—and who were all shaped in one way or another by the experience of neorealism—addressed aesthetic concerns that more often than not led them to revisit ethical and sociopolitical questions similar to the ones faced by their neorealist predecessors. In some cases the shadows cast by neorealism over these auteurs were direct: Antonioni's definition of the real and Pasolini's theories of cinematic poetry return us to major concerns of the neorealist period. Other times the neorealist precedent is distant or obscure (for example, in the rhetorical strategies of Bertolucci and the postmodern critique of the later Fellini). In all cases, however—and above all in the films from the epilogue—the auteur director's confrontation of cinematic realism and its sociopolitical implications raises concerns that were to a large degree expressed during a neorealist movement that remains ever-present in Italian film—even when it is spoofed, as in Nanni Moretti's ironic take on the inaccessibility of Stromboli, physically and cinematically, in *Caro diario* (*Dear Diary* [1993]).

This book is the first to situate Italian cinema in the context of poetry and poetics, a subject outside the purview of such magisterial histories as those by Peter E. Bondanella and Gian Piero Brunetta, as well as the rich body of works on the film and literature connection in Italy.[18] In discussing cinema's relation with issues derived from the history and practice of poetry, my book contributes to the limited material on a topic that, even outside of Italy, has only been approached indirectly, most often by filmmakers themselves.[19] Recent studies have explored the exchanges between cinema and other art forms, and the relation between literature and film has become a vibrant academic field with its own journals, textbook, recent theoretical meditations by leading scholars, even a dedicated *Cambridge Companion*.[20] My book contributes to this thriving literature but with a critical difference: it is the first to consider the advent of film within ancient traditions in the arts. By analyzing Italian cinema in connection to such questions as the afterlife of the Greek tragic chorus, the literary prehistory of montage, and the cinematic applications of poetic apostrophe, I intend to bring Italian film studies into dialogue with fields outside its usual purview. There have been notable recent contributions on the intermedial nature of Italian film, as well as a welcome study of the influence of Italian neorealism in world cinema.[21] *A Cinema of Poetry: Aesthetics of the Italian Art Film* seeks to offer something new and needed to this critical literature because it is the only book to consider the advent of film in the context of aesthetic questions that stretch back to Homer.

That the above group of films, from Rossellini and De Sica to Frammartino and Giordana, should be so deeply interconnected with the destinies of earlier art forms—and so concerned with the cinematic masterpieces that preceded them—is not surprising. The Italian nation has one of the most vaunted legacies in the visual arts, especially painting and sculpture, and has historically been one of the countries in Europe—indeed, the world—most open to experimenting with visual form.[22] Moreover, Italy's traditions in the iconography and religious painting of the Renaissance exerted a strong gravitational pull on the construction of the cinematic image.[23] The related phenomenon of a single artist working in different fields—the putative Renaissance man—includes many Italian filmmakers who were also active practitioners of other art forms. For example, Pasolini was one of Italy's most prominent poets before he made his first film, and Visconti continued to work professionally in the opera and theater throughout his prolific career as filmmaker. Even those directors who professed to be "pure" cineastes, most notably Fellini and Rossellini, were adept at realizing cinema's intermedial reach, especially in film's link to literature. Late in his career Rossellini abandoned directing for the screen to embark on an encyclopedic project featuring made-for-television biographies of some of the more versatile and well-known of Italy's original "Renaissance men," including Lorenzo de' Medici. The Italian film industry was a haven for many artists, intellectuals, and writers (for example, Edmondo De Amicis and Pasolini) for whom film provided steady pay and the chance to present their work to larger and more diverse audiences than usual.

From film's beginnings, Italian filmmakers were active in drawing on the other art forms in establishing the legitimacy of the new medium, which many considered capable of synthesizing into a single form the abstraction of music, the choreography of dance, the imagery of the visual arts, the language of literature, and the mise-en-scène of theater.[24] Looking back on this cross-fertilization, Brunetta emphasizes the role played by literary models, as one might expect in a nation whose major poets have historically held great cultural and political influence. Among all the national cinemas, he writes, early Italian film hewed most closely to the structures and legacies of literary history, a situation he describes as a "grande migrazione" ("great migration") of genres from literature to the screen (*Cent'anni* 50).[25] In an original take on the well-traveled "literature to film" critical topos, my book considers how literature operates within actual films not just as a "source text" but as a mode of aesthetic expression.[26]

Pasolini brings the intermedial tendencies of Italian cinema and its adaptive capacities to a high point. Despite its idiosyncrasies, his essay "A 'Cinema of Poetry'" established the gold standard for understanding the connection between film and poetry.[27] The "Italian" component of Pasolini's definition of the *cinema di poesia* draws on a tradition of defining poetry in transmedial terms going back centuries and encompassing figures as diverse as Vico and Croce. Pasolini's importance for this study extends past his views on cinematic poetry and into his transformative stance toward neorealism. He believed that neorealism was a glorious failure, doomed to fall short of the expectations it had created because of its untenable desire to reorganize society through cultural means rather than the underlying economic, political, and social conditions that generate culture in the first place.[28] Despite his well-known critique, Pasolini, like so many of his auteur peers, developed his cinematic vision through an ongoing negotiation with the postwar documentary-style movement. By translating neorealism into his own aesthetic and ideological agenda, Pasolini gave the moment new life even as he proclaimed its demise.

Pasolini, of course, was not the only Italian filmmaker to look back critically and creatively on neorealism. For him and many of his peers, filmmaking became a form of translation: how to recreate the elusive term *realism* in a way that neither copied their cinematic fathers nor lost their capacity to train their lens on the state of the nation. A haunting version of this cinematic dialogue with the past occurs at the conclusion of Antonioni's *L'avventura*, the story of the fruitless search for the disappeared Anna that results in the union between her best friend, Claudia, and Anna's lover, Sandro. Late in the film Claudia spends a sleepless night waiting for Sandro to return from a party. After a desperate search through their luxury hotel, she finds him in the arms of a prostitute. The couple then shed copious tears, emblems of a sad love story now contaminated by betrayal. Figuratively speaking, their grief relates to the film's larger message about the loss of the ideals associated with neorealism.

The ending of *L'avventura* may have been "announced," to quote Bertolucci's epigraph, nearly a decade earlier in the enigmatic conclusion to Rossellini's *Voyage to Italy*. After that film's main characters, Alex and Katherine Joyce, encounter the lovers ensconced in the lava of Vesuvius and decide to divorce, they drive into the middle of a Neapolitan religious procession, where they will have an unexpected reconciliation at film's end. One can draw instructive parallels between this controversial ending and the conclusion of *L'avventura*: like Rossellini, Antonioni ends his film with a sudden and dramatic emotional rapprochement between two characters locked in an emotional stalemate. As in *Voyage to Italy*, the private and domestic nature of the conflict at the conclusion of *L'avventura* marks a distance from the more public, historically inflected, and politically charged subject matter in that same postwar cinematic milieu that had inspired Rossellini and Antonioni

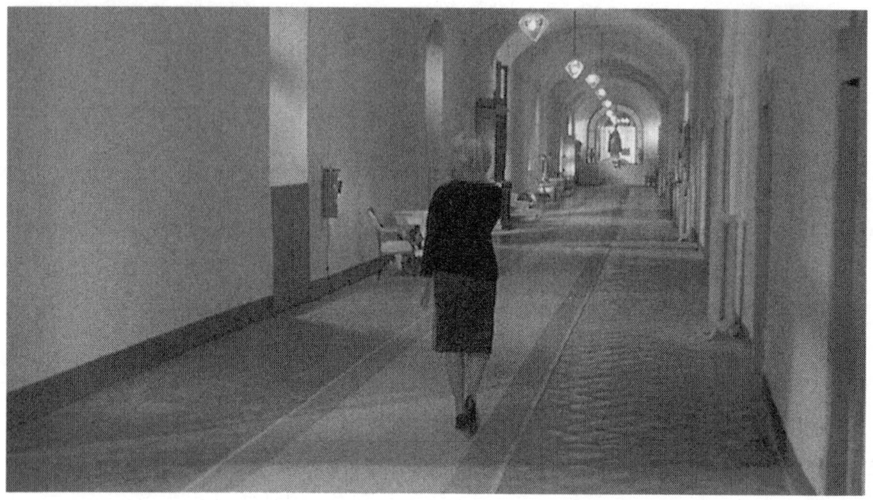

Figure 1 Claudia searches for Sandro in a long hotel corridor, one of the many objects Antonioni exploits for its symbolic resonance *(L'avventura)*.

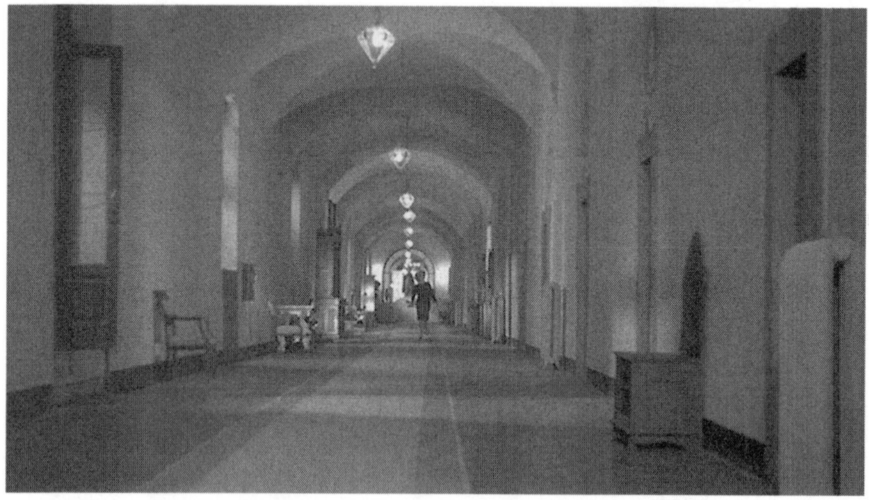

Figure 2 Claudia reenters the frame in the opposite direction from figure 1, thereby jumping the line of the traditional 180-degree film axis *(L'avventura)*.

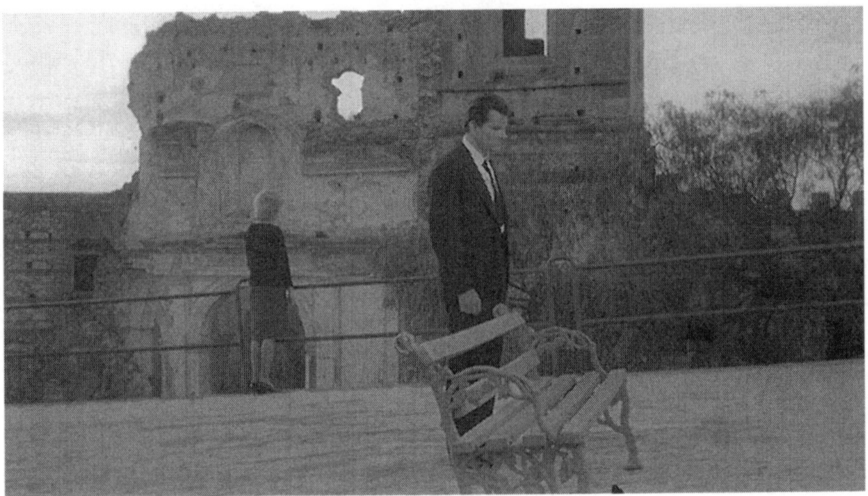

Figure 3 Antonioni places Claudia and Sandro in disjointed spatial relation to call attention to the frame's abstract compositional arrangement *(L'avventura)*.

in the 1940s. Indeed, Antonioni follows Rossellini in using this final scene to suggest the distance he had traveled from the neorealist themes of his early aesthetic development and its documentary-style cinematography. In the finale of *L'avventura* the abstract expressionism of Antonioni's compositions breaks free from the naturalist editing typical of neorealism, as do the self-conscious violations of the 180-degree axis that occur when Antonioni, in the blink of a camera's eye, has Claudia enter the hallway screen right but then leave it screen left (figures 1 and 2).

When Claudia reaches Sandro on the promontory overlooking the stark Sicilian waters, we feel as though we are back in the neorealist world, as the rugged, deep-focus landscape recalls Visconti's mythical Sicily in *La terra trema*.[29] But this hint of a neorealist landscape dramatically gives way to the awkward planar dispositions of the weeping Sandro and Claudia placed mid- and fore-frame (figure 3), a blocking that would have been inconceivable in the naturalist idiom of engaged postwar film.

As in the reconciliation scene in Rossellini's *Voyage to Italy*, Antonioni's final sequence in *L'avventura* shows how private dramas and emotional intricacies overwhelm any matter of communal and public consequence. The crepuscular light from *Voyage to Italy* that Bertolucci saw refracted in *L'avventura* heralded the birth of a new cinematic poetics born from the passing of neorealism. Because of cinema's singular relationship to commercial, political, and social structures—and because of its unique technological properties—it could transform existing aesthetic debates in ways inconceivable to earlier artists. So the finale of *L'avventura* takes part in a dialogue over cinematic poetics and aesthetic issues that not only recall the neorealist moment but stretch back, as Antonioni claims in his "Cannes Statement" on *L'avventura,* "all'epoca di Omero" to the times of Homer.

PART ONE

NEOREALIST RHETORIC AND NATIONAL IDENTITY

CHAPTER ONE

The Chorus of Neorealism

We ask for a choral cinema that would keep pace with the problems and aspirations of our souls.

—Giuseppe De Santis

"Non ho formule e preconcetti," Roberto Rossellini claimed when asked to look back on his fabled postwar cinema; "ma se guardo a ritroso i miei film, indubbiamente vi riscontro degli elementi che sono in essi costanti, e che vi sono ripetuti non programmaticamente, ma, ripeto, naturalmente. Anzitutto la *coralità*. Il film realistico, in sé, è corale" ("I do not have formulas or preconceptions. If I look back, however, on my films, I undoubtedly encounter elements that are a constant in them, and that are repeated not programmatically but, I would stress, naturally. Above all, I find a *chorality*. The realist film per se is choral") (*Il mio metodo* 88). Echoing Rossellini, commentators on the history and practice of neorealism have often invoked the word *coralità* as one of its defining characteristics.[1] Indeed, this concept emerges as one of the most illuminating rubrics for fathoming the nexus between aesthetics and sociopolitical engagement during the neorealist period, as varying notions of the chorus rallied seemingly disjoined creative minds in a common struggle. For all the distance separating, say, Rossellini's Christian humanism from Visconti's operatic realism, their exploration of chorality in the late 1940s reveals a militant commitment to using art to rebuild a disgraced nation, while highlighting their respective understanding of the aims and theories of neorealism.[2]

Whether in the Italian *coralità* or its English equivalent, *chorality*, the word *coralità* draws on its link to the root *chorus* to denote acting in concert or speaking with one voice. The provenance of *coralità* invokes associations with the ancient Greek tragic chorus, whose two chief functions continue to inform the term's afterlife: singing and witnessing. In fifth-century BCE Attic tragedy, "the chorus were 'interested spectators,' sympathizing with the fortunes of the characters, and giving expression, between the 'acts,' to the moral and religious sentiments evoked by the action of the play."[3] The mandate of the chorus for sung testimony was incorporated into the architecture and landscape of the Greek theater itself, where "the constant presence of a choral group as witnesses to the action contributed to the public character of the events portrayed" (Easterling 1540). Thus ensued a contradictory role for the chorus that shaped its later manifestations in the neorealist tradition: although the Greek tragic mode "could deal with intimate subject-matter," it also "depended on large effects of gesture and movement that could be 'read' by very diverse audiences" (Easterling 1540). In its capacity as the intermediary between the private lives depicted onstage and the public interests of the audience, the chorus ensured the popular and antielitist appeal of Greek tragedy by translating the themes of the drama into a lyrical shorthand accessible to all.[4]

The design and function of the chorus became a platform for mythmaking in the quest by later cultures for roots, actual and imagined, in the ancient world. The most influential modern treatment of the ancient chorus, Friedrich Nietzsche's *The Birth of Tragedy,* argues against both August Wilhelm Schlegel's view of the chorus as an abstract "idealized spectator" and Friedrich Schiller's notion of it as "a living wall that tragedy constructs around itself in order to close itself off from the world of reality" (*Tragedy* 57–58). In contrast, Nietzsche proposes a radically participatory role for the chorus, which becomes the key to his binary distinction between the Apollonian and Dionysian aspects of human nature. The Greek tragedy, he writes, remained true to its beginnings as a ritualistic, Dionysian musical chorus—Greek tragedy originally consisted *only* of the chorus—even when it later developed into its more classic, discursive theatrical forms in the Attic and Athenian drama. In high Greek tragedy, according to Nietzsche, the general theme is the ultimate failure of an Apollonian hero who cannot rise above the constraints of his individuality.[5] But for all the devastation these tragedies depict, the chorus in ecstatic Dionysian unity remains onstage after the hero's destruction, a testament to the "metaphysical comfort . . . that life is at the bottom of things, despite all the changes of appearances, indestructibly powerful and pleasurable" (Nietzsche, *Tragedy* 59).[6] The depiction of suffering and woe in Nietzsche's tragic stage raises the chorus member into a higher state of being, where the boundaries separating one human from the next collapse, and all other "Apollonian" forms of detachment beholden to sovereign selfhood dissolve. Thus, the Nietzschean chorus does not "observe" or "watch" the spectacle before them; they virtually reenact it and share its consequences, to such a degree that their own consciousnesses come to fuse with forms of being outside of the self. This transformation can only occur within the liminal space of artistic representation—in Greek drama, on and around the stage—because only in the rapture of aesthetic form (the supreme embodiment of which, according to Nietzsche, was the Dionysian mode of music) may Apollonian detachment and individuality be shattered and transcended ("Art saves [the choral member], and through art life saves him" [*Tragedy* 59]). Independent of the accuracy or lack thereof of Nietzsche's historical claims, the brilliance of his understanding of chorality rests on his provocative phenomenology and accompanying genealogy of the process by which an external group generally considered peripheral to the action "onstage" (the chorus) blends with tragedy's victims through a ritual trumping of selfhood.

The metaphysics of the Nietzschean chorus provides a useful philosophic perspective for analyzing neorealist chorality; but the most visceral choral legacies for postwar filmmakers came from sources closer to home. The films during the Ventennio, the two decades of Benito Mussolini's rule from 1922 to 1943, offer abundant representations of formerly disconnected human beings massed into a single unit, often under the spell of a demagogue.[7] Although this explicitly political and often violent behavior may be the most infamous manifestation of the corporatist impulse of Fascism, choral representation was a staple of Italian film even before the Fascist apotheosis. Many of early Italian cinema's historical blockbusters relied on the use of hundreds of extras organized into groups on massive and lavish sets. In Giovanni Pastrone's *Cabiria* (1914) the choral effect appears in, among other scenes, the failed sacrifice of the abducted Roman girl Cabiria to the Carthaginian god Moloch. Arrayed in a diorama-like tableau of fanatical worship, the hysterical Carthaginians move in syncopation to the musical score while their terrified victims cower at their imminent death by fire.[8] Angela Dalle Vacche writes that the representation of crowds in *Cabiria* influenced the mise-en-scène of such officially Fascist films as Carmine Gallone's *Scipione l'africano* (*Scipio Africanus* [1937]), which Mussolini's regime backed because of its celebration of Italian imperialist actions in Ethiopia (*Body* 39). In both *Cabiria* and *Scipio Africanus* an aggressive nationalism prevails, and the architectural forms that house the crowds are the grandiose corollaries for these expressions of an esprit d'état.[9] Such crowds, Gian Piero Brunetta argues, "spell out an ideal image of an orderly body politic that does not exist," by presenting "circumscribed, exhilarating moments of unification within an overall pattern of quasi-anarchic behavior" (qtd. in Dalle Vacche, *Body* 39).

In contrast to the Fascist and proto-Fascist "crowd," in neorealist film the chorus remains peripheral, in the etymological sense of this word, "of the circumference," away from the center. Whereas the Fascist crowd or masses react in usually predictable and brutal fashion, the neorealist chorus provides an aesthetic analogy (and thus analysis) of the scene at hand even as it is swept along by its action. The opposition between neorealist chorality and Fascism's vaunted aesthetics of the masses is distilled in the decision by neorealist filmmakers to divest their choral imagery of the force, violence, and coercion that defined the scenes of crowd behavior in the cinema from previous generations. Neorealist chorality, however, remained just as political as that of its Fascist predecessors: whereas the images of collectivity in films sympathetic to Mussolini in the 1930s evoked the corporatist principles of his regime, those of class solidarity in works by directors including Visconti and De Sica sought to express the age's popular Marxist tenets. But the difference in neorealist chorality rests in a quality that Nietzsche diagnosed in his writings on the Greek tragic stage: the capacity of the chorus for bearing witness.

Especially in Rossellini, this capacity for choral testimony often assumes a Christian component that did not exist in the decidedly pagan views on the chorus by the anti-Christian Nietzsche.[10] Rossellini considered neorealism to be more of a moral than an aesthetic position, and he believed that making the neorealist film meant "following someone with love and watching all his discoveries and impressions"—a view that recalls Cesare Zavattini's influential notion of *pedinamento,* the camera's "shadowing" of everyday reality.[11] Crucial to Rossellini was the waiting, for there the supposedly nonrealistic elements eschewed by many neorealists (mise-en-scène, scripted dialogue and scenario, well-defined narrative and plot) were dissolved by the director's Christian desire to plumb the psychological depths of his subjects.[12] His notion of waiting for the moment in which the soul of his actor emerges before the camera recalls the lyrical testimony borne by the chorus upon the Greek tragic stage. Many pivotal scenes in Rossellini's oeuvre of the postwar period depend on bearing witness to tragedy in an act of duty, homage, or ritual. The composition of these acts often emphasize the Christian nature of Rossellinian testimony, as one sees in the visual Crucifix created by the sign "Partigiano" ("Partisan") spread lengthwise across the standing, black-shrouded soldier in the Po River episode of *Paisà,* when a group of Resistance

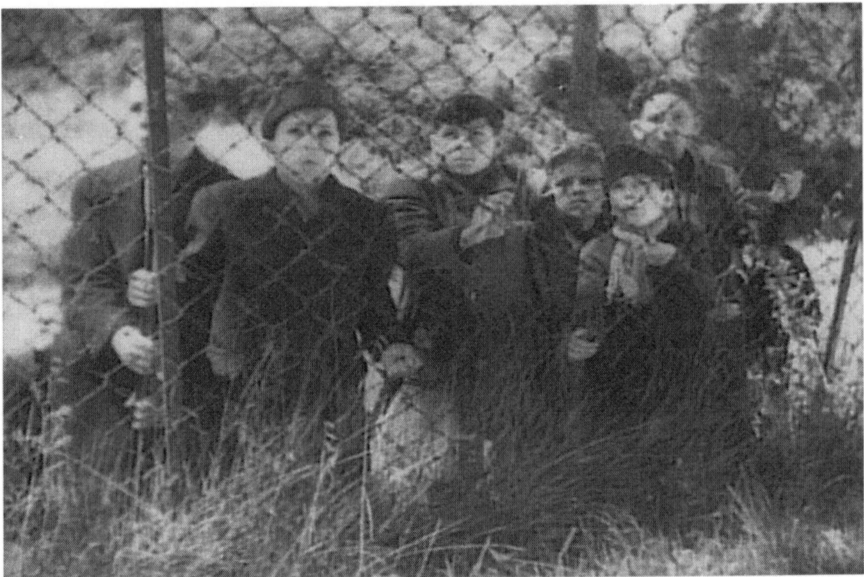

Figure 4 A chorus of partisan youths bears witness to Don Pietro's impending execution *(Rome, Open City).*

fighters bands together in vigil over a fallen comrade. A similar effect obtains in *Rome, Open City* in the prayerful disposition of Don Pietro's body as he kneels before the Christlike figure of the tortured partisan Manfredi, later scornfully referred to as a Giovanni Episcopo (John the Baptist) by the onlooking Gestapo. Fittingly, these spiritual images comment in one way or another on the embattled quest for *italianità* by a nation struggling to define itself in the wake of war.

The religious inflection of bearing witness to the nation in Rossellini's films pervades the scene of the partisan Don Pietro's execution in *Roma, città aperta*. While the priest is read his last rites, the children in his flock stand by to observe and pit their whistles in univocal solidarity against the Latin drone of the clergy (figure 4). Meanwhile, the Christian believer Don Pietro sits alone in his thoughts and prayers (figure 5). In its solemnity his death occasions none of the fury or hysteria of Nietzsche's chorus; it inspires instead the resigned and melancholic funereal march of the young witnesses toward a Rome that must be rebuilt. Despite its despair, this unified troop serves as a stark contrast to the failure earlier in the film of the Italian people to act in unison against their German oppressors, especially in the pivotal scene where the Nazis gun down the partisan heroine Pina as she runs after her

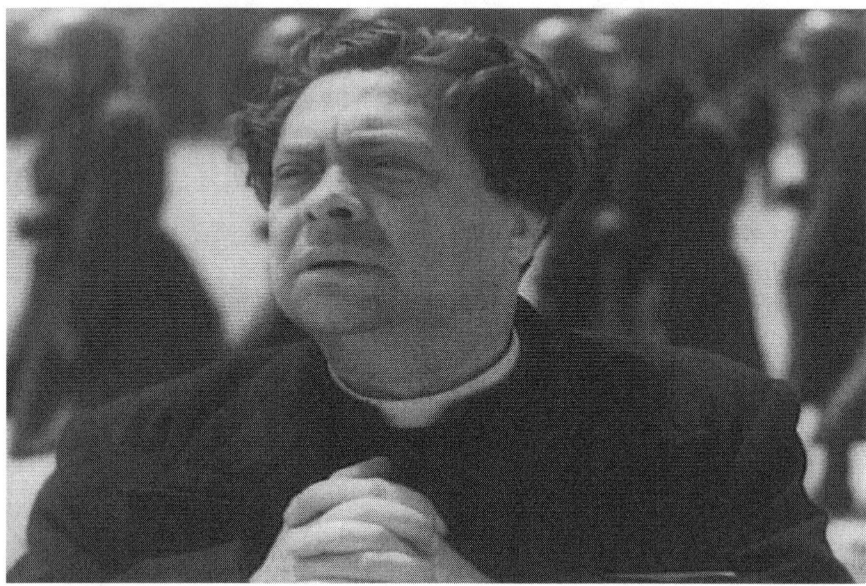

Figure 5 Rossellini's Don Pietro filmed alone in prayerful disposition as a visual counterpoint to the choral imagery in figure 4 *(Rome, Open City).*

captured fiancé Francesco. Held back by the German guard, the crowd passively watches as Pina begins her fatal solitary sprint.

A succeeding image, of Don Pietro holding Pina's corpse just as the Virgin held Christ in her arms in Michelangelo's *Pietà,* recapitulates one of the most intimate and antichoral icons in Christianity to underscore the private tragedy of the partisan family (Pina's son will join Don Pietro beside the corpse) (figure 6).[13] The image transforms a staple of religious iconography into a political allegory: the dead body of Pina represents the ultimate sacrifice made on behalf of the Resistance movement.[14] Rossellini's filming of the partisan youths is choral by his own definition of the term, for they whistle, act in unison, and are transformed by the event at hand. The youths are peripheral to the event, yet they assume its consequences, as they stand aside and watch the grim ritual of the priest's execution. Unlike the representation of crowds in Fascist film, which was often done with grandiose aerial shots or deep-focus pans that linked the multitudes to the surrounding militarist environs, Rossellini's more fluid camera grants his chorus autonomy in the rough Roman landscape—a bland no-man's land that the youths traverse in a sequence that will culminate in the magnificent final shot of St. Peter's looming above a destroyed Rome awaiting restoration if not resurrection.[15]

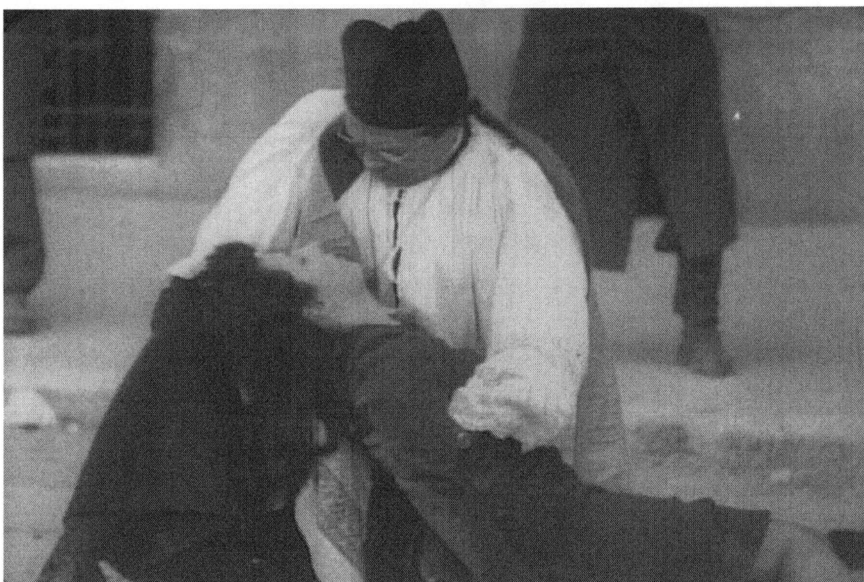

Figure 6 Don Pietro cradles the murdered partisan heroine Pina in Rossellini's homage to Michelangelo's *Pietà,* to underscore the breakdown of chorality during her fatal sprint *(Rome, Open City).*

Although less political in scope than *Roma, città aperta,* Rossellini's *Stromboli* (1950) also registers choral moments, such as the villagers waiting in prayerful ritual for the appearance of the tuna during the annual *mattanza,* a bloody harvest in the local waters. During the sequence Ingrid Bergman's character, Karin, stands apart, filmed in one anguished close-up after another in a visual allegory of her inability to transcend her individuality and join in the elemental activity that ensures the survival of the villagers and deepens their connection to their harsh landscape. By film's end she, like Don Pietro, will lie metaphysically naked and alone, sprawled before the awesome explosions of Stromboli's volcano and filled at last with a religious awakening in her hitherto bankrupt spiritual life.

Rossellini's contemporary De Sica exploited the tension between individuality and chorality by making categorical designations like the "Roman people" and the "working class" into characters in *Bicycle Thieves.* The difference between the two filmmakers, according to André Bazin, was that Rossellini's passion for his characters "envelops them in a desperate awareness of man's inability to communicate," whereas De Sica's love "radiates from the characters themselves. They are what they are, but lit from within by the tenderness he feels for them" ("De Sica" 64). De Sica's characters channel their director's affection into images of choral expression devoid of Rossellini's deferral to the private nature of religious experience. An early sequence in *Ladri di biciclette* translates domestic choral imagery into a public, class-inflected montage of the proletariat going to work during Rome's morning rush hour. Antonio and Bruno Ricci are shot in unison in a tender evocation of family and work life, an image then inserted into its broader choral context of cycling fellow laborers who jockey for position in the morning traffic. Still, Bazin writes, De Sica is a pessimistic director: neither Rossellinian Catholicism nor any other transcendental principle rescues the characters from the trials that ensue after the theft of Ricci's bike. Yet the viewer "can never be grateful enough to [De Sica] for [his pessimism]," Bazin notes, "because in it resides the appeal of the potential of man, the witness to his final and irrefutable humanity" ("De Sica" 74). Bazin's emphasis on De Sica's propensity for witness is corroborated by the filmmaker himself, who claimed that his "films are about the search for human solidarity," however fleeting, before it dissolves into the inevitable incommunicability (De Sica, "De Sica on De Sica" 38–39). Although Rossellini and De Sica diverge in their methods of achieving cinematic testimony, each waited by reality's side for a defining moment or trait to emerge from what De Sica called the "ruined morality" of postwar Italy (De Sica, "De Sica on De Sica" 31). Moreover, both directors were aware of the *negative* and not just the positive aspects of chorality: for Rossellini the failure of the Roman crowd to aid Pina during her death sprint in *Città aperta* and the hostile "double chorus" of nature and the villagers that thwart Karin throughout *Stromboli;* for De Sica the angry crowd jostling Antonio in Via di Panico when he finds the thief of his bike and the unforgiving mob that derides him after his own theft at the end of *Ladri di biciclette*.[16]

Another major supporter of neorealist chorality was the pioneering director Giuseppe De Santis, whose emphasis on choral cinema in the early 1940s established an important precursor for the neorealists.[17] One of the critics and filmmakers associated with the innovative journal *Cinema*—a group that included Visconti and Antonioni—De Santis championed Verga's writing in the influential article he coauthored with Mario Alicata in 1941: "Verità e poesia: Verga e il cinema italiano."[18] He argued that directors should follow Verga in putting characters into dialogue with the landscape, an effect he achieves throughout his best-known film, *Riso amaro* (*Bitter Rice* [1949]),

one of the more difficult "neorealist" films to categorize because of its unusual
blend of documentary-style techniques with commercial elements, including
a melodramatic plot and open display of female beauty. The film's opening
sequence tracks the *mondine* (women rice workers) as they take to the fields
to start the day's labor, in a massive grouping according to economic function
that recalls the predawn rituals of Visconti's fishermen in *La terra trema,* another film that uses the dialectic between choral units and their natural landscape to convey a sociopolitical message predicated on leftist ideology. After
the panoramic view of the *mondine,* an announcer from Radio Turin appears
in close-up to describe—much in the same way as the narrative voice-over
in *La terra trema*—the "lavoro duro e immutabile" ("hard and unchanging
work") that the *mondine* have engaged in for centuries, thus evoking gender
concerns as an overhead tracking shot captures the annual migration of this
singing and chanting female chorus.[19]

The notion of chorality was not limited to cinema: the poet and Nobel
laureate Salvatore Quasimodo joined his neorealist contemporaries in linking *coralità* and *italianità.* In his view the trauma of war either negated or
reduced to ironic detachment a people's sense of self, as existential concerns
necessarily gave way to practical ones, and the question became no longer
why but rather *how* one lived.[20] His writings on the place of the poet in the
postwar polity epitomized the view of many neorealist directors, especially
Visconti and his description of a communist-inspired "anthropomorphic cinema," in which the artist was merely one worker among others in a communal
structure that "authored" a film as much as the actual filmmaker ("Anthropomorphic Cinema" 83).[21] Looking back on World War II in 1953, Quasimodo
used choral terms to describe his switch from an interior hermeticism to a
postwar neohumanism:

> La posizione del poeta non può essere passiva nella società: egli "modifica" il
> mondo. . . . Le sue immagini forti, quelle create, battono sul cuore dell'uomo
> più della filosofia e della storia. La poesia si trasforma in etica. . . . Scrivere
> versi significa subire un giudizio: quello estetico comprende implicitamente le
> reazioni sociali che suscita una poesia. . . . La guerra ha interrotto una cultura
> e proposto nuovi valori dell'uomo; e se le armi sono ancora nascoste, il dialogo
> dei poeti con gli uomini è necessario, più delle scienze e degli accordi tra le na-
> zioni, che possono essere traditi. La poesia italiana, dopo il '45, è *di natura co-
> rale,* nella sua specie; scorre per larghi ritmi, parla del mondo reale con parole
> comuni; talvolta presume all'epica. ("Discorso sulla poesia" 291; my emphasis)

The position of the poet cannot be passive in society: he "modifies" the world. . . . His forceful images, those that he creates, beat on the heart of man more than does philosophy or history. Poetry is transformed into ethic[s]. . . . To write verses means to undergo judgment: and implicit in the aesthetic judgment are the social reactions to which a poem gives rise. . . . War has interrupted a culture and proposed new values for man; and though the weapons have been laid aside, the dialogue of the poets with men is necessary, even more than the sciences and the agreements between nations, which can be betrayed. Italian poetry after 1945 is—in its kind—*of a choral nature.* It flows with spacious rhythms, speaks of the real world with ordinary words; sometimes it presumes to the epic. ("Discourse on Poetry" 14)

Quasimodo's Olympian depiction of the poet as the modifier of the world follows the rhetoric of the *poeta vate* (poet-prophet) tradition that influenced the cultural and political life of Italy from Dante to the Risorgimento and beyond. By flowing with "larghi ritmi" ("spacious rhythms") and laying bare the "mondo reale con parole comuni" ("real world with ordinary words"), Quasimodo's notion of the choral combines the musical expressivity of lyric with a vernacular dialect attuned to the quotidian experiences of a populace in crisis. Similarly, many neorealist films aimed to capture the everyday idiom of the Italian people by employing nonprofessional actors who spoke their native dialects onscreen. Though Quasimodo describes this collective expression in terms of chorality, the popular languages he mentions are filtered through the consciousness of the poet, who, he claims in deference to the *poeta vate* paradigm, shapes the world with images that beat upon the heart of man more forcefully than rational forms of knowledge do. Quasimodo's notion of choral poetry follows the Bakhtinian distinction between poetry and prose: "no matter how many contradictions and insoluble conflicts the poet develops within [a work], it is always illumined by one unitary and indisputable discourse" (Bakhtin, "Discourse in the Novel" 286). Thus, with Quasimodo we end up with a chorus, but it is a chorus of one (the *poeta vate*) that stands worlds apart from the Nietzschean model: according to *The Birth of Tragedy* the essence of the chorus resides in its capacity to transcend the *principium individuationis* in the name of a Dionysian unity. From the perspective of Nietzsche's theories and the collectivist impulses of much neorealist film, a problem with Quasimodo's Dionysian chorus was that it sang to the Apollonian lyre of the self.[22]

Even more than eliciting thoughts of Rossellini, De Sica, De Santis, and

Quasimodo, the word *coralità* in the Italian cultural history of the two world wars is most likely to evoke the names of Visconti and his predecessor Verga.[23] Noa Steimatsky identifies the "choral" mode by which Verga blends the different literary registers of his hybrid verismo style into an organic whole that does not attempt to hide its stitching and seams. For Steimatsky, Visconti's recapitulation of Verghian chorality entailed an "appeal to a fully wrought, legible landscape, in which 'man and nature' are chorally bound. . . . Visconti boldly grafts diverse visions, scales, spaces, narrative and historical orders in a resonant chorale, embracing the traditions of which his films must partake and to which it now contributes" (*Italian Locations* 105).[24] Indeed, if there were a father of the chorus as it shaped neorealist film, it would be Verga. In his pioneering study of *I Malavoglia*, Luigi Russo stresses the omnipresence of "un coro vero e proprio, che viene compassionando o contrastando alle pene dei protagonisti" ("an actual and true chorus, which comes to sympathize with the protagonists or compare its sufferings with them") (169). By invoking Verga's reinscription of the ancient Greek chorus as the bearer of collective lyrical witness to calamity, Russo suggests the novel's competing historical trajectories, which set in dialogue two versions of Sicily: one that contains in its landscapes and customs the mythic residues of Homeric epic, another that represents the impoverished southern province of a recently unified Kingdom of Italy.[25] "Alle sventure dei poveri partecipano tutti quelli del paese" ("Everyone in the village participates in the woes of the poor"), Russo writes of a social chorality that extends to the linguistic sinews of the text, whose countless proverbs and homespun expressions reflect not "massime verbali" but "massime vissute" ("lived" rather than "verbal" maxims) (166).

Verga eschewed background description of any kind in reporting his characters and their relations with one another and the natural world, thereby achieving what Mikhail M. Bakhtin called the "heteroglossia" of a detached fictional world. Like Bakhtin's archetypal prose author, Verga "does not express *himself* in [his characters]. . . . Rather, he *exhibits* them as a unique speech-thing, [and] they function for him as something completely reified" (Bakhtin, "Discourse in the Novel" 299). Verga's novel conveys this process through the dialect speech patterns and proverbializing of the inhabitants of Aci Trezza, orchestrating what Bakhtin labels the "stratification of language" to express the worldviews of his characters and, more implicitly, the author's own "intentional theme" ("Discourse in the Novel" 299). This theme of *I Malavoglia* is clear from the author's celebrated preface, which promises "lo studio sincero e spassionato del come probabilmente devono nascere e svilupparsi nelle più umili condizioni, le prime irrequietudini pel benessere" ("a sincere and dispassionate study of how the first anxious desires for material well-being must probably originate and develop in the humblest social conditions") (*Malavoglia* 177; *Medlar Tree* 3). Verga uses proverbial discourse to submerge his narrative voice within the linguistic folds of the community of Aci Trezza, whose illiterate and rhetorically unsophisticated citizens communicate via clichés and commonplaces handed down over the centuries.[26] Russo's shrewd perception of the conflation of theological and domestic discourses in the speech of the paterfamilias of *I Malavoglia*—"padron 'Ntoni è, non soltanto il patriarca del santuario, ma anche l'umile salmista di quella sua religione della casa e della famiglia" ("Master 'Ntoni is not only the patriarch of the hearth but also the humble psalmist of the household and familial religion" [167])—underscores that no form of inner or outer life is possible for Verga's characters independent of the choral contexts. The family structure, at once a metaphor and metonymy for Aci Trezza, becomes a choral collective-in-miniature, with laws and protocols that reflect and uphold the anti-individualistic ethos binding the village's inhabitants. Chorality is, moreover, the ideological and epistemological ground on which every element in Verga's novel is based, since no idea or precept is advanced without first being filtered through familial approval, communal discussion (even gossip), and the sanction of tradition.

A keen student of the Southern Question that Verga's novel embodies, Antonio Gramsci once wrote that when the *questione della lingua* surfaces, a series of related sociopolitical problems tends to follow.[27] In Gramsci's view matters like the formation and enlargement of the governing class and the need to establish better relations between the national administration and the popular masses had a linguistic component, because the cultural hegemony of Italy was bound up with the ascent of a local literary dialect (Tuscan) to the status of national language. Though statistics vary, it is likely that at the time of the unification in the 1860s less than ten percent of the country could write or speak this Tuscan-derived "Italian"; by the early 1990s, just thirty-eight percent communicated exclusively in Italian, while another fourteen percent still spoke only or mostly in dialect.[28] Clausewitz's dictum that a language is nothing but a dialect with an army might be restated in the Italian case, with language being a dialect with a prestigious hendecasyllable of Dantesque provenance (Tuscan). The linguistic chorality developed by Verga was likely to have a lasting impact on neorealist filmmakers, since they often followed the Sicilian author in using dialect speech to test cultural memory.

The most notable translation of Verghian proverbial discourse to the screen was Visconti's adaptation of *I Malavoglia* in *La terra trema,* which conflates an anthropological documentary of the speech patterns and social conduct in Aci Trezza with a communist-inspired critique of the prevailing modes of production. Moreover, *La terra trema* offers a much different version of the national chorale than the Christian Rossellini: in Visconti the only "religion" present is a secular one based on Marxist economic principles. In visual choral groupings focused on labor and class solidarity, Visconti critiques the idea of the nation for its social disparities, to remind the audience at every turn that, as the voice-over narration announces at the opening of the film, "l'italiano non è la lingua dei poveri" ("Italian is not the language of the poor").[29]

The acclaimed opening scene of the film uses deep-focus cinematography to present, well before the narrator explains what is happening, the dawn rituals of the Sicilian fishermen with the sounds of their buoys, the preparation of their fleets, and the domestic chores of their women.[30] Scholars have emphasized the aural quality to this choral opening of Visconti's film, whose "intimate musical rhythm" lends a "religious and fatal tone of ancient tragedy" to the humble occurrences of everyday village life, and whose operatic structure unfolds its action "slowly, in a series of tableaux, with its choruses, solos, and duets."[31] The criticism has also considered Verga's recourse to the Homeric subtext for archetypal themes and visual iconography, most famously in the twin *faraglioni,* the rocks reputedly hurled by the Cyclops after the fleeing Ulysses. More than physical boundaries, the rocks delimit the horizon of the characters' worldview, since the stones divide the familiar world of tradition from an uncomprehending modernity, seductive in its promises but cruel in its offerings ('Ntoni states that, beyond the *faraglioni* the current is likely to destroy). At the conclusion of the film the humiliated 'Ntoni is forced to accept work at the Cyclops Company, Transportation and Sale of Fish, a narrative development that stands as an ironic allegory for the breakdown of Visconti's attempt at epic adaptation: in contrast to Homeric epic, in Visconti the figuratively invoked monster (and the capitalism associated with his name) triumphs over the wayfaring protagonist, instead of vice versa. In emphasizing class above all other concerns, Visconti swerves from Verga, as well as Homer, in his attempt to put epic and naturalist narrative modes in the service of his dialectical materialism.[32]

In line with Verghian chorality Visconti's interplay between word and image permeates the scene before 'Ntoni's fall from grace. After 'Ntoni's early triumph with the purchase of the family boat and lucrative harvest of an-

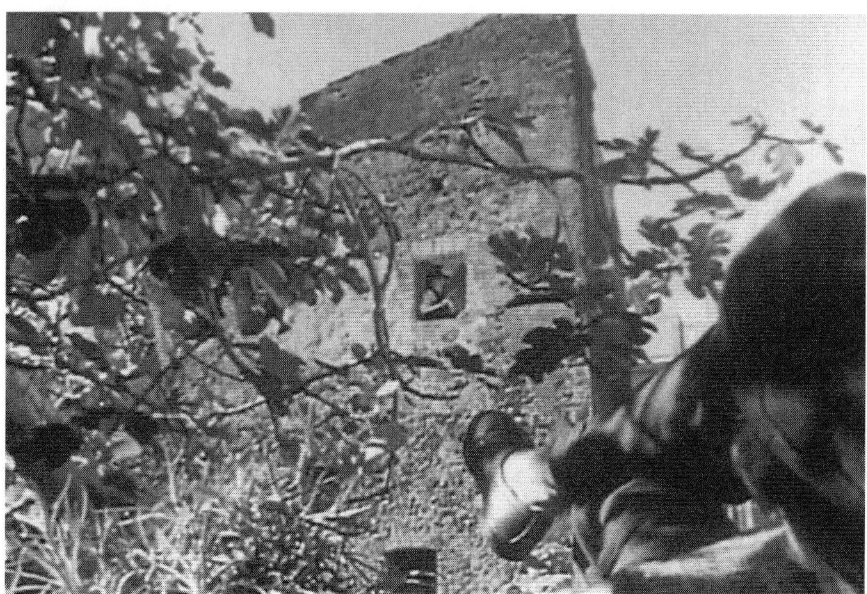

Figure 7 Visconti employs a low-angle shot to suggest the tension between 'Ntoni's perspective and that of his neighbors *(La terra trema).*

chovies, he strolls into town on the way to visiting his beloved 'Nedda. The Verghian chatter and gossip of daily village life follow him with unsolicited lessons in humility, praise for his industry, and warnings about fate, all in the form of the familiar proverbs. At one point he is told to be careful of his neighbor's words, for "Neighbors are like roof tiles: water flows from one to another."[33] The scene recalls the hum of Verga's chorus, which comments on the action at hand in the only "art" it knows, that of gossip and storytelling, to which Visconti gives a Marxist spin by making labor into the privileged focus of his choral narrative.[34] Visconti visualizes the proverb by filming first the tiles of a roof, then the water jugs with the neighbor alongside them. The next image, a low-angle shot of 'Ntoni peering up at this monitory neighbor, appears on the heels of 'Ntoni's words: "If things go well, I look after my neighbors" (figure 7). By introducing the perspective of 'Ntoni into the otherwise impersonal deep-focus pans of daily village life, Visconti reveals his protagonist's struggle to impose his subjective views on an environment resistant to his entrepreneurial vision. The villagers express their ill will toward 'Ntoni through such expressions as "He can't stop singing and laughing and spitting at people" and "He's become conceited." In this same low-angle shot of 'Ntoni's upward glance, a villager peers down to suggest that a punishing fatalism from above can strike him down at any moment, and soon enough it will. Despite his claims to the contrary ("I'll be happy because from now on I'll work for myself"), 'Ntoni never manages to escape the choral forms that Visconti captures here in verbal and visual force.

Together, Verga's and Visconti's representations of mythic Sicilian life recall Bakhtin's distinction between epic and novelistic discourses. Bakhtin defines the epic as representing the absolute past, at once "monochromic and valorized (hierarchical)," a dimension of cultural expression "walled off absolutely from all subsequent times, and above all from those times in which the singer and his listeners are located" ("Epic and Novel" 15–16).[35] To overcome this linguistic wall separating the absolute past of the epic from the present, the novelist introduces elements of linguistic heteroglossia, multiplicity of point of view, and competing ideological perspectives, which work together to vitiate what Bakhtin calls the closed circle of epic, inside of which everything "is finished, already over" ("Epic and Novel" 16). Thus, the epic represents a "discourse handed down by tradition" and "does not permit an individual, personal point of view or evaluation" (Bakhtin, "Epic and Novel" 16). More than any single hero, whose passivity and public-mindedness have been emphasized by critics ranging from Voltaire to Georg Lukács, the true protagonist of epic is the language of tradition. Much of the force of *I Malavoglia* rests on Verga's capacity to create a latter-day epic discourse in which the Bakhtinian touchstones of hierarchy, piety, and tradition speak through the choral univocity of the novel's sources of authority and law (the paterfamilias, the community, and, more ominously, the work's legendary fatalism). The eventual breakdown of the Malavoglia family, the novel's main narrative trajectory, occurs in the text's transition from being an epic of Aci Trezza's fishermen to a novel of the younger 'Ntoni's self. In failing to respect what he calls the "chiacchiere senza sugo" ("insipid talk") of the old, 'Ntoni shatters the linguistic covenant binding him to earlier generations of Malavoglia (*Malavoglia* 322; *Medlar Tree* 165). His quest for personal identity—he shares his grandfather padron 'Ntoni's name but not his worldview—becomes a linguistic struggle against the proverbs of his elders (*gli antichi*) and the family dead (*i morti*). He dares to interpret where interpretation is forbidden, and his hermeneutic transgression transforms the epic narrative surrounding his family for centuries into the tragic, discursive openness of his failed bildungsroman.

As with the proverbs in Verga—reified figures of speech much like Dante's metaphors of *contrapasso* in *Inferno*—Visconti's images of chorality in *La terra trema* represent immutable cultural practices that stand to revive an epic past threatened by a modernizing world and its novelistic discourses, which find a spokesperson in the "antichoral" 'Ntoni. Like Verga's proverbs, Visconti's choral imagery reveals the hermeneutic covenant binding the generations by historicizing the visual discourses associated with Sicily's mythic past and its sacred clichés. That class should trump nation in the visual choral discourses of *La terra trema* squares with the general leftist slant of most neorealist cinema, but with a difference: in focusing on the mythic elements of Sicilian life and landscape, Visconti's epic cinematography infuses his ideological message with the lifeblood of high cultural forms—especially Homeric literature—that locate his representations in Bakhtin's "absolute past . . . walled off" from the present. Thus, and as one might expect in so theatrically minded a director, Visconti's chorus comes closest of all to the modes and motifs of its original Greek tragic form. By combining the timelessness of epic with the pointed social commentary of the Verghian chorus, *La terra trema* bears witness to rebuilding an Italy that has one foot in and one foot out of history, with both squarely set in the international class struggle.

All told, the choral imagery in neorealist film stemmed from a sense of commitment beholden more often than not (especially in Visconti) to leftist discourses about the political function of the artist. That chorality in modern Italian art became associated with cinematic neorealism and the discourse of *italianità* suggests the degree to which the choral was thought to have found its supreme expression in the emerging medium of film, the total art especially poised for sociopolitical intervention. What is remarkable about this aesthetic postwar chorality is that, despite its marriage to the newest and most technically advanced of the sister arts (film), it still shared many characteristics with the notions of tragic and dramatic chorality that had made the concept seminal in ancient Greece. Tellingly, the filmmaker who labeled his work choral and created the images that first linked the concept to neorealism, Rossellini, eventually moved away from these representations of solidarity and collective testimony. After completing the last film of his postwar trilogy, *Germania anno zero* (*Germany, Year Zero* [1948]), Rossellini made a series of interior, psychological films with Ingrid Bergman in the early 1950s that one could describe as *antichoral,* because of their emphasis on interior life and failed human interaction. Just as the so-called economic miracle ended Italy's material crises of the postwar period, the new generation of neorealist-trained filmmakers—including Michelangelo Antonioni, Federico Fellini, and Pier Paolo Pasolini—became associated with an auteurist style whose private and inchoate symbolism left little space for the nationalist and class-inflected choral imagery that defined much classic film of the 1940s. In a retraction of the previous generation's choral ethos, Antonioni announced in 1958 that the era for films about "stolen bikes" had ended, an ironic commentary on the persistence of films made in the spirit of De Sica's *Ladri di biciclette*. Not incidentally, Antonioni's remarks appeared just a short time after Rossellini proclaimed in 1954 that it was no longer possible to make films in "bombed cities."[36] But the subsequent freedom to explore what Bazin labeled the "neorealism of the person" in 1950s Italian cinema would have been inconceivable without the rich fund of choral concepts and forms created by those artists, Rossellini and Visconti supreme among them, who had sought to resurrect a national spirit ravaged by total war.[37]

CHAPTER TWO

Beyond Beauty

Cinematic Allegory and the Question of Italy

Soleva Roma, che 'l buon mondo feo,
due soli aver, che l'una e l'altra strada
facean vedere, e del mondo e di Deo.
(Rome, which made the world good, used to have two suns that made us see
different paths, one of the world and the other of God.)

—Dante, *Purgatorio* 16

That cinema appeared so much later than its sister arts had, as one might expect, both advantages and disadvantages. Because film lacked the authority of poetry, painting, and music, it faced the ongoing challenge of establishing its aesthetic value to its predecessors. The challenge was intensified by the widespread prejudice that cinema, the offspring of technology and capitalism, was the least humanistic and most commercial of the arts—and so, the refrain went, it lacked the "aura" of less-mechanized forms.[1] Yet the early perception of its artistic shortcomings also had a liberating effect: the medium could enter into some of the most acrimonious aesthetic debates with lighter baggage. Few skeptics could accuse early directors of, say, the cultural elitism often associated with the rarefied modes of neoclassical aesthetics or contrapuntal composition. Nor were many pioneering filmmakers charged with the ideological *mauvaise foi* of the introverted romantic artist contemplating his lonely, lovely hills. Moreover, the late arrival of their medium enabled filmmakers to address, self-consciously or not, age-old crises in the history of art with a wealth of information and clarity of principles unavailable to their earlier counterparts. Cinema's fabled contribution to the discourse of realism, for instance, was both anticipated and nourished by the emergence of the historical novel in Victor Hugo, Alessandro Manzoni, and Walter Scott, as well as by the development of literary realism proper in such novelists as Honoré de Balzac, Gustave Flaubert, and Émile Zola.

It is striking, however, to note the often-unexpected manner in which the concepts and motifs of the predecessor media have resurfaced in film. For example, the free indirect style associated with the historically referential realist novel reemerged in Pier Paolo Pasolini as the means of an antinarrative, dreamlike, and "poetic" mode of filmic exposition ("Cinema of Poetry" 175–78). Similarly, the richly descriptive techniques to which Roland Barthes attributed *l'effet de réel* became for Sergei Eisenstein a source of inspiration for metaphorical and nondescriptive visual representation: the montage. Thus, cinema, like Minerva's owl, took to the air late in the day, but the earlier hours did little to help one predict its patterns of flight.

The relation between symbol and allegory, a matter of contention in literary interpretation since at least Homer, represents an instance in which the arrival of film dramatically reconfigured the terms of an aesthetic debate.[2] Of the two rhetorical figures, allegory is the older, with a definition stretching back to the ancient Greek for "speaking otherwise than one seems to speak" and with etymological roots in the Greek for "speaking in public" (*allos*, "other," plus *agoreuein*, "to speak," originally "to harangue"; from *agora*, "marketplace" or "site of assembly").[3] Allegory entails an instrumental or didactic message made public, as it were, by a signifier that proclaims a direct though not necessarily open or transparent relationship with its signified, often by linking together figures of speech for thematic effect in a process that Quintilian describes as sustained metaphor.[4] Whereas allegory denotes a particular meaning, the symbol (the term derives from a Latin neologism based on the Greek compound for "to throw together") conveys its meanings without explicit connection.[5] During the romantic age in particular, a critical mass of aesthetic thinkers argued that the symbol was the more aesthetically refined of the two figures, because it was believed to have a figurative valence—or "translucence," according to Samuel Taylor Coleridge—that the purportedly more abstract and less poetic trope of allegory did not.[6] Thus, a value judgment ensued and endured until the linguistic turn in the criticism of the 1960s and 1970s, with "symbolism being good and [allegory] bad."[7]

In Italian cultural history, however, allegorical representation enjoyed a privileged position, especially during the fraught drive for Italian political unity during romanticism and the Risorgimento. In the nineteenth century, discussions of allegory were often connected with issues surrounding Italian national character, as we see in the heated polemics stimulated by the French author Germaine de Staël, with her notorious critique of the Italian preference for neoclassical and mythological rhetoric in the essay "De l'esprit des traductions" ("The Spirit of Translation" [1816]). The fierce rebuttals her essay received, including the unpublished reply of the adolescent Giacomo Leopardi, emphasized that allegory and myth were native cultural idioms that connected Italians to their great literary heritage of antiquity and the Renaissance. Another potent reason motivated many Italians to resist the romantic vogue of the symbol and rejection of allegory. Since Dante, Italian poets have often enjoyed pride of place in the discourse of national identity in the figurative Italian *agora*.[8] Many are the names working in this tradition—Dante, Petrarch, Vittorio Alfieri, Ugo Foscolo, Alessandro Manzoni, Giacomo Leopardi, Giosuè Carducci, Gabriele D'Annunzio—and many are the texts they produced that are read as allegories for the Italian quest for unification, actual and metaphorical. For example, Foscolo's poem "Dei sepolcri" ("On Sepulchers" [1807]), an approximately three-hundred-line hymn on the phenomenology of mourning and the role of sepulchers in forging cultural identity, is remembered primarily as the vehicle of the Florentine Santa Croce's transformation into the allegorical Italian pantheon and not as a graceful meditation on the shelters we erect to house the dead. The case of Foscolo recalls the fate of many of the above authors (especially Dante), as well as of other artists, including Rossellini, whose fictional *Rome, Open City* many Italians falsely consider to be an actual documentary of the heroic partisan struggle.[9]

Despite the potential limitations in such nationalist readings, Foscolo underscored the potential utility of allegory: "Ridiculous as allegories may appear to metaphysical critics, they have been, nevertheless, the finest and most useful materials for artists to work from; and the disrepute into which they have now fallen has arisen from the injudicious use that has been made of them, and from the bad taste of their modern inventors: for every allegory is, in truth, only an abstract idea personified, which, by thus acting more rapidly and easily on our senses and our imagination, takes a readier hold of the mind" ("Dissertation" 144). This eminently Italian tendency to promote the didactic potential of allegory, especially for political reasons, permeated Italian cinematic culture after World War II, a time when Italian filmmakers took the lead in creating discourses of national identity. Though cinema had been central to constructing *italianità* before World War II—Mussolini had created Cinecittà in 1937 amid great fanfare[10]—during the reconstruction the phrase "rifare l'Italia" ("remake Italy") became a popular refrain for directors who vowed to reject the false optimism and escapism of the Fascist era. Most famously, the new realism or neorealism, many believed, should promote sober story lines anchored in Italy's difficult postwar realities, which filmmakers could represent through natural lighting, lengthy shots, dialect-based speech, the use of nonprofessional actors, urban and unadorned sets, and ideological (often communist-inspired) incisiveness.

Of course, the actual films associated with neorealism produced a wealth of approaches that make it difficult to reduce them to a single formula. Despite this diversity, a defining characteristic of neorealism that shaped subsequent cinematic movements was its self-conscious development of a poetics of national allegory. In a reversal of the hero-mongering of films produced in support of Mussolini,[11] neorealists elevated to the level of character and even protagonist previously underrepresented social classes, including the diverse partisan groups of Rossellini's *Rome, Open City* and *Paisà,* the teeming unemployed proletariat of Vittorio De Sica's *Bicycle Thieves,* and the Sicilian fishermen of Luchino Visconti's *La terra trema.* A recurring theme in much neorealist cinema that became a touchstone in the following decades was the critical interpretation of Italian history.[12] By rejecting the send-ups of a glorious Italian past from many films in the interwar period and ascribing war-related guilt and culpability to where it was deemed merited, neorealist films translated chronic problems of Italian history—its *questione della lingua,* regional fragmentation, political corruption, and class struggles—into cinematic imagery that drew on allegorical principles similar to those that had inspired authors of the Risorgimento.

A decisive issue in the postwar debates about neorealism was, not surprisingly, the question of the literary—a controversy that evoked many of the concerns of the romantic symbol-allegory debate. On the one hand, film purists argued for the preservation of intrinsic differences between the two media, cinema and literature, and claimed that to combine their forms was the aesthetic equivalent of mixing oil with water. The following words from 1952 by Vittorio De Sica's acclaimed scriptwriter and a committed Marxist, Cesare Zavattini, distilled the politically inflected animus against literary narrative: "The most important characteristic, and the most important innovation, of what is called neorealism, it seems to me, is to have realised that the necessity of the 'story' was only an unconscious way of disguising a human defeat, and that the kind of imagination it involved was simply a technique of superimposing dead formulas over living social facts" (Zavattini, "Some Ideas" 217). Some purists also questioned the idea of the author itself, claiming that the emphasis on a guiding creative hand bespoke a bourgeois, politically suspect nostalgia for a cult of the artist that an industrializing and proletarian-centric Italy should no longer tolerate. On the other hand, the literary promoters of film, in line with the influential platform developed by Mario Alicata and Giuseppe De Santis in the Fascist era, countered that since all artistic media are representations of some kind, the key for directors was to base their work on that aesthetic form that conveyed the most effective message, which Alicata and De Santis located in Verga.[13] They write: "Giovanni Verga non ha solamente creato una grande opera di poesia, ma ha creato un paese, un tempo, una società: a noi che crediamo nell'arte specialmente in quanto creatrice di verità, la Sicilia omerica e leggendaria dei *Malavoglia* . . . ci sembra nello stesso tempo offrire l'ambiente più solido e umano, più miracolosamente vergine e vero, che possa ispirare la fantasia di un cinema il quale cerchi cose e fatti in un tempo e in uno spazio di realtà, per riscattarsi dai facili suggerimenti di un mortificato gusto borghese" (217). ("Giovanni Verga not only created a body of poetry but also a region, an epoch, a society. To those of us who believe in art, especially as a creator of truth, the Homeric and legendary Sicily of *I Malavoglia* [and other works by Verga] seems to us to offer simultaneously the most solid and human, most miraculously virgin and true environment that can inspire the fantasy of a cinema that seeks things and facts in a time and space of reality, in order to rescue itself from the facile suggestions of a moribund bourgeois taste.")

Alicata and De Santis's choice of Verga is instructive, because it was indeed this Sicilian author who performed the most rigorous revision of the romantic notion of allegory and its role in fostering the discourse of national identity. Critics have traditionally viewed Verga as a locus classicus for gauging the legacies of Italian romanticism: his early literary formation bears the traces of a patriotic and romantic sensibility in works including *Amore e patria* (*Love and Country* [1858]), *I carbonari della montagna* (*The Carbonari of the Mountain* [1861–62]), and the *Ultime lettere di Jacopo Ortis*-like *Sulle lagune* (*On the Lagoons* [1863]).[14] The mature Verga's subsequent turn to a more impersonal, positivist, and scientifically conceived style—especially in his study of a poor Sicilian fishing family in *I Malavoglia*—led him to counter the allegorical projections of national identity typical of Italian romanticism.[15] His later work promotes a poetics of the fragmentary and local, wherein regionalism assumes priority over national unity, dialect over language, and received wisdom over abstract knowledge.

For example, in *I Malavoglia,* the story of a poor Sicilian fishing family, Verga's miniature catalogue of ships deconstructs the abiding premises of romantic allegory in the landmark novel *I promessi sposi* (*The Betrothed* [1827]), by Alessandro Manzoni. The ship of the Malavoglia family, the *Provvidenza,* both acknowledges and subverts the providential historicism that underwrites Renzo and Lucia's overcoming of the obstacles to their contested marriage in Manzoni's narrative. Verga's deference to Manzoni rests in his depiction of a dignified family whose humility and piety find a suitable analogue in the name of its ship, whereas the irony derives from the family's relentless lack of actual fortune in both the spiritual and the economic sense. Early in the novel, the patriarch Master 'Ntoni purchases an order of lupin beans on credit and orders his son Bastianazzo to transfer them to market in the *Provvidenza*. A storm, however, claims both the ship's cargo and Bastianazzo's life, negating any allegorical fulfillment suggested by the ship's name, which becomes the occasion of bitter wordplay. After it is pulled from the sea, some of the villagers kick the personified ship's belly while the pharmacist, Don Franco, announces, "Bella provvidenza che avete!" ("A fine providence you've got!"), a phrase that echoes his earlier taunt, "Bella *Provvidenza,* eh! pardon 'Ntoni!" ("Some Providence, eh, Master 'Ntoni?") (*Malavoglia* 224, 207; *Medlar Tree* 56, 35).[16] The punning on this Manzonian keyword culminates in the passages devoted to the death of the middle child, Luca, who is the mirror image of Bastianazzo, just as the eldest, prodigal son 'Ntoni is the headstrong parallel to his namesake and grandfather, Master 'Ntoni.[17] Word reaches the village of the destruction of Luca's battleship *Il Re d'Italia (The King of Italy),* an allegorical ship of state that embodies the new national identity foisted on the inhabitants of this remote Sicilian island of Aci Trezza in the form of compulsory military service, onerous tax burdens, and labyrinthine bureaucracy. Verga's resistance to any form of providential design results in a work that defines itself negatively against the Manzonian precedent, while seeking new avenues for construing regional identity based on ethnographic description rather than transcendental faith.[18]

Verga's "epic" sense of national allegory would have a profound effect on his most influential adapter, Luchino Visconti, in *La terra trema.*[19] Following Verga's text, in Visconti's film the Valastro vainly look out to sea for their family and ship (figure 8). In a mise-en-scène that Guglielmo Moneti ties to Visconti's long-standing investment in opera (139), a choral element is in full effect as the women bear witness to a reenactment of ancient tragedy: the death at sea of those seeking to provide for their kin. The women's broad generational composite suggests the recurrent nature of the deathwatch, a sad fact of life for the female villagers. The ancient accents of the mise-en-scène find further expression in the Homeric landscape bounded by the omnipresent *faraglioni,* the legendary rocks that separate Aci Trezza from the modern world. By remaining visually fixed in the domain of legend, the film's pictorial

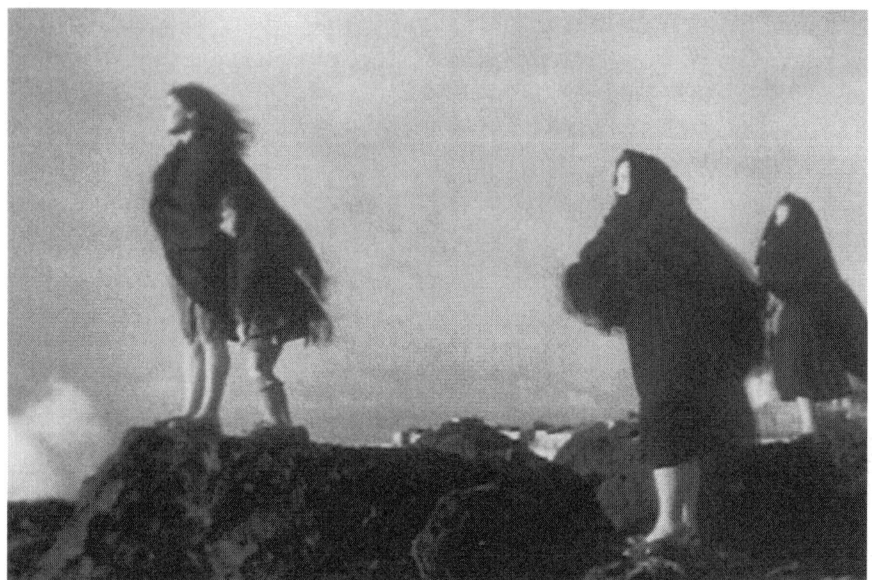

Figure 8 The Valastro women look out to sea for their men as Visconti combines mythic and naturalist elements *(La terra trema).*

dimension reinforces the thematic point made at the beginning by the narrator, who remarks that the language of the fishermen is not Italian but the humble dialect of poor workers whose story is told throughout the world, wherever and whenever men exploit other men. Thus, Visconti's antinationalist, class-inflected bias mirrors Verga's intransigent stance against the recently created nation ironically invoked in the name of Luca Malavoglia's sunken ship, *Il Re d'Italia.*

In her study of the literary master narratives of cinematic realism, Lucia Re adduces a less likely influence alongside Verga: Manzoni (108, 110–12). Both Manzoni's *I promessi sposi* and Rossellini's *Rome, Open City* probe the effect of foreign oppression on the lives of two poor engaged couples (respectively, Renzo-Lucia and Francesco-Pina) and translate their trials into the plight of an entire nation. I would go further and suggest that Rossellini's *Rome, Open City,* in line with Manzoni's religious vision, conflates Christian and socialist discourses in the interests of national allegory.

It is a widely held view that the temporal and thematic center of Rossellini's film, the death of the partisan Pina at the hands of the Nazi occupiers of Rome, shifts it into the tragic mode and horizon of historical concerns typical of the neorealist movement.[20] Before this scene the film's documentary

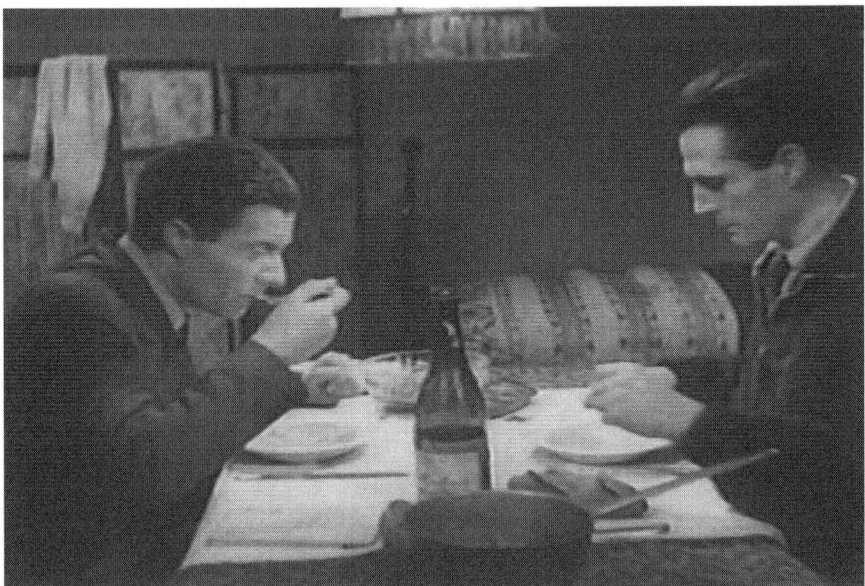

Figure 9 Rossellini sets political and religious symbolism in dialogue as the intellectual Manfredi (left) and proletarian Francesco (right) break bread together during the Resistance *(Rome, Open City).*

gravitas is leavened by comic images, including the priest Don Prieto playing soccer with a group of boys. In the first half of the film a meeting takes place between Manfredi, an Italian intellectual who represents the elite left of the Resistance, and Francesco, who embodies in Gramscian terms the organic proletarian vanguard in the ongoing class struggle. Their first encounter is over dinner, and the ensuing imagery is rife with symbols. They break bread in a frame of starkly symmetrical composition (figure 9), as a bottle of wine divides the screen in perfect halves and functions as an emblem both of conviviality and, through a dramatic configuration of Rossellini's adherence to ritual Catholicism, the blood of Christ. Iconically, the bottle serves as evidence of Rossellini's subsuming of social progressivism in Christian faith, thus linking him in a tradition of intellectual forebears that culminates in the romantic Manzoni.[21] In breaking bread together amid this religious visual rhetoric, Manfredi and Francesco consecrate a political bond, a parallel to the imminent domestic union of the *promessi sposi* Pina and Francesco. Yet the objects in the scene retain their individual symbolic resonance without lapsing into overt allegorical didacticism: they are palpable and manifest narrative entities in and of themselves as markers of wartime poverty and

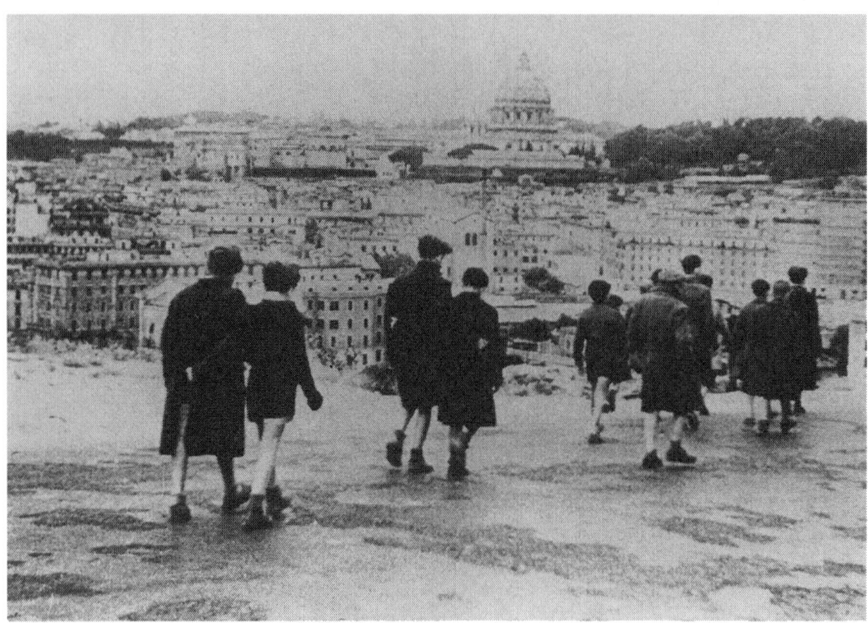

Figure 10 Partisan youths march toward St. Peter's after witnessing the execution of their leader, the priest Don Pietro *(Rome, Open City)*. Excelsa / Mayer-Burstyn / The Kobal Collection.

simple proletarian furnishings. Rossellini's ethical, a priori refusal to impose a directorial worldview onto the camera's eye prevents the bottle and bread from slipping into a purely thematic and denotative register that would render them immaterial means to a doctrinal end.[22]

The rhetorical dialectic, however, switches gears after the death of Pina. Henceforth the allegorical meanings become explicit and at times heavy-handed, for in Rossellini's lens the liberation of Italy, if not the soul of the nation, is at stake. During a visit to a restaurant by Francesco and Manfredi after Pina is shot, the Germans lead actual lambs to slaughter, and it takes little interpretive energy to substitute the Italian people as the sacrificial lambs. The film's didactic motion culminates in the execution of Don Pietro, who faces his killers with a mixture of stoicism and Christian resignation. Have strength, he is told, as he is led to the firing squad. "O non è difficile morire bene," he answers; "è difficile vivere bene" ("Oh, it's not difficult to die well; it's difficult to live well"). At this point the film's supreme allegorical emblems enter the frame: the youngsters who have formed a guerilla squad of anti-Fascist resistance under their leader, Romoletto, namesake of the eternal

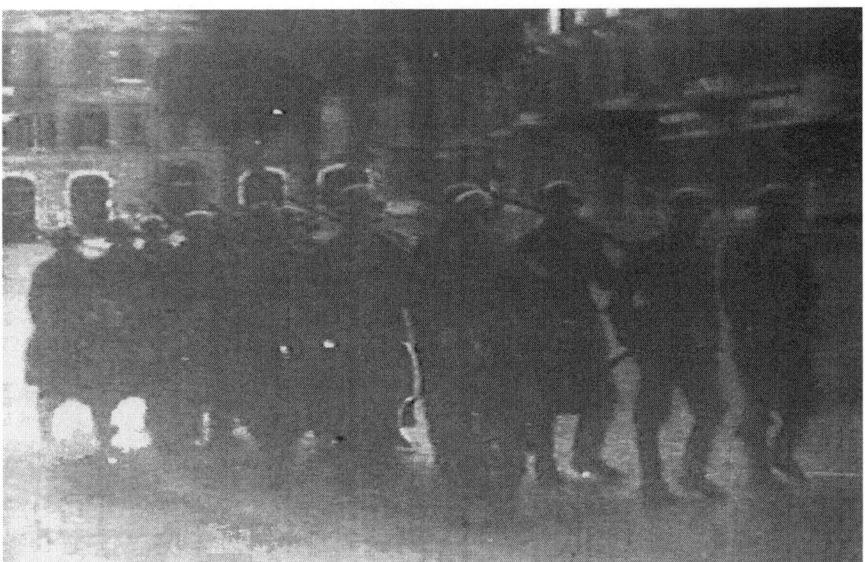

Figure 11 Rossellini's opening scene, a documentary shot of marching German soldiers, points allegorically to the similar march of partisan youths at film's end in figure 10 *(Rome, Open City)*.

city's founder, Romulus. Following the execution, the youths march away as emblems of the eventual triumph of the Resistance over Nazism, with the Rome that must be rebuilt in front of them and the dome of Saint Peter's looming on the horizon (figure 10).

The scene, in Walter Benjamin's spirit, allegorically fulfills the opening shot of the film, which was of German soldiers on a similar marching path (figure 11).[23] Rossellini's young heroes deliver a hopeful and militant message, perhaps at the expense of the symbolic freedom of the film's first half but in the name of a morally renewed and allegorically *rifatta* (remade) Italy. Fittingly, Benjamin described allegory as "beyond beauty" (*German Tragic Drama* 178), because of its capacity to sacrifice the pretense of pure reference in order to redeem a concept or doctrine, which in Rossellini's case assumes the form of a Dantesque overture to the twin master discourses of the Italian cultural tradition, the Roman history and Catholic faith from *Purgatorio* 16.

The shift from neorealism to more auteurist modes of filmmaking remains a hotly debated point in film criticism in Italy and abroad. Luciano De Giusti sums up the transition of what he calls a "fall from neorealist utopia": "Il movimento riesce a soppravviere scendendo a patti con le convenzioni dei generi e la forza seduttiva del divismo. Accetta di integrarsi rinunciando ad alcune prerogative, ibridandosi in testi che si presentano come vere e proprie 'formazioni di compromesso.' Se sono relativamente pochi gli autori e le opere che tengono fede all'ispirazione originaria e ancora possono dirsi a pieno titolo neorealisti, sono molti i film infiltrati, attraversati, nobilitati o magari sporcati dal neorealismo" (21). ("The [neorealist] movement managed to survive by slowly adjusting itself to the conventions of genres and the seductive force of the star system. It agreed to integrate itself by renouncing some of its prerogatives, becoming a hybrid in works that presented themselves as true and proper 'structures of compromise.' If few were the number of filmmakers and films who remained faithful to the movement's original inspiration, many were the films infiltrated, permeated, and elevated—or perhaps dirtied—by neorealism"). It was precisely this mixed type of film, with one foot planted in the traditions of neorealism and the other in new cinematic pathways, that produced some of the most groundbreaking results of Italian cinema of the 1950s and 1960s. Neorealism, in short, became a contested heritage that inspired directors to translate its successes into new forms while shedding some of its more doctrinal and formulaic elements that the passing of time—and the changing sociopolitical milieu—had rendered less relevant if not obsolete.

Much in the same way that Verga dealt with his romantic legacy, Federico Fellini and Michelangelo Antonioni negotiated their neorealist inheritance by finding a new aesthetic idiom for Italian national identity through a re-envisioning of allegory. The title of Fellini's *La strada* (1954), the story of the traveling strongman Zampano and his eccentric companion, Gelsomina, suggests a trope in the organic and Coleridgean "translucent" sense, for the film is an actual road *(strada)* trip through the marginal Italy of vagrants, performers, and other misplaced figures. In this seminal example of auteur film, the dialectic between symbol and allegory is most prevalent in the so-called parable of the pebble involving Gelsomina and the Fool, Zampano's mortal enemy. "Tu non ci crederai, ma tutto quello che c'è a questo mondo serve a qualcosa" ("You won't believe it, but everything in this world is good for something"), says the alternately angelic and demonic Fool, even the pebble he picks up from the ground when he visits Gelsomina after provoking Zampano's arrest.[24] When Gelsomina asks him which stone, he says that it does not matter: every stone has its purpose, even the slightest. When Gelsomina questions him further, the Fool answers: "No, non lo so a cosa serve questo sasso qui, ma a qualcosa deve servire. Perché se questo è inutile, allora è inutile tutto—anche le stelle" ("No, I don't know what it's good for, this pebble, but it must be good for something. Because if this one is useless, then everything else is useless—even the stars"). The Fool's teaching offers an allegorical lesson in interpretation with regard to both the autobiographical narrative of Gelsomina and to Fellini's personal journey "beyond neorealism."[25] By collapsing the distance between the pebbles and the stars, the Fool reminds Gelsomina that her thoughts need not be confined to the depressing material realm of her homely appearance, unbearable relationship, and financial poverty. In metacinematic terms the imbuing of the stone with magical and mysterious powers implies the distance Fellini had traveled from his early days of neorealist tutelage (he was a scriptwriter for Rossellini's *Rome, Open City* and *Paisà*).

The seeds of Fellini's ultimate break with many touchstones of the neorealist tradition were sown in his early collaboration with Rossellini. Much like his assistant Fellini, and much to the chagrin of more sociopolitical-minded critics, Rossellini often went beyond the documentary and historical elements of his films to explore the type of spiritual and metaphysical terrain covered in *La strada*. By linking the naturally allegorical stars to the more grounded and open symbol of the stone—the slate synecdoche for the *strada* itself—Gelsomina attests to Fellini's reinterpretation of the didactic and politically charged allegories that had come to be associated with neorealism. Yet he does not lose the neorealist commitment to fathoming national identity. For the course of Fellini's narrative *strada* meanders through much of Italy: from the coast, where Gelsomina is born; to the mountains, where Zampano abandons her; back to the coast, where she dies. Fellini, however, directs his camera not at the sites of historical and public importance but at the spatial and temporal interstices where the everyday lives of his characters are played out, beyond the grand narratives and public debates of neorealism proper. The mantle of the polemicist was never one that Fellini wore comfortably. All told, the cinematic allegory in *La strada* offers a nonideological view into the state of a nation's soul in all its aesthetically productive neurosis and incongruity.

A similar practice of linking together individual symbols in the interests of national allegory appears in Antonioni's film *Il deserto rosso* (*Red Desert* [1964]).[26] In the manner of a Eugenio Montale, whose Hermetic poetry in *Ossi di seppia* of the 1920s told Italians "ciò che *non* siamo, ciò che *non* vogliamo" ("what we are *not*, what we do *not* want"), Antonioni's highly stylized and often impenetrable film sequences reveal the unease and sense of

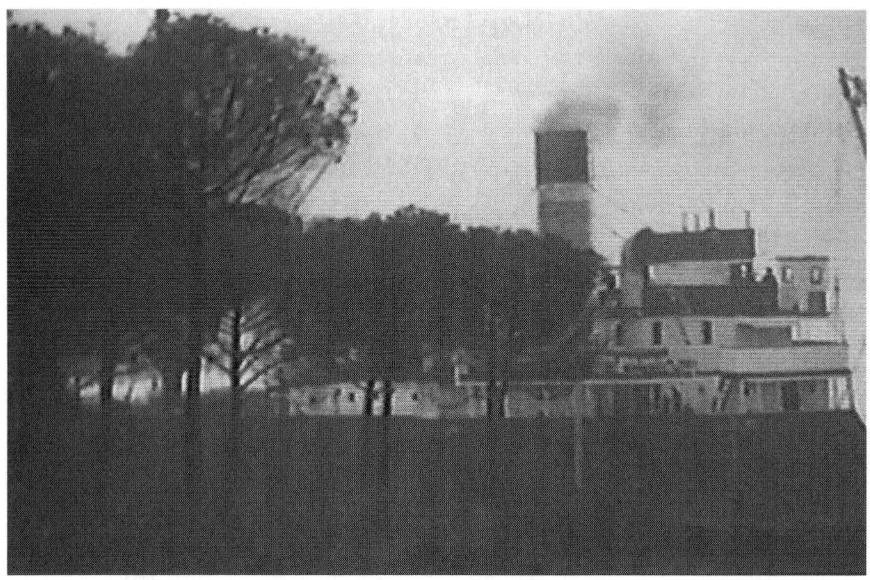

Figure 12 Antonioni's omnipresent ship occupies a range of symbols, from the ecological to the existential, for the troubled protagonist Giuliana *(Red Desert).*

loss permeating the rebuilt Italian middle and upper classes of the 1950s and 1960s.[27] In narrative terms *Deserto rosso* tells very little. The industrialist Corrado visits Ravenna to recruit workers for a manufacturing endeavor in Patagonia and, during his stay, falls in love with his friend and business partner's wife, Giuliana, recently released from a mental home where she was committed after attempting suicide. Antonioni leaves her illness vague enough to suggest that Giuliana suffers not from a specific medical condition but from a general malaise. Part of her problem is hermeneutic, for she cannot distinguish between what is and is not important in her life. Open to everything, she is overwhelmed by the most banal forms of the quotidian (her child's toys terrify her, and her husband's embrace repels her). The world has too much meaning for her: love one thing, she recalls her doctor telling her, but not everything.

As Fellini does with the pebble, Antonioni condenses the symbolic mysteries of his film into a single object, an omnipresent ship (figure 12). This ocular and sonic analogue to Giuliana's troubled perceptions assumes a range of associations: an escape from the industrial wasteland of Ravenna and neurotic landscapes of her mind, the domineering technology that threatens her relationship to natural realms like the sea and her body, even the random intrusion of external elements that thwart narrative causality in this strangely paced film. The viewer perceives the polyvalent ship through the neurotic filter of Giuliana's consciousness via Antonioni's recurrent use of the free indirect point-of-view shot adduced by Pasolini as a supreme example of the "cinema of poetry" ("Cinema of Poetry" 178–80). In this "painterly" film, the camera registers Giuliana's perceptions in a variety of tonal and chromatic scales, with near eclipse of natural lighting.[28] The ship's referential intransigence culminates at film's end in a dialogue between Giuliana and a Turkish sailor, as neither can understand a word of the other's speech. "Se Lei mi punge, Lei non soffre" ("If you pinch me, you do not suffer"), she says to him. He stares at her uncomprehendingly and chatters on in his own parallel linguistic universe.

For all its symbolic openness, however, the ship ultimately fits within the larger allegorical structure of Antonioni's representation of a reconstituted Italian middle class deaf to the hard-hitting messages of the neorealist period and its nationalist metaphors.[29] Early in the film Corrado alludes to principles reminiscent of neorealism's, which he cheapens by proclaiming an empty and unconvincing overture to universal justice when Giuliana asks him about his politics: "È come domandare in che cosa credi," he tells her. "Sono parole grosse" ("It's like asking what you believe in. Those are big words"). After hearing Corrado's weak pledge to a hodgepodge of humanity, progress, and social reform, Giuliana's ironic conclusion, "Hai messo insieme un bel gruppetto di parole" ("You've strung together some nice-sounding words"), indicates that the allegorical meanings of the engaged cinema of the postwar era, once felt in the blood, now roll off the skin. To echo Marx's dictum, the crises that first appeared as neorealist tragedy ultimately resurface as auteur farce.

In a manner reminiscent of Verga's critique of romantic allegory, Fellini and Antonioni transformed the moral and historical claims of postwar film into less explicitly political national allegories responsive to the failures, regrets, and spiritual yearnings of both a rebuilt society (Antonioni) and its disenfranchised populace (Fellini). Since I have treated the relationship between allegory and national identity in both text and image, I close this chapter by mentioning an arresting scene from ancient literature that partakes of the verbal as well as the visual and encapsulates much of my argument. In book 3 of the *Aeneid,* Aeneas relates to Dido how he left a burning Troy with his father and household gods on his back and leading his son by the hand. The image establishes many of the subsequent terms for Italian allegorical representation: the hero bears on his shoulders the burden of the past in the form of his father, along with his spiritual behest embodied in the Penates, while he shepherds a future generation (his son) into an uncertain political realm and an unforged nation. A poet haunted, I believe, by this passage was Dante, who sought a solution to its challenges in the two suns thesis quoted in this chapter's epigraph, expressing his view that the emergence of Rome as an imperial center was the divinely ordained precondition for its ultimate ascent to the seat of Christianity. In postwar Italian cinema, memories of Italian empire struck an ominous and unwelcome chord as the residue of an oppressive Fascist ideology and militarism. For the neorealists and such predecessors as Verga, however, the task established by Aeneas remained: how to reconcile the demands of "remaking Italy" in both a secular and a spiritual sense. Rossellini, Visconti, Fellini, and Antonioni negotiated this challenge within the confines of allegorical discourses whose burdens placed them into the contested question of Italy and, in Benjamin's words, beyond beauty.

PART TWO

CINEMAS OF POETRY

CHAPTER THREE

Rossellini's Cinema of Poetry

Voyage to Italy

Though the vast bibliography on Roberto Rossellini contains relatively few items that address the issue of adaptation, his work during the so-called Ingrid Bergman years (1949–55) anticipates and synthesizes many of the era's concerns about film's interrelations with literature. The critical lacuna is not surprising, given Rossellini's abiding reputation as a cinematic purist who disdained the shooting script in favor of ad hoc and improvisational techniques.[1] Moreover, the legendary debates over adaptation during neorealism associated Rossellini's work with the antiadaptation school organized around Cesare Zavattini's call for "story-less" films in his manifesto "Some Ideas on Cinema" from 1952, a distillation of the neorealist principles from his collaboration with Vittorio De Sica in films including *Sciuscià*, *Bicycle Thieves*, and *Umberto D.*[2] Any influence by Rossellini here was paradoxical, for he never pronounced on adaptation with the polemical edge of Zavattini and the pro–Giovanni Verga adapters Mario Alicata, Giuseppe De Santis, and Luchino Visconti; nor did he dedicate himself to the philosophical discussions that piqued the interest of Carlo Lizzani and other young filmmakers whom Rossellini helped rally to the neorealist cause. Thus, it was more Rossellini's works than his words that directly and indirectly shaped the approach of a generation of filmmakers to adaptation. For example, just one year after Zavattini's essay, Rossellini's future assistant François Truffaut condemned the adaptive strategies of the French "cinema of quality" tradition and promoted instead the highly personal *écriture* of such works as Robert Bresson's adaptation in 1951 of George Bernanos's novel *Journal d'un curé de campagne* (*Diary of a Country Priest* [1936])—a style of filmmaking that for many directors of the French New Wave reached its apotheosis in work that one critic called a "grande cine-poema" ("great cinematic poem"): Rossellini's *Voyage to Italy* (1954).[3]

As is typical, the polemics of Zavattini and Truffaut centered on the adaptation of the novel, whose elements of characterization, plot, and narration have historically made it the most quarried of all literary genres by filmmak-ers.[4] Despite Zavattini's incendiary remarks, novelistic sources permeated neorealist cinema, which Alberto Asor Rosa described as representing a "trionfo del narrativo" ("triumph of narrative").[5] Though its horizon of concerns loomed a world apart from these contemporary Italian and European debates, an event held in New York in October 1953 illuminates film's interrelations with literature in the light of the often-overlooked category of lyric poetry. The symposium entitled "Poetry and the Film" questioned the aesthetic principles of the "poetic" film, the relation between the visual and verbal in the arts, and, most quixotically of all, the definition of poetry and its cinematic equivalents. The event's participants, which included the filmmaker Maya Deren, playwright Arthur Miller, and poet Dylan Thomas, produced no clear theoretical agenda or systematic program on poetry's link to film, but they did provide useful analytical tools and the seeds of a critical vocabulary for approaching this generally overlooked problem in the history of aesthetics.[6] Indeed, the connection between film and lyric poetry remains one of the more vexed among the sister arts.[7] With the notable exception of works by early pioneers D. W. Griffith, Joseph Moncure March, and many artists associated with French surrealism, relatively few lyric poems have been adapted for the screen,[8] even though film's belated arrival made it appealing to avant-garde poets and artists seeking to expand the formal reach of their respective fields.[9] This relative paucity of "poetic adaptations" applies principally to lyric poetry, since dramatic, epic, and narrative poems have served as constant sources for filmmakers going back to the origins of cinema. Yet the fluidity and capaciousness of the terms involved have created a surplus of theoretical confusion about just what "poetic cinema" signifies.[10] For Pier Paolo Pasolini, the subject's most influential exponent, the *cinema di poesia* meant capturing the unfiltered, prelinguistic unconscious of his characters through the free indirect point-of-view shot; for Sergei Eisenstein the visual rhythms of montage were the equivalent of metrical verse, a formula that allowed him to discern the protocinematic elements in poets including John Milton and Alexander Pushkin; and for artists as diverse as Derek Jarman and Stan Brakhage the lyric film translated into a symbol-laden revolt against traditional narrative.[11]

Voyage to Italy, a film released in 1954 and made the same year as the "Poetry and the Film" symposium (1953), establishes a unique position in the film-poetry relation while also signaling important new developments in Rossellini's oeuvre. Its story centers on an estranged British couple, Alex and

Katherine Joyce, who travel to Naples by car to attend to an inheritance left to them by their Uncle Homer, an eccentric expatriate who made Italy his home during World War II.[12] The trip is the first time, Katherine tells Alex, that the two have spent much time alone together, away from their comfortable society life in England. The results are hardly fortunate. They backbite, bicker, and upset one another to such a degree that they eventually decide to divorce, only then to have their ambiguous reconciliation at film's end. Like the earlier films *Francesco, giullare di Dio* (*The Flowers of Saint Francis* [1950]) and *Europa '51* (1952), *Voyage to Italy* references a range of literary works that appear and disappear as randomly as the events and nonevents in this deliberately nondramatic and meandering film.[13]

In a break with his films from the mid 1940s, the Rossellini of the late 1940s and 1950s drew increasingly on literary sources and worked in collaboration with some of the leading authors in European literature, most notably the key figure in the film-poetry relationship at the time, Jean Cocteau, who wrote the screenplay for Rossellini's *Una voce umana* (*A Human Voice* [1947]).[14] The most obvious literary debt of *Voyage to Italy* is to James Joyce's tale from *Dubliners,* "The Dead" (1914), which provides the motif of a tragic young admirer who courts—and, in a sense, dies for—the lead female character before she settles into the stalemate of her marriage and its main palliative, nostalgia. Beyond this structural conceit, Rossellini borrowed from Joyce the haunted atmosphere that blurs the lines between the past and present and keeps characters at the awkward impasse between memory's aura and the bitter shortcomings of lived events. The film was supposed to have been based on Colette's *Duo* (1934), which also narrates the disintegration of a marriage owing to a crisis of intimacy. Yet when Rossellini failed to secure the rights to Colette's story, he was forced to abandon the project and accept his favorite situation of all: the lack of script and story. He and his collaborator, Vitaliano Brancati (the Sicilian author to whom much of the film's literary qualities are due), actually composed an ersatz poem that was to have provided the initial impulse for the tensions driving Katherine and Alex apart before their sudden reconciliation.[15] Though the poem never made it into the film, its themes of the living dead and the dead living suffuse the cinematic narrative.

It would be reductive and misguided to describe Rossellini's use of these sources as "adaptations" per se, because the poem that figures so centrally in *Voyage to Italy* is a make-believe one and therefore not a literary source in the technical sense. Moreover, *Voyage to Italy* never sets in motion the dialogue between a classic text and its cinematic representation in the manner of, say, Pasolini's version of Giovanni Boccaccio's *Decameron,* a relationship that Dudley Andrew describes as "intersecting" ("Adaptation" 99).[16] In this sophisticated form of adaptation the film provides insight into the complexities of adaptation while also emphasizing the status of cinematic and literary works as two distinct aesthetic forms. Nor does Rossellini's use of literary sources in *Voyage to Italy* contain the sustained reading or interpretation that one finds in more conventional adapters, most notably the Visconti who produced films based on a range of major European authors. For Rossellini the literary text functioned, more often than not, as *pretext:* a bearer of some hint, suggestion, or theme to be prodded and teased out in the name of a goal or ideal of which he himself, as an emphatically intuitive filmmaker, was often not wholly aware.[17] With Rossellini the source text, just like any other figure, incident, or object, is deprived of its a priori conceptual and figurative ballast as it is incorporated into the film.[18] To invoke André Bazin's famous metaphor, for Rossellini literary texts are not, like the bricks of a house, sacrificed in the name of a larger unity or structure; they remain instead like the rocks that one uses to ford a river—the means to an end yet also as distinct and unassimilated as the individual blocks of stone.[19]

Just as it would be a mistake to label Rossellini's use of the film's imaginary poet, Charles Lewington, as an adaptation in the conventional sense, so, too, would it be misguided to consider his "cinema of poetry" to be the work of a director who coveted so-called poetic effects and the aesthetic prestige they can confer. Rossellini, in fact, refused to accept the epithet *poet;* nowhere, in the films of the Bergman years or, for that matter, any other of his works, does one find instances of what might be termed "art for art's sake."[20] More likely, Rossellini dedicated himself to film because he believed it was uniquely capable of discovering those new forms of knowledge that led him to pursue an encyclopedic project spanning four decades, more than fifty films, and a variety of genres. The "poetic" element in his work invokes the etymological sense of the term as a *poesis* (making)—a stance reminiscent of Pasolini's view that the natural fusion of cinema and poetry leads to the attainment of nonlinguistic, irrational forms of knowledge beholden to film's capacity to access directly the images of the unconscious and their montage-like modes of articulation.

Early in the film Alex learns that Katherine, prior to her marriage, had a young admirer, the expatriated writer Lewington, who had lived in Italy and authored the following verses that Katherine cites for Alex: "Temple of the spirit, no longer bodies but pure ascetic images, compared to which mere thought seems flesh, heavy, dim." I have explored elsewhere how Rossellini's citation of Lewington's verses forms part of his critique of the romantic myth of Italy created by foreigners during the age of the Grand Tour and perpetrated for centuries afterward (*Romantic Europe* 49–52). Katherine Joyce embodies a stereotypical, latter-day Grand Tourist enchanted by the passions of Italian life and splendor; Alex is the tritely rational workaholic northern visitor who disdains Italian laziness and somnolence ("I must say, one sleeps well in this country," he remarks); and Lewington represents the typically "romantic" poetaster both in his physical makeup ("thin, tall, fair, so pale and spiritual," Katherine describes him) and his verse, an allegorical and mystifying set of images that might have been written by any of the awestruck literary émigrés who transformed Italy into Percy Bysshe Shelley's "paradise of exiles." Following James Buzard's typology, we see that Katherine yearns for the individual, spiritual Italian itinerary of the "traveler," whereas Alex is content with the commoditized clichés of the "tourist" (18). She is keen to "travel south" and immerse herself in the anticipated splendors of Mediterranean art, but her northern mate desires only to return to his ordered English habitat.[21]

The verbal aura of Lewington's poetry is heightened by the solemn manner in which Katherine intones his lines, half asleep in the sun while the Bay of Naples stretches out behind her. After her recitation Katherine visits the imagined "temple of the spirit" that Lewington's verses celebrate, the Archaeological Museum of Naples. Katherine's reactions to the statuary of ancient Italy submits the themes invoked in Lewington's poetry and its accompanying pseudoromantic tenets to the manipulation of Rossellini's visual strategies. Each time she peers at one of the relics, Katherine feels frightened and overwhelmed, a response Rossellini exploits through unusual camera angles. In one image Katherine and the guide are dwarfed by a high-angle shot of the statue of the Farnese Hercules (figure 13); in another, a claustrophobic close-up and reaction-shot of Katherine suggests her discomfort before the menacing, decidedly nonascetic and un-Lewingtonian statuary (figure 14).[22] Moments later, a statue seems poised to pounce on its pale Nordic visitor, as the diminutive boy is amplified by Rossellini's foreshortened angle to encroach uncomfortably into the personal space of Katherine and her jocular, nonplussed Italian guide.

Rossellini's visual reworking of Lewington's poem allows Italian culture to look back through inanimate eyes and gaze on those same foreign presences that had historically objectified it. Italy, Rossellini claimed, was anything but

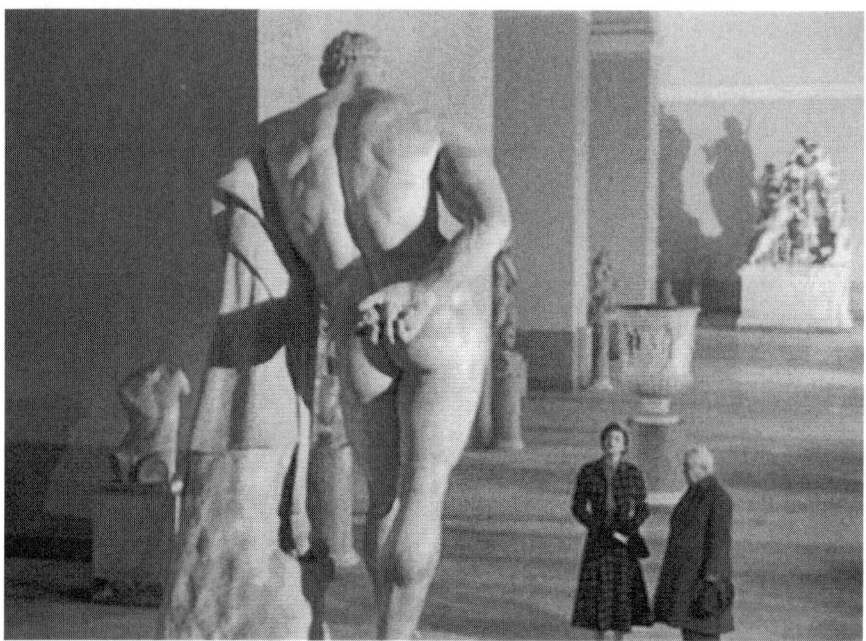

Figure 13 A high-angle shot of the Farnese Hercules by Rossellini as his subjective camera work captures Katherine Joyce's point of view *(Voyage to Italy)*.

the funereal landscape that Katherine, Alex, Lewington, and others believed it to be: "C'è quel falso poeta che lei cita sempre, che parla dell'Italia come di un paese di morte. Paese di morte, l'Italia! Non esiste, perché la morte diventa una cosa tanto viva che mettono le coroncine ai teschi. Cioè, è differente il senso delle cose. Per loro la morte ha valore archeologico, per noi ha valore vitale. Ed è un altro tipo di civiltà" ("[Katherine] is always quoting a so-called poet who describes Italy as a country of death—imagine, Italy a country of death! Death doesn't exist here, because—it's so much a living thing that they put garlands on the heads of dead men. There is a different meaning to things here. To [the Joyces] death has an archaeological meaning, to us it is a living reality. It's a different kind of civilization") (Rossellini, *Il mio metodo* 335; Rossellini, "Interview with Roberto Rossellini" 155).

During Katherine's visit, Rossellini provides a group of portraits whose monumentality, intensified by the fixed position of the statues, imbues an epic quality to these intrusively animate forms. They may be stationary, but in Katherine's view they seem capable of movement. At one point, the chiaroscuro effect that surrounds the vicious dogs highlights the frame's violent

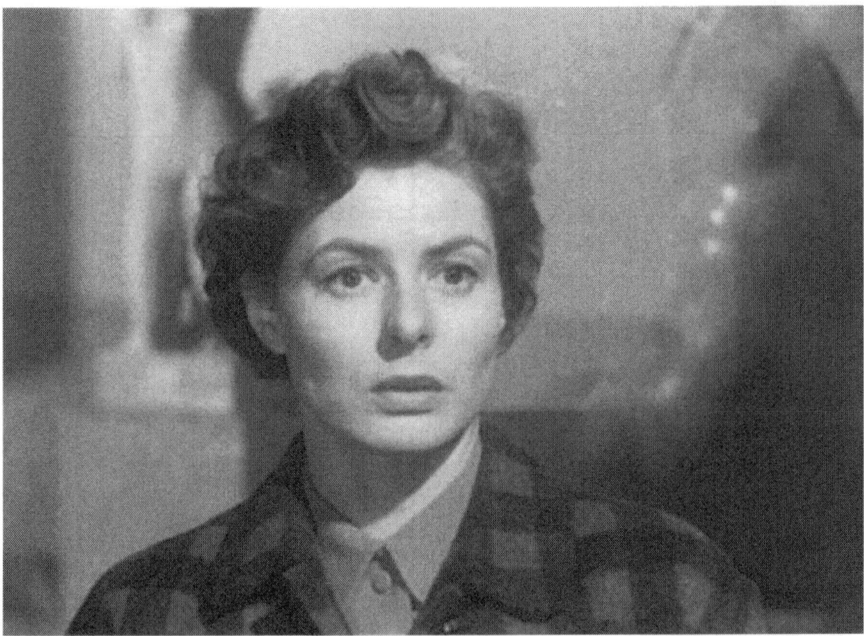

Figure 14 One of the many shots that finds Rossellini's protagonist, Katherine Joyce, overwhelmed by her perceptions at the Naples Archaeological Museum *(Voyage to Italy)*.

energy and establishes an emotional correlative to Katherine's troubled perceptions (figure 15). The audience perceives the statuary through the filter of her consciousness. So, in line with Pasolini's notion of the free indirect point-of-view shot, Rossellini achieves a "cinema of poetry" by employing the signs of reality—that is, the objects, feelings, and sensations of Katherine's perceptions—to project a human consciousness without the mediating skein of language or other forms of description. The leitmotif of Katherine's discomfort rhymes with reactions of hers in later excursions, especially her anxious visit to the city's teeming catacombs, and recalls the contrasting shot of her serene declamation of Lewington's verses.

The disjunction between what Lewington writes and what Katherine sees recalls a perennial impediment to comparing poetic and cinematic modes: the perceived intrusion of the raw material of literary discourse, language, into film's visual imagery. Historically, the question of whether literary or poetic language belongs in film was intensified by the belief that cinema, in its silent period, was more open to nonnarrative and image-based experi-

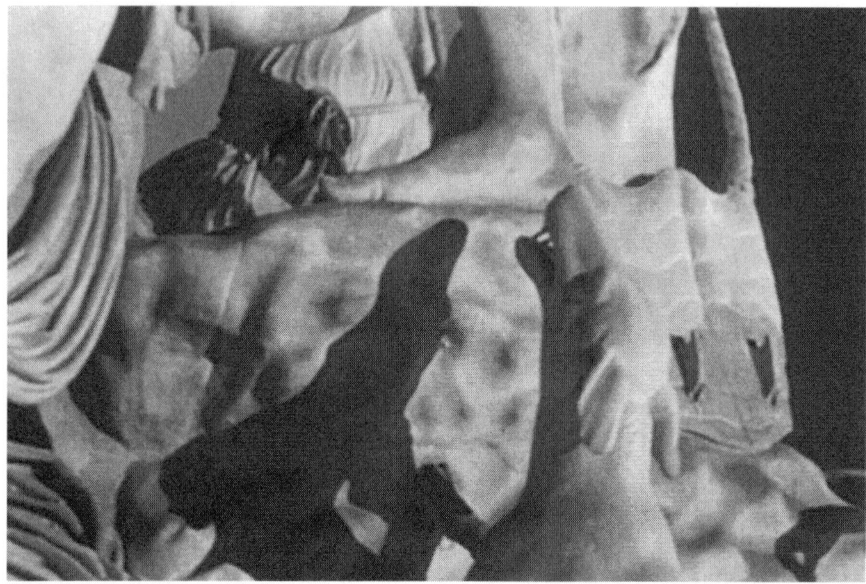

Figure 15 The fierce chiaroscuro imagery reflects Katherine's perceptions, anticipating Pasolini's free indirect point-of-view shot and its "cinema of poetry" (*Voyage to Italy*).

mental forms than during its narrative apotheosis in the age of sound. Silent cinema often quoted actual lines of poems as the text or intertitles for the accompanying visual exposition, though some silent filmmakers avoided citing lines that were so well known as to need no explicit mention. With the advent of sound some film purists perceived a threat to the integrity of the film image and its capacity for nonlinguistic expression.[23] Later, in Pasolini, the direct access of cinematic imagery to the unconscious, devoid of linguistic mediation, formed the basis for his view of the medium as the most naturally "poetic" of the arts. In the Archaeological Museum sequence, Rossellini makes the sound of Lewington's verse—and the memories it incarnates—into an unconscious haunting of what Katherine sees as she reaches out to Italian culture. To access her inner realm, the film channels Lewington through James Joyce, whose short story "The Dead" provides *Voyage to Italy* with its most important technical element: the dialectic between sound and image in a haunted female consciousness, which Rossellini translates into a mode of cinematic exposition that Pasolini later described in terms of the free indirect point-of-view shot.

Joyce's "The Dead" is a story of aural ghostliness. The annual dancing party hosted by the Misses Morkan is devoted to feasting and songs that evoke a bygone way of Irish life, a nostalgia enforced by the wistful chords of folk songs like "The Lass of Aughrim" and the protagonist Gabriel Conroy's dinner toast to the *"generation that is now on the wane"* (192; italics in original). Gabriel, a creature of high rhetoric given over to musings on the likes of Robert Browning and William Shakespeare, admits the failure of his "orating to vulgarians," which is overpowered by the musical strains of "The Lass of Aughrim" that flood his wife, Gretta, with memories of Michael Furey, the young man who died not long after courting her with this song. Gabriel realizes that Furey's words have lain dormant in his wife's heart; their resurfacing as the echo of a passionate love stands as the antiphonal counterpoint to what he describes as his own "fatuous" speech ("He had a very good voice, Michael Furey," Gretta remarks) (220–21). A phrase from Gabriel's review of Browning suggests the story's larger theme of how his wife's melancholy is fueled by the aura of Furey's undying voice: *"One feels that one is listening to a thought-tormented music"* (192; italics in original). The initial conversation between Alex and Katherine Joyce about Lewington lacks the tenderness and understanding of the Conroys' tête-à-tête about Furey in their hotel room at story's end. Yet it, too, stages the resurgence of a voice from the past that has apparently never left the female lead's most intimate memories. After reciting Lewington's verses, Katherine denies ever having loved him, telling Alex only that they "got on terribly well together" (a direct allusion to Joyce's "The Dead") and that, on the eve of her marriage, he showed up shivering beneath her window, just like Furey.[24] Though Katherine repeats Lewington's lines, in reality it is the verses that speak through her, since her encounters with Italian art are structured by her responses to the images of this fictitious poem. Even if the Italy Lewington wrote of does not exist ("Poor Charles," Katherine later tells Alex; "he had a way of seeing things all his own"), it is the dream of Lewington's highly sublimated Italy—the corollary for the pure love he evidently felt for Katherine—that leads her along, his verses the mantra that might save her marriage and her soul.[25]

In a study of John Huston's adaptation of Joyce's story in the film *The Dead* (1987), Luke Gibbons notes that contrary to received wisdom, "film may often be at its most visual when images carry the intonations of the voice, allowing us to read between the lines of the script," and that in cinematic adaptations "the visual architecture of a film may ventriloquise apparently absent voices," especially when it renders the textures of inner speech (128).[26] Rossellini's representation of aural haunting differs from Huston's because of the Italian director's greater reliance on the inner, silent citation of Lewington's verses by Katherine, a woman given neither to song nor to the more erotic, extroverted charge of affection that defined Gretta's relations with Michael Furey. The tension between the sound of language and the visual elements of the image is heightened in *Voyage to Italy* by the superimposition of Lewington's words onto Katherine's ocular perceptions, to create the chiastic impression that while Katherine sees in the light of her admirer-poet's words, she also grafts his verbal discourse onto the film's visual imagery.

In addition to the dialectic between the linguistic and the visual, a second issue in the film-poetry relation that Rossellini's film accounts for is the potential obstacle posed by ocular vision to the nonmimetic insights of the film medium. At the risk of a tendentious allegory, one could argue that the notorious eye-slashing scene at the opening of the best-known surrealist film, Luis Buñuel's *Un chien andalou* (*An Andalusian Dog* [1929]), represents the overcoming of natural sight by the dreamlike connotations of the film image—a cornerstone both of Pasolini's notion of cinematic poetry and Miller's view of montage at the "Poetry and the Film" symposium (Pasolini, "Cinema di poesia" 169; Deren et al. 8). Rossellini offers his own version of the relation between visual perception and unconscious vision by granting Katherine increased insight into Italian culture as she distances herself from Lewington's verses. During her first cultural excursion to the Archaeological Museum, Lewington's words are prominent and, correspondingly, her cultural exchanges the least illuminating. As the narrative progresses, however, Katherine's insights increase, most notably in her decisive final visit to Pompeii, when she witnesses the unearthing of two ancient lovers in the lava. The less Katherine actually *sees,* the more she is able to glean from her encounters with Italian art. Lewington's verses promise Katherine "temples of the spirit" and "pure ascetic images," neither of which is available to the human eye. Though Katherine initially misunderstands the impetus toward sublimation motivating these verses, in time she begins to attain the kind of vision evoked by the name of the individual who brought her to Naples in the first place: Uncle Homer, namesake of the iconically blind epic seer who, along with James Joyce, serves as an ironic cultural avatar for the British couple's decidedly nonepic journey south to settle a will.

Many believed that the third and greatest obstacle that stood between filmmakers and the creation of a cinema beholden to the forms of lyric poetry, broadly defined, was linear and logically articulated narrative. Underscoring cinema's provenance in "elementi irrazionalistici, onirici, elementari e barbarici" ("irrational, oneiric, elementary, and barbaric elements"), Pasolini writes that "storicamente . . . la tradizione cinematografica che si è formata sembra essere quella di una 'lingua della prosa,' o almeno di una 'lingua della prosa narrativa'" ("historically . . . the cinematographic tradition which has developed seems to be that of a 'language of prose,' or at least that of a 'language of prose narrative'") ("Cinema di poesia" 172; "Cinema of Poetry" 172). The shift from a cinema of poetry to one of narrative prose, according to Pasolini, was "una violentazione . . . inevitabile" ("an unavoidable . . . rape"), because—and here the capitalist critique of his essay is most explicit—the powers-that-be immediately realized the capacity of narrative, escapist cinema to bring in "una quantità di consumatori inimmaginabile per tutte le altre forme espressive" ("a number of consumers unimaginable for all other forms of expression") ("Cinema di poesia" 172; "Cinema of Poetry" 172). Yet, he continues, the volatile, antinarrative, and noninstrumental poetic language of film persists, even in the cinema of narrative prose. This visual poetry, however, is forced below the realist surface and granted a supporting role as an "elemento inconscio di urto e di persuasione" ("subconscious [element] of shock and persuasion"), subordinate to what Pasolini calls the "inutili e pseudo-critici paragoni" ("useless and pseudo-critical comparisons") between film and its narrative kin, the theater and the novel ("Cinema di poesia" 172; "Cinema of Poetry" 172). In telling and prophetic fashion Pasolini emphasizes the adoption by art-house films of this language of prose narrative, deprived of "punte espressive, impressionistiche, espressionistiche" ("expressive, impressionistic, and expressionistic highlights") ("Cinema di poesia" 173; "Cinema of Poetry" 172). Before and after Pasolini, and especially in Hollywood, one finds many examples of the art-house film—for example, costume dramas based on nineteenth-century literature in the Merchant-Ivory mold—that remain principally "literary" in their articulation, since they rely on complicated plot structure, detailed representation of milieu, development of character, and especially the prepackaged authority of a prestigious source text.[27]

The type of threat to avant-garde and engaged cinema described by Pasolini shares the polemical edge of the neorealism of De Sica and Zavattini, who argued that the conventional story lines of mainstream film represented a weakening of ideological will. In their view the truly "anthropomorphic" cinema (Visconti, "Anthropomorphic" 83)—one consistent with communist principles—had no need of an individualistic, authorial (and implicitly bourgeois) guiding narrative hand (Zavattini, "Some Ideas" 217). They could make a film, they pledged, of a woman buying a cheap pair of shoes. The Rossellini of the late 1940s and 1950s was also less invested in traditional narrative: in the late 1940s, because it would detract from an unmediated, documentary-like, and "choral" effect (*Il mio metodo* 88); in the 1950s, because an exterior roll of events could flatten the psychological textures beholden to the improvisational performances of his deliberately uninformed actors. The proverbial eclipse of traditional narrative in *Voyage to Italy,* for which no extant script exists and whose characters were allegedly directed from notes scribbled onto Rossellini's shirt cuffs, allows the symbolic resonance of Lewington's verses to surface and resurface, unimpeded by the forward momentum of the plot.[28] As has been noted, the film lacks a set beginning and end, as the audience initially encounters the main characters in medias res on the road to Naples, and the concluding image of Alex and Katherine's fraught embrace gives way to the random image of a policeman conducting an orchestra.[29] With the absence of a beginning and an end there can be no middle. This lack of narrative core gives the film the feel of a lyrical exploration of time itself, whose synchronous effects find their perfect analogue in a palimpsestic Naples, a city of memory reminiscent of the overlapping topographies in Sigmund Freud's Roman metaphor of the memory trace.[30]

Nothing is erased in human or natural history in Rossellini's Naples, and through a philology that is at once cultural and visual his camera unearths, in the archaeological sense of returning to origins, the traces of predecessor civilizations and codes of behavior. *Philology* is an apt term because of its link to a word often associated with Rossellini, *humanism,* which like philology involves the reestablishment of contact with ancient cultures through the discovery of their sign systems and forms of expression. In *Voyage to Italy* this rediscovery is visual rather than textual. Yet the goals of the film are consistent with those of many Renaissance humanists: to recuperate the past as an antidote to a present crisis, through a historicist program born out of a distrust for systems of abstract thought divorced from lived reality, whether the metaphysics of the philosophers or the doctrines of the theologians. This palimpsest-like film is over- and underwritten by a wealth of texts, from Joyce and Colette to the imaginary Lewington and the aforementioned invisible poem by Brancati (see note 15), all of which are left as traces in a film that disavows the script. The unreciprocated overtures that Katherine makes to the statuary in the Archaeological Museum signify the rift between what Rossellini called *drappeggiate* (draped or toga-wearing) and modern *cucite* (sewn-fabric) civilizations. The word *text* shares a common etymology in the Latin forms for something written and something woven, so in coming down

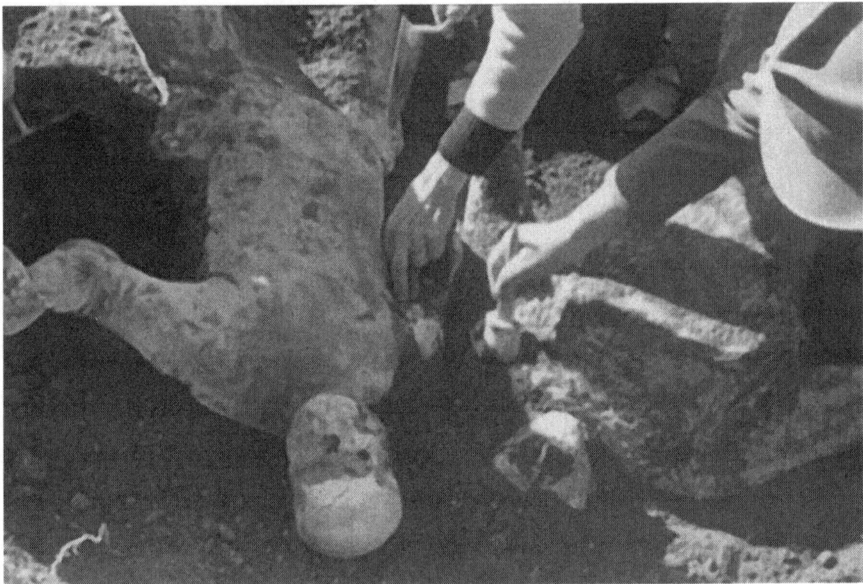

Figure 16 A couple in Vesuvius's lava captured in a plaster injection that parallels the imprinting of light on the film negative *(Voyage to Italy)*.

on the side of the *drappeggiate,* Rossellini by implication favors looser textual forms that can be transformed and refitted at will. Over and against the more tightly wound *cucito* world of stable textuality, *Voyage to Italy* refuses to monumentalize either the past or its art. The ancient forms in the film are too alive to be savored by the connoisseur, catalogued by the antiquarian, or sublimated by the aesthete.

In Katherine's final visit to Pompeii the capacity of ancient culture to look back on those reaching out to it assumes its most dramatic force. Just after Katherine and Alex decide to divorce, they are called to the destroyed city, where they witness the recovery of a couple that had lain submerged in the lava for centuries (figure 16). Katherine stares at the plaster molds of the figures and realizes that her own marriage pales in contrast to their eternal embrace. Like Shakespeare's Claudius, who storms out after Hamlet's staging of a regicide, Katherine responds not to the actual death of her marriage but its representation (figure 17).

Laura Mulvey reads the unearthing of the lovers through a plaster injection into the cavities their bodies created in the lava of Vesuvius as an allegory for Rossellini's eternal realist desire to capture the "imprint" of the human

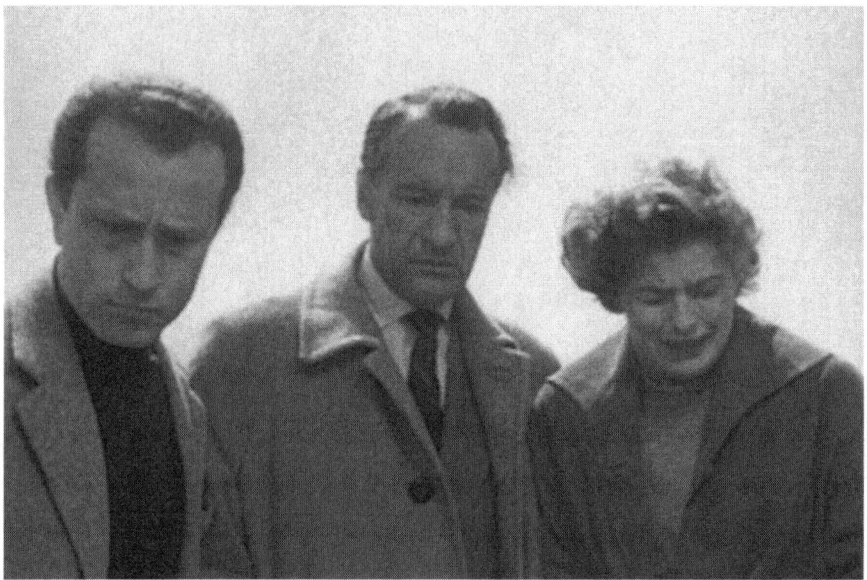

Figure 17 Katherine reacts to the physical evidence of her own failed marriage: the unearthed couple of Vesuvius *(Voyage to Italy)*.

figure on the celluloid materiality of film—which in this episode, she argues, "sets up a relation between materialism and the supernatural: the trace of the physical figure meets the mystery of death, the point where religion and superstition become indeterminably entwined with human belief systems" (98). Raymond Bellour notes that the plaster figures represent a kind of "photograph . . . formed from the real itself" (110), akin to Bazin's notion of the realist image as an index of the place and time of its registering ("Ontology" 13–14). Because the bodies, Bellour notes, are "developed" like a photograph, the original lovers form the putative negative that generates their representation for the bewildered Katherine and Alex. The plaster figures are also "negative" to the modern British couple in that they are presumed to embody all that the Joyces lack, as their "mummified" passion, to invoke Bazin ("Ontology" 15), emerges as an ominous sign of life's fleeting nature ("Life is so short!" Katherine shouts to Alex after seeing the couple). The plaster lovers reveal that it is Alex and Katherine who are immobile, embalmed, and sterile, incapable of movement or reproduction, whereas the ancient figures, in turn, brim with imaginary passions. The vision of the bodies, like Rossellini's integration of Lewington's poem in the Archaeological Museum montage, serves as a cinematic parable for the power of the image to confront the perceiving subject with a truth that, however unpleasant, he or she must acknowledge. By imbuing the inert couple with a life narrative, Rossellini's Orphic gesture fulfills the meaning of verses that neither their author, Charles Lewington, nor their declaimer, Katherine Joyce, is able to grasp. The unearthed lovers truly are "no longer bodies but pure ascetic images," compared to which Katherine's thought seems "flesh, heavy, dim."

Alex and Katherine's unexpected rapprochement at film's end continues to elicit a range of impassioned and contradictory interpretations. On one hand, Truffaut claimed that the Joyces' reconciliation was no less than a "consecration" and that henceforward all would be "without defect" for them (qtd. in Gallagher 414). On the other hand, most tend to view the reconciliation as a momentary ceasefire and prelude to continued strife. Even Rossellini's understanding of the ending changed over the years, culminating in his well-known description of its "bitterness" in 1965.[31] The sum of the responses asks, as so often occurs in Rossellini, whether an isolated moment has the potential for *durée*—for example, will the partisan youths at the end of *Roma, città aperta* (*Rome, Open City* [1945]) march toward a better Italian future after the degradations of world and civil war? Will the religiously enlightened Karin at the conclusion of *Stromboli* (1950) return, purified of turmoil, to the village she despises? Can Irene's social epiphanies in *Europa '51* (1952) continue to bear spiritual fruit during her institutionalization? Framed in terms of genre, the ending of *Voyage to Italy* becomes an issue of whether the lyrical moment can spread out into narrative and develop into a "story" in its own regard. The audience will never know whether the momentary burst of passion triggered during San Gennaro results from the Joyces' fear of being alone, the complicated sentiments associated with companionship, or even the miraculous potential of the religious festival at hand. Yet since so much of *Voyage to Italy* is about perspective (optical, cultural, and otherwise), it seems fair to say that Rossellini's vaunted "objectivity" can accommodate, indeed invite, a multiplicity of viewpoints on the couple's final embrace.[32] Independent of one's take on the scene, it remains the lone moment in the film where emotions similar to the ones that had inspired Lewington's lines (and their subsequent haunting of Katherine) overtake the two main characters, who appear in entirely new guises and dispositions: an Alex in hot pursuit of his jostled wife; a Katherine who clings to her rescuing husband.

Éric Rohmer once claimed that Rossellini transfigures his material just as the single puff of a cigarette releases a massive cloud of vapors during Katherine's initial visit to Vesuvius. Through this metaphor of ionization, Rohmer implies the underlying aesthetic principles and structures of Rossellini's film-making in the Bergman years, especially as they relate to his manipulation of poetic source material in *Voyage to Italy*. In an interview with the directors of the New Wave Rossellini insisted that he tried to avoid close-up shots for fear that he would keep them in his films and that he worked inversely to the standard model of establishing a connection between the subject and his or her environment and then gradually moving closer to the actor through medium shots and the culminating close-up. Rossellini described instead his method as beginning with the close-up and then moving out toward the longer, deeper, and immobile *plan-séquence* (uninterrupted sequence) that was his visual signature. As we see in the transition from, say, the initial close-ups of the rowing fishermen in *Stromboli* to the panoramic filming of their annual ritual slaughter of tuna *(la mattanza)*, the movement of his camera is often inductive rather than deductive, with a tendency to shift from the part to the whole in the manner of synecdoche. A form of visual ionization structures his use of Lewington's poem in that it, like the literary sources in *Francesco, giullare di Dio,* sets a sequence of events and images into visual registers neither anticipated nor suggested by the text itself, just as the ionized atom releases its energy and converts into a different state of matter when activated by an external stimulus of a complementary charge. Rohmer's scientific analogy is apt considering that Rossellini's main preoccupation in the last decade of his life was to bridge the gap between what one might term the opposite charges of knowledge, the humanistic and the scientific, and that his last unedited film consists of a series of interviews with scientists from Rice University about the threat of atomic war, a lethal example of energy improperly harnessed.

Though Rossellini never directly weighed in on either adaptation or the role of lyric poetry in film, his work in the 1950s after his acclaimed neorealist trilogy differs from that of most fellow filmmakers in that he actually incorporated poetic material, albeit fictive, into his films.[33] His technical innovations in this area, as in so many others, outpaced the conceptual insights of his contemporaries and created aesthetic forms that the existing lexicon had yet to name. The multiplicities of viewpoint and conflicting definitions about the relation between film and poetry may suggest, pace Pasolini, that the link between the two is impossible to reduce to a coherent theory. Yet the dialogue persists, and in *Voyage to Italy* Rossellini manages to achieve a *cinema di poesia* by alternately citing and silencing an imaginary poet in a makeshift adaptation and by employing a montage of visual rhymes, symbolic references, and pictorial glosses on these declaimed verses. No member of the debates on literary adaptation in the early 1950s mentioned either Rossellini's name or his film *Voyage to Italy*. But, as Bazin suggests, the gauge of artistic brilliance is never merely a question of the relationship between genres and, by extension, media; it can be instead a matter of the way one artist relates to another.[34] In *Voyage to Italy* Rossellini creates an idealized poetic voice (Lewington) whose verses channel centuries of foreign views on Italy and, by extension, the pantheon of foreign artists who formed them. In Rossellini's representation of Lewington and the imagery surrounding his verses, he provides a rare aural and visual commentary on a relationship between film and poetry that we have only begun to understand.

CHAPTER FOUR

Poesis in Pasolini

Theory and Practice

Not surprisingly, the early reception of Pier Paolo Pasolini's notions on the *cinema di poesia* (cinema of poetry), first elaborated in a paper at the Pesaro Film Festival in 1965, was divided to the extreme.[1] The most common resistance regarded Pasolini's positing of an identity between the language of the unconscious, which he believed that cinema was uniquely qualified to capture, and the discourse of "reality" itself.[2] In a departure from the position taken by such theorists as André Bazin, who had written that the cinematic sign follows photography in its capacity to "index" the external world by mechanically registering its imprint in time and space, Pasolini argued that film could capture a nonmimetic reality beholden to memory, dreams, and other manifestations of the unconscious.[3] Stephen Heath's representative critique dismissed what he called Pasolini's "natural attitude" to film: "In the context of a cinesemiotics [Pasolini's thinking] can only lead to the denial of cinema as a semiotic system: cinema becomes not a process of the articulation of meaning, but direct duplication of some Reality; it represents 'reality' with 'reality'" (109). Heath's remarks square with the acid commentary of Umberto Eco, who in the words of one scholar "blacklisted" Pasolini's cinesemiotics (Bruno 98).[4] Pasolini, according to Eco, "contrasts . . . the most elementary aim of semiotics, which is to reduce the facts of nature to cultural phenomena and not to retrace the facts of culture to natural phenomena" (142). Never one to back down from a polemic, Pasolini retorted:

> Un giovane biondo, caro Eco, avanza verso di te. Non ne senti l'odore. Forse perché non ce n'ha; o perché è lontano, o perché altri odori formano un diaframma tra te e lui, o forse perché tu hai il raffredore. Strano, perché un certo odore dovrebbe averlo, addosso. . . . Caro Eco, le cose stanno esattamante al contrario di come tu le interpreti. . . . Tutte le mie caotiche pagine su questo argomento (codice del cinema uguale codice della realtà, nell'ambito di una

Semiologia Generale) *tendono a portare la Semiologia alla definitiva culturiz-zazione della natura.* ("Codice dei Codici" 277, 279; Pasolini's italics)

A blond young man, my dear Eco, advances toward you. You do not sense his odor, perhaps because he has none; or perhaps because he is far away, or because other odors divide him from you. Or perhaps because you have a cold. This is strange, because he certainly should have a certain odor about him. . . . Dear Eco, things are exactly the opposite of how you interpret them. . . . All my chaotic pages on this topic (that the code of cinema equals the code of reality, within the context of a general semiotics) *tend to bring semiotics to the definitive transformation of nature into culture.* (trans. Bruno 98)

This quotation adduces the aporia separating the poet and theorist of cinema. From a rational perspective, Eco is of course correct in reminding Pasolini that the natural world will always resist human attempts to render it a pure cultural construct.[5] Yet, from Orpheus onward, a dream of poets has been to animate the inanimate or at least give voice to the voiceless. No doubt aware of the quixotic nature of his claims, Pasolini persisted in offering them in the name of the mythopoetic aspects of his craft.[6] Film, he believed, could write with things instead of words.[7]

Pasolini believed cinematic language to be ontologically poetic, even though he agreed that, historically, the discourse of film had been relegated to the province of narrative and prose by political and commercial corruptions.[8] Yet Pasolini insists in "Il 'cinema di poesia' " that the poetry of cinema will out, and along with it the irrational nature of the medium. This occurs, he argues, despite the fact that the oneiric quality of film was tamed, submerged, and reduced to modes of narrative-based intelligibility because of cinema's mass appeal and commercial value. The undeniable ascendancy of narrative film, in Pasolini's view, led to all manner of absurd comparisons between the cinema and the theater, as well as the novel. His critique of the novel as a false cinematic analogue is consistent with his distinctions between the so-called cinema of poetry and its eclipse by the rampant adaptation of novelistic sources for the screen.[9]

The key to understanding this discrepancy between the language of poetry and prose in Pasolini's film theories lies in his notion of the *stile indiretto li-bero* (free indirect style), which allows the author to penetrate the spirit of his characters and adopt their worldview and psychology. According to Pasolini, Michelangelo Antonioni achieves this with his protagonist Giuliana in *Red*

Desert, as does Bernardo Bertolucci through the character Fabrizio in *Prima della rivoluzione* (*Before the Revolution* [1964]), just as Dante had done with Francesca da Rimini in canto 5 of *Inferno.* But Pasolini finds free indirect style or discourse more powerful in film than literature because it is unmediated by language. In film, free indirect discourse permits the director to express, through *im-segni* (im-signs or image-signs), the undiluted consciousness of human experience, which the audience perceives just as the character expresses and perceives it—that is, in the unfiltered and highly metaphorical, thus poetic, world of memory and dreams.

This brief rehearsal of Pasolini's "Il 'cinema di poesia'" prepares us to approach perhaps the greatest theoretical challenge, if not paradox, posed by his essay: the method promoted by Pasolini as the means for arriving at poetic cinema, free indirect discourse, is commonly understood by most to represent the supreme technical innovation of the realist *novel* in the nineteenth century. In short, Pasolini's theories on the supposedly innate visual poetry of the free indirect style contrast with the pervasive view that links this technique to prose, especially the high realist novel. For example, drawing on Émile Benveniste's distinction between "story" and "discourse," Franco Moretti foregrounds the link between the free indirect style and what he diagnoses as the "eternal yesterday" of the realist novel:

> In fully consistent historical narration, [Benveniste claims that] "even the narrator is no longer there. The events are announced as they are produced in their appearance along the horizon of the story. No one speaks: the events seem to tell themselves on their own. The fundamental tense is the aorist, which is the tense of the event outside the person of the narrator."
>
> The combined use of the aorist and the third person induces us, therefore, to see the world through a symbolic form that no longer has anything in common with discourse, with the "here and now" of the dialogue between an "I" and a "you." . . .
>
> . . . With the realistic novel a new attitude towards life and history has been generated—the "narrative" attitude. And this attitude has severed all links with comment and judgement. (*Way of the World* 123–24)[10]

Moretti provides a more traditional and accepted view of the free indirect style than Pasolini, who answers his own rhetorical question ("Come è teoricamente spiegabile e praticamente possibile, nel cinema, la 'lingua della poesia'?" ["Is the 'language of poetry' theoretically explicable and practically possible in cinema?"]) by amending it to: "È possibile nel cinema la tecnica del discorso libero indiretto cinematografico?" ("Is the technique of free indirect discourse possible in cinema?") ("Cinema di poesia" 175; "Cinema of Poetry" 175). He answers yes and then offers the following definition of how the *stile indiretto libero* makes poetic cinema possible:

> Esso è semplicemente l'immersione dell'autore nell'animo del suo personaggio, e quindi l'adozione, da parte dell'autore, non solo della psicologia del suo personaggio, ma anche della sua lingua. Casi di discorso libero indiretto si son sempre avuti, in letteratura. . . . Il "libero indiretto" è più naturalistico, in quanto è un vero e proprio discorso diretto senza le virgolette, e quindi implica l'uso della lingua del personaggio. . . . Il discorso diretto corrisponde, nel cinema, alla "soggettiva." Nel discorso diretto l'autore si fa da parte e cede la parola al suo personaggio, mettendola tra virgolette. ("Cinema di poesia" 176)

> [Free indirect discourse] is, simply, the immersion of the filmmaker in the mind of his character and then the adoption on the part of the filmmaker not only of his character but also of his language. Cases of free indirect discourse have always existed in literature. . . . Free indirect discourse [in literature] is more naturalistic [than interior monologue] in that it is an actual direct discourse without quotation marks and thus implies the use of the language of the character. In cinema direct discourse corresponds to the point-of-view shot. In direct discourse the author stands aside and cedes speech to his character, putting what he says in quotation marks. ("Cinema of Poetry" 175–76)

Despite their discrepancies, Moretti's and Pasolini's conflicting views share a belief in, first, the disappearance in the free indirect style of the "author" or "narrator," to create the appearance of a purely objective narrative utterance (or, in Pasolini's case, *antinarrative* discourse); second, the illusion for readers/audiences that they have direct access to the consciousness of the characters in the fictional representation. Unlike Moretti, however, Pasolini elaborates on the ideological corruptions that language enacts on the supposed objectivity of free indirect discourse:

> Quando uno scrittore "rivive il discorso" di un suo personaggio, si immerge nella sua psicologia, ma anche nella sua *lingua:* il discorso libero indiretto è dunque sempre linguisticamente differenziato, rispetto alla lingua dello scrittore. Riprodurre, rivivendole, le lingue diverse dei diversi tipi di condizione sociale, è reso possibile allo scrittore dal fatto che esse ci sono. Ogni realtà linguistica è un insieme di lingue differenziate e differenzianti socialmente: e lo scrittore che usi il "libero indiretto" deve avere soprattutto coscienza di

questo: che è poi una forma di coscienza di classe. ("Cinema di poesia" 178; Pasolini's italics)

> When a writer recreates the speech of one of his characters, he immerses himself in his psychology, but also in his *language.* Free indirect discourse is therefore always linguistically differentiated when compared to the language of the writer. The writer has the possibility of reproducing the various languages of the different types of social conditions by reanimating them because they exist. Every linguistic reality is a totality of socially differentiated and differentiating languages, and the writer who uses "free indirect discourse" must be aware of this above all—an awareness which in the final analysis is a form of class consciousness. ("Cinema of Poetry" 178)

Thus, for Pasolini literary free indirect discourse depends on a level of mediation, through language, that establishes an ideologically inflected distance between author and characters—the very distance that the free indirect discourse was meant to elide.[11] When Pasolini alludes to "class consciousness," he claims that writers, in wishing to present the unmediated reality of their characters, try to write themselves out of their own narratives by speaking in the language of their fictional creations. But in establishing their own authorial indivisibility and, by extension, filtering the consciousnesses of their characters, authors must do so linguistically and perforce descend into the political.[12] This occurs because language is a fundamentally class-inflected medium, whether or not an author wishes to imitate the language his characters would think or speak in, and whether or not he wishes to neutralize the representational voice so that it would seem as though the "narrative itself" were speaking. Because humankind has codified language to reflect the realities of political power, language necessarily carries with it the human stain of (in Pasolini's view, a suspect and capitalist) ideology. The anticapitalist animus of Pasolini's essay extends to the film industry: to his mind the cinema of prose was based on the classical editing conventions of spatiotemporal continuity that were perfected in Hollywood.

Pasolini's filmmaker, like his putative realist novelist, faces problems of his own with regard to the language of politics and the politics of language. For although the film image has a pregrammatical quality that liberates it from some of the more class-inflected problems of linguistic representation, the organizing directorial *sguardo* (gaze) upon this image-object is subject to the same forms of ideological contamination as language.[13] Pasolini diagnoses the difference between the worldview of the director and that of his characters in terms of an imposition of the director's *stile* (style) in implementing the free indirect point-of-view shot: "Lo 'sguardo' di un contadino—magari addiritura di un paese o di una regione in condizioni preistoriche di sottosviluppo—abbraccia un altro tipo di realtà, che lo sguardo, dato a quella stessa realtà, di un borghese colto" ("The 'gaze' of a peasant, perhaps even of an entire town or region in prehistoric conditions of underdevelopment, embraces another type of reality than the gaze given to that same reality by [a cultured bourgeois]") ("Cinema di poesia" 178; "Cinema of Poetry" 178). Unlike the linguistic difference separating character and author, the image or visual distance between filmmaker and character cannot be institutionalized—that is, reduced to a grammar or translated through linguistic mimesis into the illusion of recreating the worldview of the peasant (which could be done in the novel, say, by the author's reproducing the peasant's language patterns or penchant for proverbial expression).[14] As has been noted, Pasolini's preference for working with nonprofessional actors should be considered part of this attempt to access a realm of authentic speech outside of bourgeois grammatical protocols.[15]

The trio of cinematic poets celebrated in Pasolini's essay (Antonioni, Bertolucci, and Jean-Luc Godard) face a set of daunting, ideologically conditioned challenges in their efforts to create a *cinema di poesia.* Although they, too, will "gaze" at the world differently than do the fictional inhabitants of their films because of class differences, the image-signs that they use to present the worldview of characters can never, because of the infinite nature and variety of the objects in the world, be reduced to a grammar. The bourgeois may, so to speak, own grammar, but the raw data of reality (which for Pasolini takes the form of unconscious images) will always escape the taxonomies and codifications of the reigning ideology: "Non esiste un dizionario delle immagini. . . . Se per caso volessimo immaginare un dizionario delle immagini dovremmo immaginare un *dizionario infinito,* come infinito continua a restare il dizionario delle *parole possibili.* . . . Insomma, mentre l'operazione dello scrittore è un'invenzione estetica, quella dell'autore cinematografico è prima linguistica e poi estetica" ("There is no dictionary of images. There is no pigeonholed image, ready to be used. If by any chance we wanted to imagine a dictionary of images, we would have to imagine an *infinite dictionary,* as infinite as the dictionary of *possible words.* . . . In other words, while the activity of the writer is an aesthetic invention, that of the filmmaker is first linguistic, then aesthetic") ("Cinema di poesia" 169–70 [Pasolini's italics]; "Cinema of poetry" 169–70).

The language of literature, he continues, derives from a utilitarian medium of exchange and is therefore instrumental. Cinema, however, is for Pasolini a noncommunicative and noninstrumental discourse: "Gli uomini comunicano con le parole, non con le immagini" ("Men communicate with words, not images") ("Cinema di poesia" 167; "Cinema of Poetry" 167). So the director must resort to a mimesis of style aimed at producing the same seamless reality effect of literary free indirect discourse. The image-sign in film, however, observes a different logic than its literary antecedent. Pasolini writes: "Egli sceglie una serie di oggetti o cose o paesaggi o persone come sintagmi (segni di un linguaggio simbolico) che, *se hanno una storia grammaticale storica inventata in quel momento*—come in una specie di happening dominato dall'idea della scelta e del montaggio—*hanno però una storia pre-grammaticale già lunga*" ("[The filmmaker] chooses a series of objects, or things, or landscapes, or persons as syntagmas [signs of a symbolic language] which, while they have a grammatical history invented in that moment—as in a sort of happening dominated by the idea of selection and montage—do, however, have an already lengthy and intense pregrammatical history") ("Cinema di poesia" 171 [Pasolini's italics]; "Cinema of Poetry" 171).

By "pregrammatical," Pasolini understood film to be oneiric, because of its "osservazione abituale e quindi inconscia dell'ambiente, mimica, memoria, sogni" ("habitual and thus unconscious observation of the environment, gestures, memories, dreams") ("Cinema di poesia" 172; "Cinema of Poetry" 172). His key word is *primitive,* which earlier he had adduced to describe the brute, prehuman, and animal-like language of cinema as irrational and beholden to memory and dreams.[16] The enormous gulf separating the theories of the realist novel in the nineteenth century and Pasolini's *cinema di poesia* is hopefully now clear: for the realist novel the structural principle of the free indirect style is of a rational nature, since the emphasis is no longer on the subjectivity of either the author or the filtering consciousness of his characters but rather on the concrete events that drive the narrative. With Pasolini the free indirect style is, by his own admission, *irrational.* He believed that by removing the ideologically contaminated filter of language separating the worldviews of characters and filmmaker, the image-sign provides access to the raw inner world of the unconscious, whose illogical and arbitrary modes of expression negate any impulse toward the historical, narrative causality of the high realist novel.

The intellectual genealogy of Pasolini's theories on the cinema of poetry stretches back to the unlikely provenance of Giambattista Vico and his notion of *poesis* as the central and seminal act of cultural "making."[17] Given his interests in aesthetics and philosophy, Pasolini had likely read Vico, though it does not appear that he was directly influenced by his theories. More likely than not, this is an instance of two distinct and powerful thinkers offering comparable meditations on a subject (poetry) that served as the key to the elaboration of their larger projects. In his seminal critique of Cartesian analytical thought, Vico writes that humans, in their error, make themselves the measure of all things. In so doing, he continues, men and women turn to totalizing abstractions—one could insert structuralist semiotics here—and neglect the fundamental contingencies and irrationalities of history, which should have taught humankind in the first place that it can only know that which it has made, a notion he condensed into a celebrated maxim, "verum factum," first elaborated in *De antiquissima italorum sapientia* (*On the Ancient Wisdom of the Italians* [1710]).[18] The link between "making" and "knowing" for Vico falls within what he terms *poiesis* (more commonly used in its Latin form, *poesis*), whose Greek root signifies "to create." For Vico all knowledge, from the historical and sociological to the philosophical and political, is embedded in the signs that a society "poetically" creates in its early irrational period, when its principal expressive mechanisms were metaphor, figures of speech, and tropological linguistic signs. Vico warns that the student of cultural history must always look behind, around, and through these signs to establish their archaeology and grasp the range of meanings encoded in their etymologies. The Vichian maxim *verum factum* represents Vico's critique of analytical Cartesian philosophy and its premise that one can know only the workings of one's own mind, distilled in Descartes's celebrated *cogito ergo sum* (I think, therefore I am) formulation in *Discours de la méthode* (*Discourse on Method* [1637]). To fathom the world, according to the Cartesian line, one needs to understand the machinations of one's own mind and the accompanying language of mathematics and science that Descartes believed to be the rational agent's natural idiom. After an early—and, given the intellectual climate of his age and milieu, inevitable—flirtation with Cartesian thought, Vico dedicated his career to anti-Cartesian stances and claimed instead that the entirety of human endeavors, from the use of language to the establishment of civil codes and communal practices, could be traced to their earliest cultural productions, all of which stood outside of the enigmatic, shifting, and elusive mind (hence his repeated defense in *De nostri temporis studiorum ratione* [*On the Study Methods of Our Time* (1709)] of that same liberal arts education diminished by Descartes).

The *verum-factum* link, with its implicit emphasis on the capacity of the poetic sign to embody the enigmas of history, resurfaces in Pasolini's theories of cinematic language, where one finds a similar promotion of *poesis* as a form of cultural and epistemological production. As for Vico, for Pasolini the image-signs that the filmmaker captures at the unconscious level of his characters are always irrational, concrete, and "poetic" in their immediacy and culturally productive state. These images are never "grammatical" (that is, codified) and never permeated with the "barbarism of reflection" that Vico locates in overdeveloped societies that have lost touch with their primitive roots. The earliest peoples, Vico writes, must have begun with a metaphysics that was poetic rather than rational and abstract, since these irrational and robust peoples conceived the foundations of civil society in figurative terms. The early poets invented sublime fables suited to popular education, perturbed to excess the sentiments of the people, and taught virtue to the vulgar (*Scienza nuova* 375). In Vico, and later Pasolini, the nature of the civilized world, as opposed to primitive and pregrammatical times, is detached from the senses; ancient minds, on the other hand, were unabstract (Vico posits that poetry arises from "l'ignoranza" ["ignorance"] [*Scienza nuova* 402]). In sum, "la sapienza poetica" ("poetic wisdom") to Vico represents a "metafisica rozza" ("crude metaphysics"), and is the "tronco" ("trunk") that yielded all the other branches of knowledge—from economics, law, and morals to history, politics, and theology (*Scienza nuova* 367–68). The early mind anthropomorphized the raw data of perception in order to better understand it with images rather than words, as humans depended on metaphor and language's connotative functions before they were able to establish more codified and abstract terms (Vico, *Scienza nuova* 429, 431).

In line with Vichian tenets, Pasolini depicted the pregrammatical and unabstract nature of the cinematic image-sign as raw, animalistic, and attuned to the gestures of brute reality. Indeed, in the semiotic writings on film produced after "Il 'cinema di poesia,'" Pasolini offers views on the primitive that are strikingly Vichian in tone and tenor, albeit with his own ideological edge: "Il barbaro non ha bisogno di illusioni *per vivere, ossia per esprimersi.* Ma dal momento in cui comincia a vivere la realtà come contemplazione . . . egli scopre la storia, cioè l'illusione. Di cui da quel momento in poi avrà sempre bisogno, e fonderà quindi su questo . . . : l'alienazione prima contadina e poi piccolo-borghese" ("The barbarian has no need of illusions *to live or to express himself.* But from the moment in which he begins to live reality as contemplation . . . he discovers history, that is, illusion. From here to that moment on he will always need, and make the base of his actions . . . : the alienation first of the peasant then of the petit-bourgeois") ("Tabella" 297 [Pasolini's italics]; Nowell-Smith, "Pasolini's Originality" 20).[19]

A central principle of Vico's *Scienza nuova* (*New Science* [1725]), both structurally (it is the third book of five) and thematically, is laid out in the section entitled "La descoverta del vero Omero" ("The Discovery of the True Homer"). The argument sets out to solve in trademark-Vichian fashion, through a series of dubious though powerful etymologies and other creative philological tools, the controversies surrounding the authorship of the foundational epics of Western literary history, the *Iliad* and the *Odyssey*. It is fitting that Vico should put so much energy into this question because in attacking the analytical certainties of Cartesian thought, he placed great emphasis on the concrete cultural productions of a given people. The key in Vico to fathoming any cultural or political belief in the present lies in tracing the development of this same belief in and through time. Thus, Vico's philologist was also a philosopher, because he alone was best equipped to discern the nexus between logos and idea that represented the codification of cultural practices and norms.[20] Moreover, as works of the imagination the *Iliad* and *Odyssey* represent humankind at its earliest and most vigorous state—when, in Vico's view, people thought in those imaginative universals that would be refined away into the precepts and codes of civil society. By analogy, Vico writes, a primitive warrior would never utter the abstract phrase, "I am angry"; he would say metaphorically, "My blood boils" (*Scienza nuova* 935).[21] Similarly, in the figurative and unrestrained language of the two Homeric epics, the heart of primitive man is laid bare. In discerning the raw emotions and early creations of a culture, Vico believed that one gains access to its mind.

Pasolini's film *The Decameron*—in which each character "communicates with his own body, his own sanguine humors, his . . . shattered teeth, sex, sweat" (Petraglia 108)—provides a visual instantiation of key Vichian principles and corporeal semiotics.[22] *The Decameron,* alongside adaptations of Chaucer's *Canterbury Tales* and *1001 Nights,* was one of three films based on classic medieval texts in the director's so-called trilogy of life—a project, in Pasolini's words, that involved a shift from the ideological to the ontological (and, by extension, from politics to narrative). In addition to producing a cinematic *écriture* with the naked human body as both signifier and signified, Pasolini's film enacts the theories of "Il 'cinema di poesia'" by engaging with its literary source in ways that implicate human corporeality.[23] Early in the film a wizened reader of the film's aulic literary source, Boccaccio's

Decameron (1349–51), sits beside the text and begins to narrate to the illiterate, boisterous audience who will actually constitute many of the Neapolitan characters in Pasolini's refashioning of the text. The literary presence of Boccaccio's Latinate Tuscan text is invoked, but then the storyteller quickly discards the work—whose language he mislabels by claiming that Tuscan is spoken in Lombardy—and begins a spirited oral narration of a licentious nun who unwittingly presents herself to her mother superior wearing the drawers of the priest she has just known intimately.[24] The shift is from Boccaccio's learned, disembodied textuality to the erotic, physical orality of the cinematic adaptation, a work that seeks to elide the author's mediating prose style by directly presenting the gestures, speech, and actions of its nonliterate subjects.[25]

In his essay on Nikolai Leskov, "The Storyteller" (1936), Walter Benjamin describes the species of the storyteller as a dying one, for the degraded nature of modern life (Benjamin wrote the piece between the two world wars) deprived people of the capacity to "exchange experiences" (83). It is not difficult to read the piece as a corollary to the thesis of his landmark essay "The Work of Art in the Age of Mechanical Reproduction," for like the artwork whose aura is negated by a mechanically reproducible, technology-driven art, the storyteller's "incomparable aura" cedes pride of place to the "rise of the novel at the beginning of modern times" ("Storyteller" 109, 87). The latter form (the novel), Benjamin argues, is distinguished from the story (as the novelist is from the storyteller) by its dependence on the book, which is utterly divorced "from the oral tradition." Whereas the storyteller "takes what he tells from experience," the novelist "has isolated himself" (87). Analyzing Pasolini's transition from leading poet to filmmaker in the last fifteen years of his life, Maurizio Viano writes that part of the impetus came from his refusal to remain sitting at his desk and "being separated from the world. . . . By choosing cinema, Pasolini rejected the relationship with the world inscribed in literary production" (48).[26] As in Pasolini's essay on the cinema of poetry, the novel's medium, literary prose, emerges as a class-conditioned and protobourgeois distancing from everyday life and labor into an aestheticized solitude from which the novelist is able to make the world whole again in written form. But by the very totality and ideological coherence of the written work—as opposed to the fragmented and evanescent nature of the storyteller's art—the novelist marks the distance separating his or her life experiences from the literary text.

Benjamin's remarks in "The Storyteller" serve as fitting commentary on

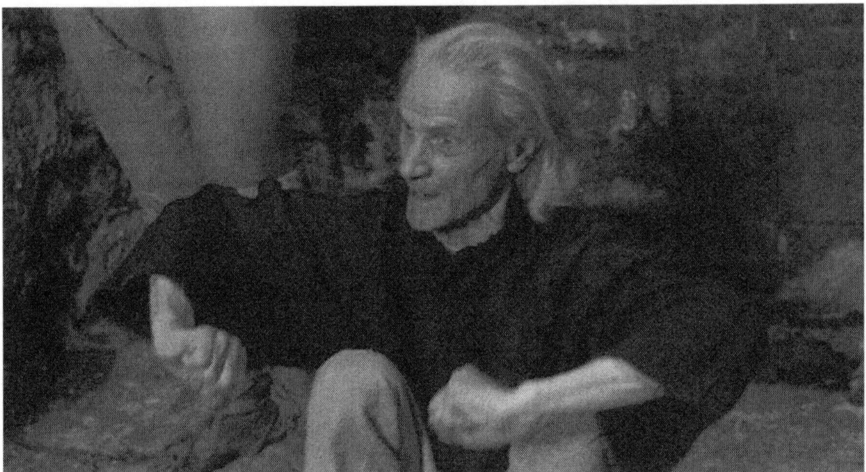

Figure 18 Pasolini's storyteller provides an "intersecting" adaptation of Boccaccio's source by translating its lofty textual rhetoric into a theatrical oral tale for the illiterate of Naples *(The Decameron)*.

Pasolini's *Decameron* because they describe the shift from textuality to orality as a desire to reclaim a lost social integration between artist and art. The essay on Leskov also underscores the disembodiment that takes place in the transition from voiced to written narration. In storytelling, Benjamin writes, "soul, eye, and hand are brought into connection. Interacting with each other"—as we see Pasolini's storyteller do here in full gesture (figure 18)—"they determine a practice. We are no longer familiar with this practice" (108). The mixture of nostalgia and despair motivating Benjamin's remarks find a similar expression in Pasolini's "Abiura della 'Trilogia della vita'" ("Rejection of the 'Trilogy of Life'" [1975]).[27] Although the three films celebrate narrative art and represent a declaration of "love to life," Pasolini writes, they were also born from a "setting aside of hope" and desire to immerse himself in the past ("Abiura" 7).[28] Thus, Pasolini's recourse to the mortal human body carries with it the eternal complement to earthly corporeality: death.

The film *The Decameron* instantiates the conceptual sympathies between Vichian *poesis* and Pasolinian free indirect style. The important scene where the actor Pasolini performs the tenets of his theory on cinematic poetry, during the visit by Giotto's most acclaimed disciple (played by Pasolini himself) to the piazzas of busy downtown Naples, might have been appended to Vico's "Discovery of the True Homer."[29] Pasolini actually frames (by making an imaginary camera of his hands) the fluid human drama before him, an act

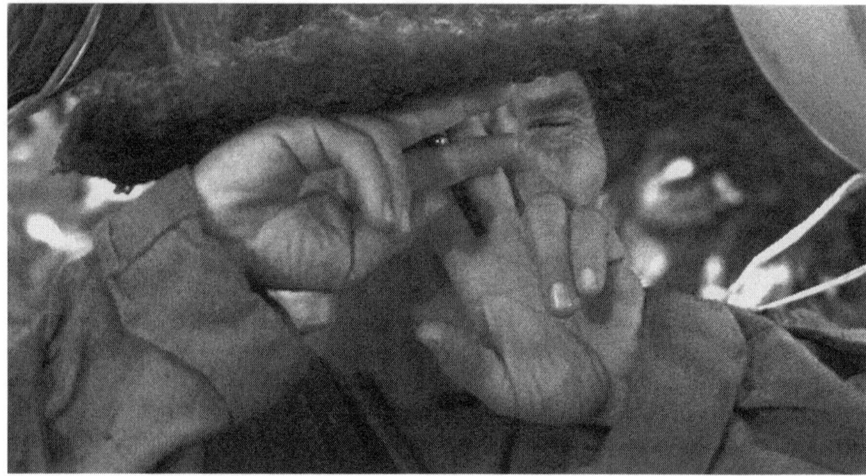

Figure 19 Pasolini frames reality as he creates the *cinema di poesia* from the unfolding events *(The Decameron)*.

that underscores cinema's ability to "write with reality" and elide the distance separating human embodiment and its aesthetic representation (figure 19). In this scene, as throughout the film, the "artist" is neither Benjamin's solitary novelist nor Pasolini's despised bourgeois auteur. Rather, to return to Visconti's notion of an "anthropomorphic cinema," he is a Marxist-conceived man among men, performing his labor with art just as others do with their various technologies, tools, and wares ("Storyteller" 83). Like Benjamin's Leskov the storyteller, Pasolini's artist experiences the life that he casts into form.

Vico's musings on Homer in the *Scienza nuova* also address the issue of cultural belatedness and its relationship with aesthetic creation by adducing proofs to establish that the *Iliad* and the *Odyssey* could not have been written by the same person. According to Vico the texts abound in anachronisms that suggest that they were compiled over centuries: "È infinita la differenza che si può osservar degli stili dell'uno e dell'altro poema omerico" ("The difference we can observe between the styles of the two [Homeric] poems is infinite") (*Scienza nuova* 853). Thus, in Vico, the word *Homer* serves as a code for the entire Greek peoples who composed and collected the rhapsodies that were later transformed into the two epics. The *Iliad,* as the book of raw passion and violent excess, marks the early heroic stages of Greek civilization; the more reflective *Odyssey* charts its reflective, melancholic, and rationalist autumn. In recording the customs, characters, and events that would go under the name *Homer,* the Greek people were collectively their nation's first historians and poets—and, as such, incapable of speculative thought. Vico writes: "La ragion poetica determina esser impossibil cosa ch'alcuno sia e poeta e metafisico egualmente sublime, perché la metafisica astrae la mente da' sensi, la facultà poetica dev'immergere tutta la mente nei sensi; la metafisica s'innalza sopra gli universali, la facultà poetica deve profondarsi dentro i particolari" ("By the very nature of poetry it is impossible for anyone to be at the same time a sublime poet and a sublime metaphysician, for metaphysics abstracts the mind from the senses, and the poetic faculty must submerge the whole mind in the senses; metaphysics soars up to universals, and the poetic faculty must plunge deep into particulars") (*Scienza nuova* 821). These words provide a fitting gloss for Pasolini's attempt in "Il 'cinema di poesia'" to establish a pregrammatical form of representation for the cinematic apparatus, which like Vico's Homer records without understanding and registers without analyzing. As we have seen in Pasolini's polemic with Eco, he hoped to bring the dogma of semiotics into the general transformation of culture, an intent that had also garnered fierce resistance to Vico's cultural philology centuries earlier. Whereas Pasolini sought to substitute the human body for the cinematic sign, Vico wished to draw attention to the corporeality of signification in those figurative words first uttered by primitive peoples whose collective "poetry" laid the groundwork for their future society's institutions.

The figure of the artist/poet in Pasolini's *Decameron* is the binder of fables who congregates in the heart of the polis, the marketplace *(agora)*, just as Vico speaks of the impoverished Homer (whose name Vico etymologically associates with "to link together") who "andò per i mercati di Grecia cantando i suoi propri poemi" ("wandered through the market places of Greece singing his own poems") (*Scienza nuova* 872). For Pasolini, as for Vico, the poetic element of the aesthetic representation in question (respectively, film and epic) derives from the everyday swirl of human activity, commerce, and energy. The "people" enjoy the capacity or right to compose the poetry of their age because the technological qualities of these two media (again, film and epic) rely more on the passive collection of figurative material than on the guiding aesthetic hand of a removed artist figure. The ensuing art for both thinkers is barbaric and prerational, as Pasolini's Neapolitan street theater emerges as the fitting analogue for the markets in Vico's Homeric Greece. For both, the poetry in question comes to life through a realistic idiom whose texture and vibrancy derive from the unmediated expression of, on the one hand, a vision of the world uncontaminated by language (Pasolini) and, on the other, a tableau of the infant stages of a raw civilization free from the abstractions of the rational mind (Vico).

Pasolini returns to illiterate, medieval Naples in *The Decameron* because like Vico he believed philology to be the key to human knowledge.[30] Earlier in his career this view led him to record the Friuli dialect of his childhood in his earliest collections of poetry. Later, as the mature director of *The Decameron,* he employed a visual philology that unearthed the bodies and sexualities of a people excluded from the aulic language of Boccaccio's classic literary text. The figure of Pasolini as the disciple of Giotto recalls Vico's Homer because, as the visual binder of fables in medieval Naples, he produces the triptych at film's end that represents his age's version of the motion picture. Moreover, the three frames of the altar, with one left suggestively unfinished, are composed by a happy workshop of artisans and laborers whose contributions are recorded in detail.

No work of Pasolini's would be complete without its contradictions, and the film's concluding statement witnesses the disappearance of Vico's primitive artist and Benjamin's storyteller. In his place stands an amalgam of the prototypical romantic artist, Vico's overly reflective modern man, and Pasolini's self-loathing bourgeois artiste. "Perché realizzare un'opera, quando è così bello sognarla soltanto?" ("Why create a work, when it's so beautiful just to dream it?"), Giotto's disciple asks (*Trilogia* 48). The line evinces a tension, which I take to be unresolvable, between theory and practice in Pasolini's views on the cinema of poetry. He emphasized again and again that, as a dilettantish semiotician, his theories had no special purchase and that moreover his dream of bringing semiotics into the general transformation of culture was just that, an unrealizable fancy. But the ideas in the essay "Il 'cinema di poesia,'" just like its accompanying scenes in *The Decameron,* point to a historical function of poetry that finds a powerful antecedent in the Vichian concept of *poesis.* In so doing, Pasolini's work squares with one of the philosophical tradition's most powerful contributions in Italy and elsewhere on the knowledge claims of the poetic mode. When Giotto's disciple stands before the incomplete triptych, he acknowledges the impossibility of a purely "collective" work, such as put forth in Vico's views on the ancient Greek peoples as the "authors" of the *Iliad* and the *Odyssey.* Such collective authorship is no longer possible in Pasolini, because—in line with Benjamin's idea that in a ruined modernity experience is no longer "exchangeable" ("Storyteller" 83)—he believed the fallen (that is, capitalist) world could no longer accommodate such expressions of aesthetic, class-free chorality. Although the film is set in the past, the problems of the present remain by the conclusion of *The Decameron*. Too morally inclined to succumb to escapism, Pasolini saddled the final scene of his *Decameron* with the class concerns of his present age. By accelerating the concerns of the past to affect the present, this anachronistic act established that, however much Pasolini wished to return to a "love of life" in the past, his conscience would not let him remain there long. The nihilistic films that immediately preceded and followed the trilogy, *Porcile (Pigsty)* in 1969 and *Salò o le 120 giornate di Sodoma (Salò, or The Hundred and Twenty Days of Sodom)* in 1975, the year of Pasolini's brutal murder, bring this last point home tragically.

PART THREE

AESTHETIC *CORSI* AND *RICORSI*

CHAPTER FIVE

Threat of the Real

Fact and Image in Antonioni

Come se fosse estate / ci siamo lasciati sorprendere / dal buio.
(As though it were summer, / we let ourselves be surprised / by the darkness.)

—Bernardo Bertolucci, "L'eclisse" (poem)

The career of Michelangelo Antonioni provides a Janus-faced perspective on the history of Italian film. As the innovative auteur whose work in the 1950s and 1960s cleared new pathways for filmmakers overwhelmed by a neorealist heritage, his films reassert the value of experimental approaches reminiscent of cinema's avant-garde heyday before the dominance of narrative film. However, as a "visual" director who guarded against linking film with nonpictorial art forms, especially literature, he stands outside the traditions of cinematic adaptation that lend Italian film its legendary intermedial reach.[1] Yet it is in this seeming impasse between the theoretical auteur and the medium-specific "visual poet" that the singularity of Antonioni's contributions to the surrounding aesthetic debates becomes manifest.[2] The centrality of his position is intensified by the fact that he, along with Federico Fellini and Pier Paolo Pasolini, stands as a major transitional figure who came of age during the neorealist era yet whose finest work is usually considered to mark a distance from this neorealist *apprendistato* (apprenticeship). A distillation of the director's lifelong dialectic with neorealist principles and practices took the form of a meditation on stolen bikes:

The neorealism of the postwar period, when reality itself was so searing and immediate, attracted attention to the relationship existing between the character and surrounding reality. It was precisely this relationship which was important and which created an appropriate cinema. Now, however, when for better or for worse reality has been normalized once again, it seems to me more important to examine what remains in the characters from their past experiences. This is why it no longer seems to me important to make a film about a man who has had his bicycle stolen. That is to say, about a man whose importance resides (primarily and exclusively) in the fact that he has had his bicycle stolen. . . . Now that we have eliminated the problem of the bicycle (I am speaking metaphorically), it is important to see what there is in the mind and in the heart of this man who has had his bicycle stolen, how he has adapted himself, what remains in him of his past experiences, of the war, of the period after the war, of everything that has happened to him in our country—a country which, like so many others, has emerged from an important and grave adventure. (Leprohon 89–90)

Thus, in an Italy "normalized" after decades of civil and world war, the Antonioni of the 1950s and 1960s believed that the new Italian cinema had no need to make films (pace Vittorio De Sica and Cesare Zavattini) about the actual if not banal goods of life. The rub in the Italy of the Economic Miracle was to capture the inner life of the individual who, metaphorical *bicicletta* in tow, sought to adjust to life in a materially though not morally rebuilt nation.[3]

The reticence to film stolen bikes—and thereby return to a mode of classical neorealism—reveals Antonioni's stake in the debates in Italian cinema of the 1950s about the image's relation to notions of realism. In Roberto Rossellini's *La macchina ammazzacattivi* (*The Machine to Kill Bad People* [1949]), the film image's contact with its real-world referent is so highly charged as to prove lethal, an allegory for Rossellini's desire to move beyond the documentary style of his postwar films and capture a version of reality that was not surface or immanent. The postneorealist Rossellini eschewed the identity between the realist sign and its signified because it left little room for exploring the hidden psychological textures that preoccupied him in the 1950s; rather than represent "reality" as such, the image in *La macchina ammazzacattivi* subsumes it. More broadly, the films that pushed the boundaries of neorealism are legion, ranging from styles and genres as diverse as the operatic return to nineteenth-century realism in Luchino Visconti's *Senso* (1954) to the psychic dramas at the margins of society and mental health in Fellini's *La strada* from that same year.[4] A critical mass of such films shares a cinematic equivalent of the Pauline biblical injunction—"the letter kills, but the Spirit gives life" (2 Corinthians 3:6)—as postneorealist filmmakers, many of whom had been nurtured by the movement into artistic maturity, came to believe that the verisimilar representation of the filmed object spelled its aesthetic failure.

The counterintuitive notion that a mimetic representation of the image could have detrimental to mortal aesthetic effect recalls a Platonic trope of significant cinematic impact. In Plato's cave, whose analogies figure richly in Bernardo Bertolucci's *Il conformista* (*The Conformist* [1970]), the images projected onto the dark wall are illusionary refractions and shadows offered by the political puppeteers for the distraction of the masses. In a pivotal scene in Bertolucci's film, the Fascist Marcello Clerici visits his former professor Luca Quadri in Paris, where the latter lives in exile as an organizer of anti-Mussolini resistance. Clerici is ostensibly in Paris to celebrate his honeymoon, but he actually has made the journey to assassinate Quadri. When their conversation turns to Plato's cave, Clerici insists that the Italian Fascists prefer the spectacles of history—those shadows on the cave walls that he uses hand gestures to recreate in Quadri's apartment—to the Platonic real, the light of truth above the corrupt citizenry's heads and beyond its moral reach. Bertolucci evokes the seductive power of the film medium by showing, through dazzling chiaroscuro effect, how the flooding of light in the cave of history can dissolve the shadows of Fascist illusion: when Quadri draws open the apartment's shutters, the visual images he created in the darkness disappear. Drawing an analogy between these Platonic/Fascist spectacles and the medium of film, Bertolucci once said in an interview that the myth of the cave, with its dependence on spectators submerged in darkness and responsive to images produced by a source of hidden light, was no less than "the invention of cinema" (21). Thus, the spectacular nature of *Il conformista*—a departure from the more rarefied and inaccessible early films the director made under the influence of *maîtres à penser* including Pasolini and Jean-Luc Godard—stands as an allegory for Bertolucci's retreat from the ideological legacies of engaged realist cinema.

It was common for filmmakers of the postneorealist era to offer Platonic-sounding glosses on their move away from the documentary slant of the 1940s, by insisting that they were seeking a new and more viable idiom for this elusive "real." For Rossellini this updated realism meant looking inside characters to access a realm that, he believed, only cinema, poetry, and the novel could enter; for Pasolini the solution lay in an ad hoc conflation of Platonic and Freudian ideas that cast the real as the "poetic" language of an unconscious that expressed itself principally in images rather than words; for Fellini, and his acclaimed "neorealism of the person" (Bazin, "*La strada*" 57), the real morphed into its putative antithesis, the realm of dream, fantasy, and neurosis. In Antonioni's most commercially successful film of the 1960s, *Blow-Up* (1966), the photographic image does not destroy in the manner of

Rossellini's machine to kill bad people—but it does portend death. The mortality that the photographer, Thomas, espies in the enlarged images from his seemingly innocent photography spree in a London park signals the end of more than the man held in fatal embrace by the cipher Jane. For the photographer's own brutally constructed aesthetic world, which for one critic is representative of Antonioni's cinematic universe,[5] is rent asunder by an image of murder that forces him to suspend his reduction of the world into glossy portraits and advertising shots. Thomas's subsequent isolation of the images from this murder into enlarged fragments requires something that this self-consumed, restless artist-of-the-moment had yet to consider: narrative. By piecing together the fragmented elements of an assassination, he gives his inchoate story a discernible beginning, middle, and end. Yet it is a narrative that nobody in his drug-addled world wishes to hear. By film's end he is back in the world of make-believe and mimes, content to abort his quest for justice and return to the imaginary games of his bohemia, which culminate in an invisible game of tennis. He thus abandons the burdens of truth and self-discovery that the violent image had foisted on him to return to a life inside the white lines of artifice.

The photographer's retreat from the realistic claims of an image associated with death recalls a leitmotif in Antonioni's films leading up to *Blow-Up*, especially the trilogy *L'avventura, La notte,* and *L'eclisse:* his desire to separate the "fact" from the "image."[6] In a small gem of an essay entitled "Il 'fatto' e l'immagine" ("The 'Fact' [or 'Event'] and the Image" [1963]), he remarks, "Un regista è un uomo come tutti gli altri. Eppure la sua vita non è normale" ("A filmmaker is a man like any other, and yet his life is not normal") ("'Fatto' e l'immagine" 50; "Event and Image" 50). The filmmaker is therefore a man among men, as Visconti also defined him in his essay "Anthropomorphic Cinema," differing only in the nature of his métier. For Antonioni the anthropological difference separating the filmmaker from his brethren derives from his particular notion of vision:

Vedere per noi è una necessità. Anche per un pittore il problema è vedere. Ma mentre per il pittore si tratta di scoprire una realtà statica, o anche un ritmo se vogliamo ma un ritmo che si è fermato nel segno, per un regista il problema è cogliere una realtà che si matura e si consuma, e proporre questo movimento, questo arrivare e proseguire, come nuova percezione. Non è suono: parola, rumore, musica. Non è immagine: paesaggio, atteggiamento, gesto. Ma è un tutto indecomponibile steso in una sua durata che lo penetra e ne determina l'essenza stessa. (" 'Fatto' e l'immagine" 50; Antonioni's italics)

Seeing is for us [filmmakers] a necessity. For a painter too the problem is one of seeing: but while for a painter it is a matter of uncovering a static reality, or at most a rhythm that can be held in a single image, for a director the problem is to catch a reality which is never static, is always moving toward or away from a moment of crystallization, and to present this movement, this arriving and moving on, as a new perception. It is not sound—words, noises, music. Nor is it a picture—landscape, attitudes, gestures. Rather it is an indivisible whole that extends over a duration of its own which determines its very being. ("Event and Image" 51)

This quotation deconstructs a lasting preconception about Antonioni's aesthetics: that his is a "painterly" cinema, the subject of much critical focus over the years, partly because of Antonioni's celebrated line that he was a "filmmaker who paints" (qtd. in Dalle Vacche, *Cinema and Painting* 44). In reality Antonioni did not privilege painting: it was to him just one art among the many that the cinematic medium synthesized in equal measure.[7] For example, although Antonioni tended to avoid the use of extradiegetic music in his films, he attributed enormous importance to the diegetic aural track, especially ambient sound and silence, which he labeled "true music," "the music that can be adapted to images" (Leprohon 100). Any notion of cinematic painting Antonioni had in mind would be akin to the concluding scene of Pasolini's *Decameron* (1971), where the disciple of Giotto (played by Pasolini himself) stands in front of an incomplete triptych in Naples's Santa Chiara cathedral. In line with Antonioni's behest of capturing a "reality that is never static," Pasolini's two paintings represent the sutured frames of the filmic image, a pictorial surface imbued both with movement (space) and *durée* (time).

The word *fatto* in Antonioni's essay can be translated as both *fact* and *event,* depending on one's emphasis. The choice of *event* draws attention to Antonioni's manipulation of figurations of temporality, whereas the technically more accurate *fact* implies the distance the filmmaker wishes to insert between real-world phenomena and their aesthetic representations. There is also a political dimension to Antonioni's essay that relates, as much in his early work does, to his relationship with neorealism. In full thrall to this latter movement Antonioni's initial films included a brief documentary about

Roman street cleaners, *N.U.* (1948), as well as an acclaimed filmic essay on the inhabitants, principally fishermen, of his native Po River Valley, *Gente del Po* (*People of the Po Valley* [1943]). But, as his remarks in 1958 on the need to move beyond stolen bikes makes clear, for Antonioni what mattered was not a typical Italian's socioeconomic status and condition (embodied in the symbol of his labor, the bicycle); rather, Antonioni was concerned with this Italian's character, "whether he is timid, whether he loves his wife, whether he is jealous, etc." (qtd. in Leprohon 90). In that indefinite and open "etc." Antonioni declared his independence from the political and ideological scope of neorealist aesthetics and his desire to separate the fact or event (the putative stolen bike) from the image (the complete portrait of the new Italian, in all his or her psychological texture and complexity).[8]

"Il 'fatto' e l'immagine" begins by describing a white sky, cold and empty sea, half-shuttered hotels, and a lone figure: "Su una delle sedie bianche della Promenade des Anglais a Nizza è seduto il bagnino, un negro con la maglietta bianca" ("On one of the white seats of the Promenade des Anglais the bathing attendant is seated, a black man in a white singlet") ("'Fatto' e l'immagine" 51; "Event and Image" 52). Antonioni continues, noting "un bagnante che fa il morto a pochi metri dalla riva" ("a single bather floating inert a few yards from the shore") and "non si sente che il rumore del mare, non si nota che il dondolio di quel corpo" ("nothing to be heard except the sound of the sea, nothing to observe except the rocking of that body") ("'Fatto' e l'immagine" 51; "Event and Image" 52). The sense of foreboding is palpable, and the drama and danger appear as anticipated: "L'urlo è breve, secco, pungente. Basta guardarlo, il bagnante, per capire che è morto" ("The cry is short, sharp, and piercing. A glance is enough to tell that the bather is dead") ("'Fatto' e l'immagine" 51; "Event and Image" 52). Though Antonioni dispatches the "event" of the above scene in the shortest space of time, the reaction caused by the tragedy has a more dilatory effect, as he provides several sentences on the inane chatter between two young children who witness the incident. At the end of the scene—"Dopo una diecina di minuti arriva la polizia, la spiaggia è sgombrata" ("After ten minutes or so the police arrive, and the beach is cleared")—we cut forward to the retrospective narrator:

> Eravamo in Guerra. A Nizza aspettavo il visto per raggiungere a Parigi Carné, del quale dovevo far l'assistente. Erano giornate piene di impazienza e di noia, e di notizie riguardanti una Guerra ancora ferma su una assurda linea Maginot. Supponiamo di dover sceneggiare un pezzo di film, sulla base di questo

movimento, di questo stato d'animo. Per prima cosa io proverei a togliere dalla scena il "fatto," a lasciare soltanto l'immagine descritta nelle prime quattro righe. In quel lungomare così bianco, in quella figura solitaria, in quel silenzio, c'è secondo me una forza straordinaria. Il fatto, qui, non aggiunge nulla, è di più. Ricordo benissimo che mi distrassi, quando accadde. Il morto funzionò da diversivo a uno stato di tensione. Ma il vuoto vero, il malessere, l'angoscia, la *nausée,* il letargo di tutti i sentimenti e desideri legittimi, la paura, la rabbia, io li riprovai quando, uscito dal Negresco, mi trovai in quel bianco, in quel niente che prendeva forma intorno a un punto nero." (" 'Fatto' e l'immagine" 51–52)

It was wartime. I was at Nice, waiting for a visa to go to Paris to join Marcel Carné, with whom I was going to work as an assistant. They were days full of impatience and boredom, and of news about a war which stood still on an absurd thing called the Maginot Line. Suppose one had to construct a film, based on this event and on this state of mind. I would try first to remove the actual event from the scene, and leave only the image described in the first four lines. In that white sea-front, that lonely figure, that silence, there seems to me to be an extraordinary strength of impact. The event here adds nothing; it is superfluous. I remember very well that I was interested, when it happened. The dead man acted as a distraction to a state of tension. But the true emptiness, the malaise, the anxiety, the nausea, the atrophy of all normal feelings and desires, the fear, the anger—all these I felt when, coming out of the Negresco [Hotel], I found myself in that whiteness, in that nothingness, which took shape around a black point. ("Event and Image" 53)

The narrator's oscillation between the description of the drowning and his self-distancing from its effect makes it difficult to say whether the scene's fore-boding derives from the gravity of the event or from the anxious emotional economy in which the incident is simultaneously recalled and repressed. The retrospective separation of the event from the image occurs in the subtle shift of focus from the tragic accident to the details that prepare the audience for the impending death. Antonioni notes that in recomposing the sense of war and foreboding in those embattled days in Nice, he would organize every-thing around those "first four lines" describing the sand and sparse sea. This pregnant dreariness in the setting of the swimmer's death suggests something ominous at hand. For the Antonioni in "Il 'fatto' e l'immagine," the visual in-auspiciousness draws on the poisoned atmosphere of a world at war; for the Antonioni of the 1950s and 1960s, the malaise linked to his imagery reflected the feelings of dissatisfaction and spiritual poverty in a materially rebuilt na-

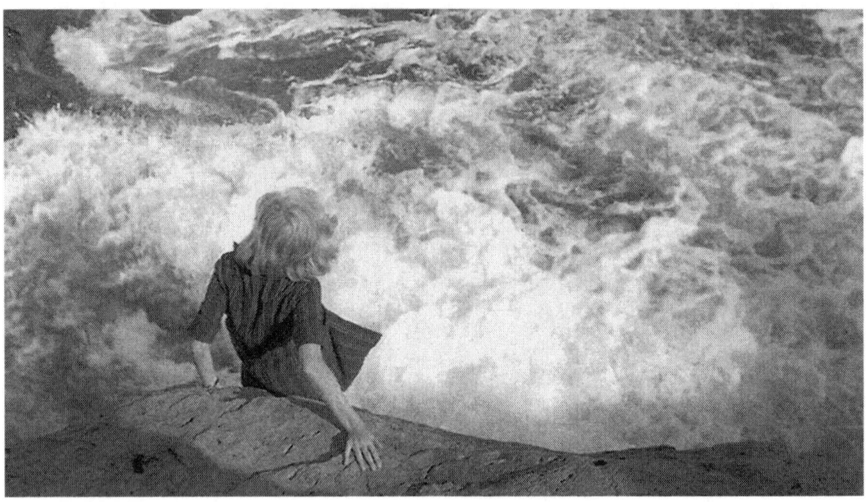

Figure 20 Claudia stares out at a roiling sea, an "image" that trumps the "fact" of her best friend Anna's disappearance *(L'avventura)*.

tion. In the scene above, the event or fact of the drowning cedes pride of place to its associative imagery of the bleak beachscape. A similar desire to separate the event/fact from the image shapes the aesthetic agenda of his acknowledged masterpiece, *L'avventura.*

The film's principal event, which is soon overwhelmed by its image-based associations, is the disappearance of Anna after a spat with her lover, the callow and wealthy philanderer Sandro. This event, moreover, becomes the "black hole" that subsumes the narrative and themes established in the earlier portions of the film. Once Anna disappears, any hope in the audience's mind for a logical exposition fades away, taking with it the possibility of fathoming the characters' underlying emotions, motivations, and thoughts. The images enjoined to Anna's disappearance emerge as the stubborn clues and signs of her memory and legacy long after she vanishes. Claudia looks out to sea for Anna (figure 20), and the white foam crashing about her is a visual emblem, or image-correlative, for her turbulent state of mind and raw emotions after her best friend's disappearance (and for her impending seduction by the predatory Sandro). The succeeding image of the hypersexual yet immature Sandro depicts him looking out over the sea into the jutting rocks on the horizon, the sparseness of the environs an analogy of his yawning yet empty egotism.

These visual themes and images return as the two play out the effects of the

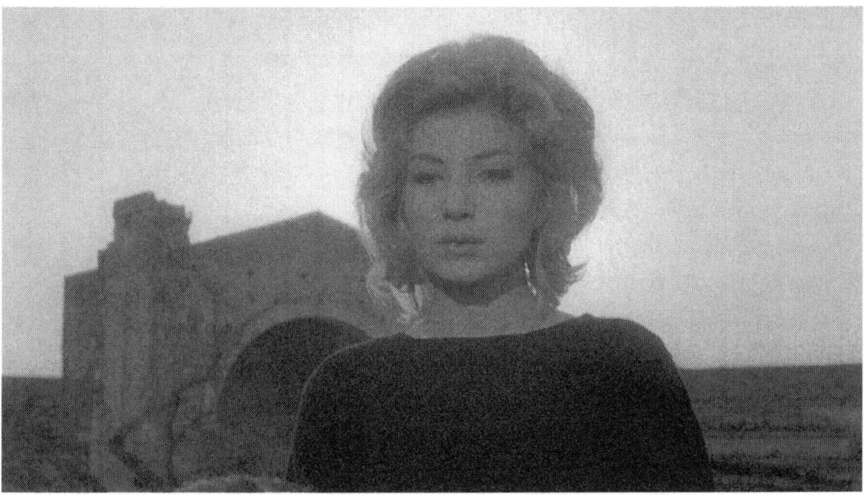

Figure 21 The divinely backlit Claudia fronts the womblike structure that is her objective correlative *(L'avventura)*.

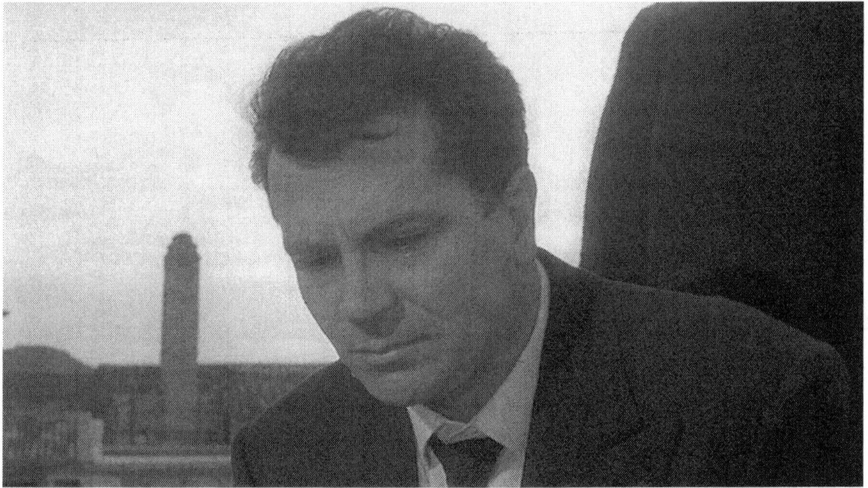

Figure 22 Sandro weeps before the phallic tower that ironically comments on his mix of philandering and helplessness *(L'avventura)*.

event of Anna's disappearance, especially in the celebrated conclusion of the film, in which Claudia's image-correlative is the holy womb of an abandoned church and Sandro's the ironically adduced phallic tower of a distant building (figures 21 and 22). The audience is prepared for this conclusion in the initial extended sequence between Sandro and Claudia after Anna's disappearance, where the physical immanence and visual associations of the objects and images take priority over the narrative development of the events and facts in a manner consistent with the ideas in "Il 'fatto' e l'immagine." In replacing the human world with one of objects, Antonioni was one of the many directors in the 1960s to use his medium to gain access to the symbolic systems and social codes of the material world.[9]

The search for Anna takes place in a landscape whose bareness deepens the characters' emotional intensity and inner turmoil. Few if any words are spoken, and when they are, the utterance only leads to miscommunication. The editing dehumanizes the landscape by shifting from tight close-ups of Claudia and Sandro to open stretches of rock and sea, a telescoping that serves to reduce the significance of the human drama at hand through a process Geoffrey Nowell-Smith describes as Antonioni's tendency to have the "physical prevail over the social."[10] The effect of the montage is thus a kind of antiromantic withering away of the subjective imprint on the landscape and an accompanying shift from the characters' various (often petty) horizons of concerns to the chilling indifference of nature, as Anna's loss is swallowed up by the drowning of human time in a cosmic rhythm.

Claudia and Sandro fall in love during this embroiled search. But tension permeates their impending union, an atmosphere Antonioni captures by having the audience hear the ocean crashing and witness the surf roiling onto the coast, beneath a leaden sunlight that barely creases the thick clouds. Similarly, in "Il 'fatto' e l'immagine" the stark images of a deserted beach and its sea and sand displace the event of the man's drowning and implicate the larger sociopolitical matrix of the scene: World War II and its rank existential atmosphere. Anna's disappearance is the Archimedean point on which balances the totality of the film's "true emptiness, the malaise, the anxiety, the nausea, the atrophy of all human feelings and desires, the fear, the anger," those same emotions Antonioni felt when confronting the event of the drowned man in "Il 'fatto' e l'immagine." When Claudia accepts Sandro and his womanizing at film's end—an act that signals the finality of Anna's disappearance—the editing returns us to the images of figures 21 and 22. Antonioni uses a medium shot to situate the characters in disparate pictorial and communicative planes, an image that rhymes with an earlier depiction of the two figures in planar disjunction. Once again, Claudia's realization that she will accept Sandro occurs against the backdrop of a visual correlative for her "feminine" acquiescence (the womb of the church in figure 21, the open sky in figure 23).

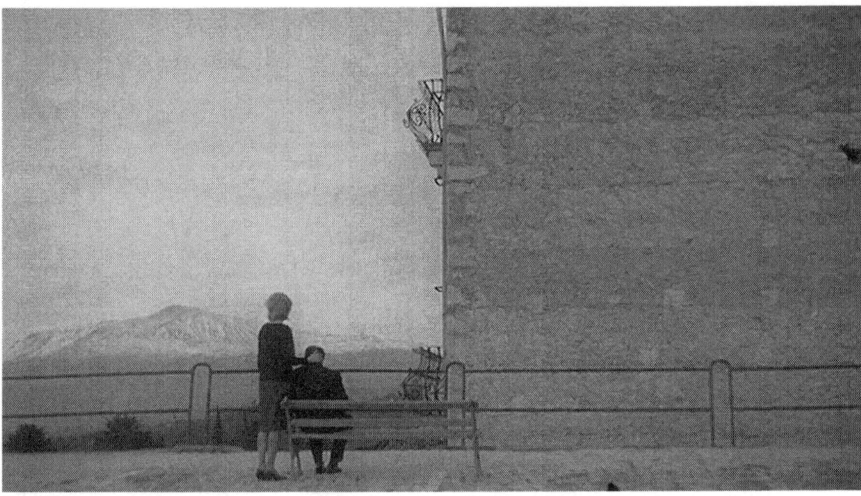

Figure 23 Once more, Antonioni links Claudia to an element—the open sea—that reveals her character, just as the stone wall to her right stands as a symbol for the impermeable Sandro *(L'avventura)*.

The separation of the realist sign from its referent in *L'avventura* draws on Antonioni's ongoing concern with the representation of time as expressed in "Il 'fatto' e l'immagine": "Ecco che entra in giuoco la dimensione del tempo, nella sua concezione più moderna. È in questo ordine di intuizione che il cinema può conquistare una nuova fisionomia, non più soltanto figurativa. Le persone che avviciniamo, i luoghi che visitiamo, i fatti a cui assistiamo: sono i rapporti spaziali e temporali di tutte queste cose tra loro ad avere un senso oggi per noi, è la tensione che tra loro si forma" ("'Fatto' e l'immagine" 50). ("[In cinematic representation] the dimension of time comes into play, in its most modern conception. It is in this order of intuition that the cinema can acquire a new character, no longer merely figurative. The people around us, the places we visit, the events we witness—it is the spatial and temporal relations that we have with each other that have meaning for us today, and the tension that is formed between them" ("Event and Image" 51). This disquisition on cinematic temporality turns on Antonioni's use of the word *modern*, which suggests the original possibilities that film, by virtue of its technology, provides for the creation of aesthetic temporality. By writing that the cinema can transcend figuration in the name of a new representational idiom, Antonioni discredits the notions of literary and pictorial realism associated with cinema's capacity to "index" human time, in the words of André Bazin.[11] The cinema, he countered, produces a new relationship between the subject and temporality that renders preexisting notions on the matter obsolete. A master of the nouveau roman, the genre to which Antonioni's films of the 1960s are often compared, Alain Robbe-Grillet offers a telling definition of Antonioni's particular version of modernity with its temporal implications: "In a Hitchcock film, the meaning of what you see on the screen is constantly delayed, but at the end of the film, you understand everything. With Antonioni, it's exactly the opposite. The images don't hide anything. What you see is very clear, but the meaning of the image is constantly problematic, and becomes more problematic as the film unfolds. When the audience leaves, the film remains open. . . . This is one of the important characteristics of the Modern" (qtd. in Chatman, *Michelangelo* 15).

In line with Antonioni's own words in "Il 'fatto' e l'immagine," Robbe-Grillet emphasizes the rift between the film's facts (which in a more traditional narrative such as Hitchcock's move the narrative toward closure) and its images (which in Antonioni are ends in themselves that "hide nothing," are always "open").[12] The audience is thus compelled to read the sequence of images as constituting a narrative of equal importance to the chain of events that form the film's story or plot. In a similar vein Gianni Celati construes the essence of Antonionian temporality in terms of attenuation: "The views [in *L'avventura*] of the island [where Anna disappears] are never offered as finished descriptions, but rather as pauses within the landscape, as tarries which produce dead moments" (219). Thus, the filmmaker is able to transform the temporal into the spatial; temporal *durée* and pictorial representation coalesce into what Celati describes as a modern and new form of "adventure," the "ineluctable present" in which "time . . . cannot be killed," an aesthetic form of "liberation" (220).[13] Robbe-Grillet's and Celati's observations on the originality of Antonioni's temporality have been corroborated by a host of critical voices, who despite their divergences acknowledge Antonioni's ability to condense the physical and temporal dimensions of human life into a single image. For Celati the closing scene of Sandro and Claudia's ambiguous reconciliation in *L'avventura* represents the "true time of waiting": "the girl [Claudia] stands in profile and the man [Sandro] sits on the bench, at dawn, while in the background there is the curtain of the sky" (220). The lines bear an eerie resemblance to those articulated by Antonioni in "Il 'fatto' e l'immagine," in speaking of the malaise before the war and its connection to the surprising tragedy of the dead swimmer at Nice: "In quel lungomare così bianco, in quella figura solitaria, in quel silenzio, c'è secondo me una forza straordinaria" ("In that white sea-front, that lonely figure, that silence, there seems to me to be an extraordinary strength of impact"). The crux of the representation lies, therefore, in hiding the real—or at least leaving it implicit—in analogous imagery that suggests a larger "off-screen" truth.

The tension between fact and image in *L'avventura* resurfaces in the montage at the end of *L'eclisse,* the story of an unusual relationship between the young Roman translator Vittoria and the swaggering stockbroker Piero. After a series of trysts, the couple arrange to meet at the "usual spot." But their rendezvous manqué takes the form of a seven-minute visual essay on the architecture, byways, and everyday scenes of an evening commute in the one-time Fascist showpiece district EUR. Mirella Joan Affron notes that while this "montage does recall to the viewer the film just viewed . . . the composition of the edited sequence and its placement in the emphatic position are such that it takes on a form and meaning of its own, tending to replace the film at the conclusion of the viewing experience as well as in its recollection" (146). The succession of unanchored images becomes, Affron notes, a "text apart," and in this drift from the main narrative a new formal economy with its own protocols of interpretation and meaning ensues. Antonioni does gesture in the direction of real-world phenomena in the sequence: it contains references to, among other things, the atomic age, an eclipse of the sun, the anonymity of modern city life, and the actual crosswalk where Piero and Vittoria have often met. Yet Antonioni avoids explicit reference through ellipsis, analogy, and, as we have seen in *L'avventura,* his trademark practice of linking objects to their objective correlatives. In *L'eclisse* the aestheticization of all areas of life blends any passing human presence into the chromatic and compositional economies of the picture frame. But the effect is not, as commonly believed, to "dehumanize" characters either absent or present. Rather, I believe that Antonioni's impersonal images create a sense of nostalgia over the lovers' disappearance from the film.

The final sequence begins where the lovers have previously reunited, a crosswalk that Antonioni transforms into a visual pun on their impending failed "crossing" or appointment. If the image can be said to be a "beginning" to anything, it is to the predominant role that composition will have in the subsequent images. The careful arrangement of vertical, horizontal, and diagonal lines establishes the architectonic feel of this concluding film-within-a-film. Antonioni, of course, has been accused of an overly rigid sense of design that can lend his images an immobile feel.[14] Yet here the stately if static appearance of these heavily designed frames is balanced by the whir-

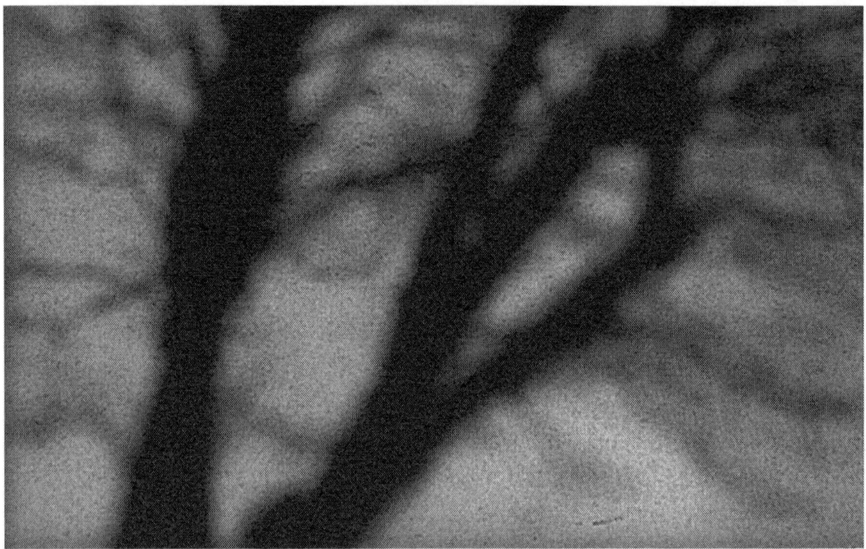

Figure 24 The lattice shadows of a tree establish the centrality of objects and formal elements over traditional narrative concerns in Antonioni's famous concluding sequence *(L'eclisse).*

ring movement of counterimages like the horse and carriage and the curving lattice shadows of a tree (figure 24). A series of portraits also softens the visual asceticism of the compositions by introducing a human element that challenges the immobility of the buildings and structures with the energy and imperfections of the human body. If there is a dialectic between things and people in the concluding sequence of *L'eclisse,* Antonioni seems a disciple of the poet Francis Ponge in taking the side of the inanimate, since his portraits include a dour-looking woman and a stern older man whose visage is fractured into oddly detailed close-ups.[15] When these anonymous presences are combined with the absence of the film's two main characters, the effacement of subjectivity writ large in the final sequence would seem to suggest the eclipse of the self in an antihumanist vision.

This occlusion of the human from the brimming cityscape recalls Stanley Cavell's description of cinema's capacity to establish an entire world independent from and outside of the human element: "A world complete without me which is present to me is the world of my immortality. This is an importance of film—and a danger. It takes my life as my haunting of the world. . . . So there is reason for me to want to deny the coherence of the world, its coherence as past: to deny that the world is complete without me. But there is equal reason to want it affirmed that the world is coherent without me. That is essential to what I want of immortality: nature's survival of me. It will mean that the present judgment upon me is not yet the last" (160). One would be hard pressed to find a more suggestive comment on a perennial theme of Antonioni's films, both in the trilogy and throughout his career: the image of one's life as a haunting of the world. In *L'avventura* the lives in the film go on after the disappearance of Anna. Yet the subsequent film narrative continually returns to Anna, reconfiguring her intimate life into new sexual and social networks in her absence.[16] In their different ways, other films of Antonioni's create this uncanny sensation of characters' capacity, in prosopopoeia-like fashion, to look back on the living from beyond the grave. In *Profession: Reporter* (1975) the haunting takes the form of the protagonist's staged death; *Il mistero di Oberwald* (*The Mystery of Oberwald* [1981]) is also a film about the blurring of identity. In *Blow-Up* the quest for a cadaver jars Thomas from an artificial world that he dominates into a destabilizing realm of vanishing evidence, troubled self-reflection, and finally willful escape to the make-believe of mimes. This pursuit for an identity fractured into duality or nonexistence finds supreme expression in the concluding scene of *La notte*. When Lidia and Giovanni admit to each other that they are no longer in love—just before they *make* love on a golf course—the key event is the recitation of a long passionate letter from one of Lidia's admirers. Giovanni asks who it was that could have written such stunning words; she answers that it was Giovanni himself—a person that both of them have forgotten, since the better part of him seems to have disappeared long ago.[17]

For Cavell, an astute interpreter of "absence" in *L'avventura* (79), both the majesty and horror of film is that, more than any other aesthetic medium, it can project a total and totalizing "world" onscreen in which the subject need not be present for that world to be complete. In Antonioni there are countless scenes in which objects enjoy the pictorial and thematic centrality independent of humans. His cinema, especially during the 1960s, was synonymous with such nonhumanistic aesthetic movements as abstract expressionism and analytical cubism. But, as is so often the case with Antonioni, appearances only tell part of the story. To return to "Il 'fatto' e l'immagine," Antonioni's representation of humankind aims to distinguish the "facts" of individual existence from its images. So he often leaves the viewer not with the person or individual as such, but rather with the set of atmospheric, environmental, and other (visually) contextual elements that correspond to the character in question. Memories of Anna, for example, return to Sandro and

Claudia in the form of the haunting Liparian musical theme, the crashing of foamy waters, and the sparse, open, unyielding sea. These images become a visual analogy for the no-longer-relevant fact of who and what Anna was and the "events" in which she partook. Similarly, in *Blow-Up,* Thomas has only the image of the dead man in the form of an amplified photographic negative. His hunt for the actual victim and the people associated with him lead to dead ends, like his thwarted sexual attraction to the mysterious Jane. But overall the quest serves to rend the veil covering what had been his sense of impermeable and eternal youth.

The ending of *L'eclisse* pushes this theoretical concern with separating the event or fact from the image to its unsettling extreme by providing an example of what Cavell describes as nature's survival of the individual. The final sequence, I believe, creates nostalgia for the subject, so that by film's end the audience senses the full weight of Piero and Vittoria's absence; they will never return. Although it may seem counterintuitive to impute to Antonioni a "humanistic" concern with subjectivity, all of the films from the trilogy—and each of the protagonist couples (Claudia and Sandro, Lidia and Giovanni, Vittoria and Piero)—are defined by an absence either actual (the quest for Anna by Sandro and Claudia, Vittoria and Piero's disappearance before the final scene) or implied (Giovanni's incapacity to recognize the link between his younger and older selves). Nature, it is said, abhors a vacuum; yet the cinematic world of Antonioni during the era of its fragile, transcendent greatness in the early 1960s thrives on the visual, emotional, and existential *buchi neri* (black holes) created by characters in search of others or themselves. However riven by figures of absence, Antonioni's films are also concerned with presence. In Antonioni, Gilberto Perez writes, the dialectic between presence and absence stands as an analogy for the relationship between the human and the nonhuman. Each exists only in relation to the other, and it is the tension between them that drives his work.[18] No wonder, then, that in a sketch for the shooting script of *L'eclisse,* the phrase "Piero and Vittoria have not yet arrived" appears three times. And in the actual screenplay the description of the suburban images, figures, and scenarios are often linked to their relationship (imagined or actual) to these two main characters.[19] In a public seminar dedicated to *L'eclisse,* Enzo Paci, a professor of philosophy at the University of Milan and the leading Italian phenomenologist of his generation, even described Antonioni's films as heralding a "return to the subject."[20]

Joan Esposito notes that the root of *eclipse* comes from the Greek *ekleipsis,* which means a leaving, a forsaking, the failure to appear at an accustomed place. The modern Italian usage of the word *(eclisse)* also entails the sudden or temporary absence of a person and, in the grammatical sense, an ellipsis (30). An eclipse traces a trajectory across the sky, as well as the eye, in an event that suggests both closure and occlusion. Peter Brooks considers the process of reading plot in Freudian terms that could be used to describe the experience of observing an eclipse: in following the characters of a book from page to page, the reader, like the stargazer, seeks fulfillment by reaching an "end that is the consummation (as well as the consumption) of its sense-making" (52). Such closure, spatial as well as temporal, can only come at the end—of the novel or of the event or phenomenon—because it is natural for the reader to defer the symbolic death (Freud's Thanatos) that comes with termination, just as he or she seeks to prolong the textual desire (Eros) that compels the forward momentum of the act of reading. In Antonioni's *L'eclisse* the narrative closure comes *before* the actual end of the film, for the disappearance of the lovers signals the culmination of their screen presence. Following their disappearance, we shift from the world of people to a world of things. Thanatos, it seems, has prevailed over Eros.

But only temporarily. After our initial shock over the disappearance of Vittoria and Piero, Antonioni's visual poetics reassert the endurance of subjectivity. A contemporary film by Alain Resnais, *L'année dernière à Marienbad* (*Last Year at Marienbad* [1961]) also tells of a failed rendezvous and a broken promise, but the eclipse of the subject defines the film from beginning to end: there is little along the lines of "character" in the film, and any human presence in the scenes and interludes serves only to instantiate various cinematic ideas, motifs, and tropes. Moreover, questions about the human—agency, meaning, and value—are nonexistent in much of the experimental imagery and forms in the kind of avant-garde film that is often associated with Antonioni (wrongly, I believe). In the conclusion of *L'eclisse,* however, the failed appearance of the characters does indeed constitute a haunting: although neither Piero nor Vittoria appears in any of the scenes, their memory, hinted at or suggested by a world of things, surges to the fore. The "event/fact" of their presence in the film has been eclipsed, but their accompanying images (the trough of water where Vittoria has dipped her hand, the sidewalk where they used to meet, the blond woman whose physiognomy visually rhymes with Vittoria's) are marshaled to create an analogue for their relationship and for themselves. The concluding montage is by no means optimistic, for, as this chapter's epigraph suggests, the warmth of the sun is about to be eclipsed by a cold moon; but the characters' spirits linger. And a world filled with spirits, however invisible and troubled, remains open to enchantment.

It is not surprising that, subsequent to his trilogy of the early 1960s, Antonioni's films became even more mannered and stylized. After the film that is often associated with the three that preceded it, *Il deserto rosso,* he seldom made films either in Italy or about Italian subjects. With the passing of the economic miracle, and with Antonioni's distancing himself from the native neorealist traditions that had occasioned his apostasy in the films of the trilogy, his once deeply felt aesthetic imperative to separate facts and events from their image correlatives seems to have diminished. It is a testament to the theoretical insights of Antonioni's essay "Il 'fatto' e l'immagine" that many of this filmmaker's most powerful cinematic moments result from his capacity to probe the pressing issues of a given period while also troubling the standard "realist" (that is, mimetic) link between facts and images. The stakes in such an operation, as Antonioni was no doubt well aware, were high, given the prestige and moral gravity that had accumulated around the legacies of neorealism at home and abroad. But, as Antonioni writes in "Il 'fatto' e l'immagine," for the filmmaker, the "necessity of *seeing*" supersedes all other concerns, whether commercial or political. By creating films whose central premise is the tension between what the surface of the image hides and what it reveals, his experimental forays into the dialectic between fact and image in the early 1960s represent some of the most provocative contributions to that single greatest issue in Italian cinematic history: the question of realism.

CHAPTER SIX

Chiasmus, Italian Style

Rhetoric and Ideology in *The Leopard* and *The Conformist*

In her study of Italian identity after political unification in 1861, Suzanne Stewart-Steinberg explores the traits that impeded the formation of a national self, including the Italians' supposed lack of interiority, their *scioltezza* or elasticity in acting and thinking, and their love of rhetoric (1–19). The latter quality brings all three together: the rhetorician must be *sciolto* in his nimble movement from one idea and topos to the next, and his use of words as performative agents tends to elide inquiry into such matters as authenticity and an interior self. For example, the Nazi officer Bergmann's claim in *Rome, Open City*, "Voi italiani siete malati di retorica" ("You Italians are addicted to rhetoric"), is intended as an insult that decries the lack of inner resolve and character that he believes renders Italians inferior to his master Aryan race. However misguided Bergmann's diagnosis—the Resistance fighters he interrogates do not speak, even under torture, thereby refuting his ascription of their "rhetoricity"—the stereotype of the suspiciously rhetorical nature of Italian political culture endures.

In a related vein Angela Dalle Vacche explores how Italian filmmakers' continual preoccupation with the past led to the projection of "corporeal entities [that] became metaphors for the Italian body politic" (*Body* 3). She goes on to argue that these "shapes of history" are not "images of social reality" but rather "reflections of an imaginary, national self" (*Body* 3). Following Dalle Vacche's cue, we find that it is not only in the manifestations of human corporeality that the "shapes" of Italian history emerge; it is also in the rhetorical figures employed by filmmakers exploring this national self. In Italian aesthetics one such figure that bridges the rhetorical and the political is the chiasmus.

Derived from *chi*, the Greek letter for *x*, chiasmus indicates a crossing over of the elements of two phrases or clauses that are parallel in syntax but whose word orders are then reversed. In Italian literary history a celebrated example of the trope comes from the opening lines of Ludovico Ariosto's *Orlando*

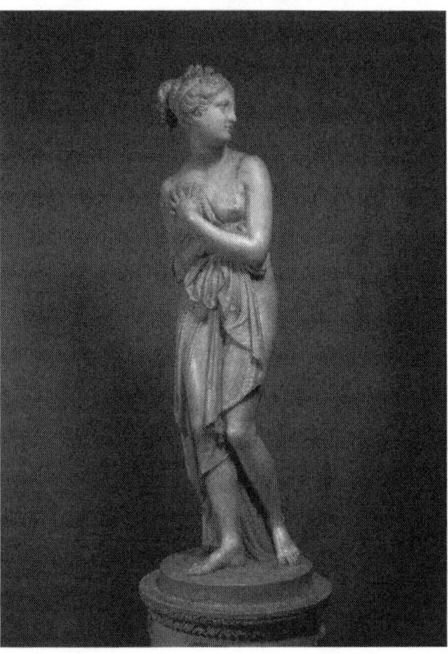

Figure 25 Canova's figure forms a visual chiasmus with her counterbalancing limbs (*Venus*).

furioso (1516), which switches the normal word order to link *donne* to *arme* and *cavellier* to *amori,* instead of vice versa: "Le donne, i cavellier, l'arme, gli amori, / le cortesie, l'audaci imprese io canto" ("The ladies, the knights, the arms, the loves / The courtesies, and the brave deeds I sing") (1.1.1–2). Ariosto thus creates a verbal irony through a *coincidentia oppositorum* that scrambles the usual ordering in this parallel structure.

For all its prominence as a rhetorical figure of speech, chiasmus also plays a prominent role in the visual arts. A staple of neoclassical aesthetics, chiasmus in painting and sculpture of this style uses counterbalancing gestures or forms to create a sense of order and harmony. For example, in Antonio Canova's *Venus* (1817–20) the bending of the goddess's left arm in the opposite direction of her gaze creates a visual *x* reinforced by her body listing in counterpoise to the right, also on an axis complementary to her gaze (figure 25). In less systematic fashion Titian's *Portrait of Cardinal Pietro Bembo* (1540) creates a visual cross between the gaze of his subject's face and the pointing of his hand to establish a sense of balance suited for the paradigmatic Renaissance man, Bembo, one of the age's most influential writers, politi-

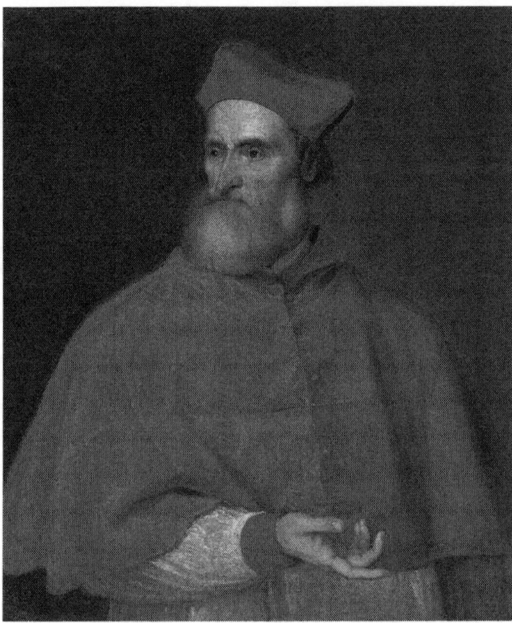

Figure 26 Titian crosses the arc of his subject's gaze with his gesturing hand to emphasize the harmonious blending of opposites in a Renaissance polymath (*Portrait of Cardinal Pietro Bembo*).

cians, and clerics—a polymath whose creative energies swirled in different but mutually reinforcing directions (figure 26). A later visual artist, Andy Warhol, was able to create chiastic effects in his multipaneled paintings and silk screens by reversing elements from one visual unit to the next, a hybrid practice that draws on ancient traditions in the plastic arts while pointing toward the frame-by-frame exposition of film.[1] As we will see, the film medium combines literature's capacity to create chiasmus through the coupling of syntactic units articulated in temporal sequence and the visual arts' ability to set in dialogue the compositional elements of a single image.

The uses of chiasmus became an important tool for Italian artists and writers seeking to express the complexities and contradictions of their nation's political life, as creative minds across the media captured what Stewart-Steinberg describes as the chiasmus's capacity to show how "opposites cross back into each other and thereby also provide each other support" (63). This oscillation between a movement away from something and a return toward it reveals the paradoxical yet practical function of the chiasmus in Italian political discourse: people and parties who would seem to be enemies end up "crossing over" to become allies, and the words of one slogan or ideology ultimately support the same position they would appear to be attacking. In this manner the chiasmus became the master trope for depicting the shape of power in all its *scioltezza* (elasticity) in two of the most important and bitterly contested episodes of national identity formation, the Risorgimento and Fascism, and in both literary and cinematic expression.

Revolutionary Stasis:
Chiasmus in Lampedusa and Visconti

Writing from the Italian periphery in his native Sicily, the author Giuseppe Tomasi di Lampedusa had firsthand knowledge of the dizzying power plays that had passed his island from one foreign ruler to the next for more than two thousand years. From his cynical perspective Italy's official transition to statehood in 1861 represented yet another move in the national chess game that, more often than not, reduced Sicily to the status of pawn. Appearing nearly a century after this watershed event, his novel *The Leopard* distilled the position of an elite class that sought to protect its position while adapting to the forces of historical change brought on by national self-determination: "Se vogliamo che tutto rimanga com'è, bisogna che tutto cambi" ("If we want things to stay as they are, things will have to change") (*Gattopardo* 32; *Leopard* 40). This famous mantra chiastically projects the past into the future while relegating the future to the past: for the nobles to retain their former privileges in the newly unified Italy, they needed to effect cynical compromises that followed the letter if not the spirit of democratic collaboration.

In Lampedusa's novel this process of *trasformismo* culminates in the fateful marriage negotiations between the upstart Don Calogero and the book's protagonist, Don Fabrizio Salina, alias the Leopard. The former needs the latter's money, and the latter needs the former's bloodline; together they broker the equivalent of a political and socioeconomic chiasmus. The event takes place at roughly the center of the novel and represents the apotheosis of Don Calogero's ascent and the Leopard's capitulation. In a masterful prelude to the decisive encounter Lampedusa writes: "Quando alle quattro e mezza precise gli venne annunciata la venuta puntualissima di don Calogero, il Principe non aveva ancora finita la propria toletta; fece pregare il signor Sindaco di aspettare un momento nello studio e, continuò, placido a farsi bello" ("When Don Calogero's arrival was announced at exactly half past four the Prince had not yet finished his toilet; he sent a message asking the Mayor to wait a minute in his study and went on placidly beautifying himself") (*Gattopardo* 83; *Leopard* 144). By forcing Don Calogero to wait for him, the prince strategizes on how to best impose his authority on a rival that in previous times he would not have deigned to acknowledge. The lush depiction reveals the Leopard's perfumed artillery:

> Si unse i capelli con il *lemo-liscio,* il *Lime-Juice* di Atkinson, densa lozione biancastra che gli arrivava a cassette da Londra. . . . Rifiutò la *redingote* nera e la fece sostituire con una di tenuissima tinta lilla che gli sembrava più adatta all'occasione presunta festosa, indugiò ancora un poco per strapparsi dal mento, con una pinzetta, uno sfacciato peluzzo biondo che era riuscito a farla franca la mattina nell'affrettata rasatura. . . . Prima di uscire prese su un tavolo un estratto delle *Blätter der Himmelsforschung* e con il fascicoletto arrotolato si fece il segno della croce, gesto di devozione che ha in Sicilia un significato non religioso più frequente di quanto s'immagini.
>
> Traversando le due stanze che precedevano lo studio si illuse di essere un Gattopardo imponente dal pelo liscio e profumato che si preparasse a sbranare uno sciacalletto timoroso; ma per una di quelle involontarie associazioni di idee che sono la croce delle nature come la sua, davanti alla memoria gli passò l'immagine di uno di quei quadri storici francesi nei quali marescialli e generali austriaci carichi di pennacchi e gale, sfilano, arrendendosi dinanzi a un ironico Napoleone; loro sono più eleganti, è indubbio, ma il vincitore è l'omiciattolo in cappottino grigio; e così, oltraggiato da questi inopportuni ricordi di Mantova e di Ulma, fu invece un Gattopardo irritato a entrare nello studio. (*Gattopardo* 83–84)

He plastered his hair with *lemo-liscio,* Atkinson's lime and glycerin, a dense whitish lotion which arrived in cases from London; . . . he rejected the black frock coat and chose instead a very pale lilac one which seemed more suited to the presumably festive occasion; he dallied a little longer to tweak out with pincers an impudent fair hair which had succeeded in getting through free that morning in his hurried shave; . . . before leaving the room he took from the table an extract from the *Blätter der Himmelsforschung* and with the rolled paper made the sign of the cross, a gesture which in Sicily has a nonreligious meaning more frequently than is realized.

As he crossed the two rooms preceding the study he tried to imagine himself as an imposing Leopard with smooth scented skin preparing to tear a timid jackal to pieces; but by one of those involuntary associations of ideas which are the scourge of natures like his, he found flicking into his memory one of those

French historical pictures in which Austrian marshals and generals, covered with plumes and decorations, are filing in surrender past an ironical Napoleon; they are more elegant, undoubtedly, but it is the squat little man in the gray top-coat who is the victor; and so, put out by these inopportune memories of Mantua and Ulm, it was an irritated Leopard that entered the study. (*Leopard* 145)

The Leopard's irritation is well founded. Holder of the keys to the kingdom, he must now grant access to a person (and a class) that normally would have been barred by high walls. In the past Tancredi Falconeri's passion for Angelica would have simply resulted in her being his mistress, with no question of the marital terms that the Leopard and Don Calogero were about to negotiate. But owing to the changing historical conditions, the Leopard refused to marry his daughter Concetta to his beloved nephew Tancredi—even though, we learn, their love was mutual—because she could provide him neither the cunning nor the cash his noble class required for survival in an Italy of "jackals."

The passage on the Leopard's ablutions reveals the obsolescence of the elegance, finery, and other class symbols of the ancien régime in the newly unified country. Whereas the Leopard's choice in pomade and frock coat may have once served him in dealings with tasteful and discerning fellow nobles, in the Italy of Don Calogero the "plumes and decorations" carried by men like the Leopard and the Austrian generals of the Napoleonic campaigns held little weight. Lampedusa suggests the futility of the Leopard's meticulous toilet by linking his masculine pretensions with feminine associations: though Don Fabrizio strides out of his toilet like a leopard looking to rend the flesh of a helpless victim, he does so with "smooth scented skin" and is soon reduced to a pretty but ineffectual simulacrum of his once-powerful person.

Since the Leopard offers Don Calogero above all genealogy, he begins the marriage negotiations by describing his and Tancredi's descent from the Peers of the Realm, Grandees of Spain, Knights of Santiago, and other illustrious forebears. However highborn the family may be, the Leopard continues, its dire economic straits are just as pronounced. Don Calogero has just the remedy, but before playing his hand he matches the Leopard in political savvy by remarking slyly: "L'amore, Principe, l'amore è tutto, e questo lo posso sapere io" ("Love, Excellency, love is all, as I know myself") (*Gattopardo* 89; *Leopard* 153). Then the bounty comes tumbling out of his mouth: "Nel contratto matrimoniale assegnerò a mia figlia il feudo di Settesoli, di salme 644, cioè ettari 1680, come vogliono chiamarli oggi, tutto a frumento; terre di prima qualità ventilate e fresche, e 180 salme di vigneto e uliveto di Gibildolce; e il giorno del matrimonio consegnerò allo sposo venti saccheti di tela con mille 'onze' ognuno" ("In the marriage contract I will assign to my daughter the estate of Settesoli, of six hundred and forty-four *salmi,* that is ten hundred and ten hectares, as they want us to call them nowadays, all wheat, first-class land, airy and cool; and a hundred and eighty *salmi* of olive groves and vineyards at Gibildolce; and on the wedding day, I will hand over to the bridegroom twenty linen sacks each containing ten thousand ounces of gold") (*Gattopardo* 89; *Leopard* 153–54). It is difficult to say whether the comment that follows the inventory belongs to the Leopard or his aristocratic descendant Lampedusa: "La volgarità ignorante gli sprizzava da ogni poro; malgrado ciò i suoi due ascoltatori furono sbalorditi" ("Ignorant vulgarity exuded from [Don Calogero's] every pore; even so, the two listeners [the Leopard and Father Pirrone] were astounded") (*Gattopardo* 90; *Leopard* 154).[2] The Napoleonic Don Calogero has vanquished the Austrian-general-like Leopard: "Don Fabrizio ebbe necessità di tutto il suo potere di controllarsi per nascondere la sorpresa. Il colpo di Tancredi era più sbardellato di quanto potesse supporsi. Una sensazione di disgusto stava per assalirlo" ("Don Fabrizio needed all his self-control not to show his surprise; Tancredi's coup was far bigger than he had ever imagined. A sensation of revulsion came over him again") (*Gattopardo* 90; *Leopard* 154).

The chiasmus emerges as the symbol for the historical substitutions of a corrupt political unification embodied in the crossing over of the Leopard and Don Calogero into each other's camp: the Leopard provides Don Calogero with the bloodline to legitimate the material basis of his ascendancy, just as Don Calogero's infusion of cash and property into the Leopard's impecunious family allows him and his noble class to remain powerbrokers. Though the actual marriage will be between Tancredi and Angelica, in a sense it is the Leopard and Don Calogero who are chiastically wed in the above scene. Each needs the other in equal and unconditional measure. As he watches Don Calogero's retreating figure "rimpicciolirsi" ("becoming smaller and smaller") after their negotiations, the Leopard is forced to admit that "quel mucchietto di astuzia, di abiti mal tagliati, di oro e d'ignoranza . . . adesso entrava quasi a far parte della famiglia" ("this little conglomeration of astuteness, ill-cut clothes, money, and ignorance . . . was now to become almost a part of the family") (*Gattopardo* 90; *Leopard* 154).

Lampedusa's literary chiasmus takes the form of an equally telling chiastic commentary on the machinations of Italian state-formation in Visconti's cinematic adaptation of *Il Gattopardo* in 1963, which appeared just a few years after the novel's embattled drive for publication.[3] Millicent Marcus writes that the renowned ballroom scene at the end of the film—which influenced, among others, the long wedding sequences in Francis Ford Coppola's *The Godfather* (1972) and Michael Cimino's *The Deer Hunter* (1978)—is "macrocosmic [because it] stands not only for the self-enclosed universe of nineteenth-century Sicilian aristocracy but also for a ceremonial reenactment of the entire plot of *The Leopard*" (*Filmmaking* 53).[4] The hour-long scene exposes the ancien régime's own hand in its downfall. At one point, while observing a group of identical young Sicilian ladies bouncing on a bed, the Leopard notes acidly that in-class breeding and marriage contracts have yielded a weak progeny that resemble monkeys about to climb the chandeliers. Yet the Leopard also cannot help but shudder when the uncouth arriviste Don Calogero comments on the impossibility of building houses like the setting of the ball, because of the rising cost of gold. The ballroom scene choreographs the movements that allow Angelica to take her place among the Leopard's family and the island's greatest ladies. Whereas the novel balances on the chiastic switch effected in a marriage contract that mixes the Leopard's blood with Don Calogero's assets, the film's plot culminates in the visual chiasmus of a waltz shared by the Leopard and Angelica.

The scene gives the impression of a dying Leopard, an extreme departure from Lampedusa's novel, where the protagonist's death does not occur until twenty-seven years after the ball. But Visconti wished to condense the novel's time frame to focus on the years of the unification that took place between 1860 and 1861, so he dispensed with the attenuated literary decline of the protagonist. The Leopard does, figuratively speaking, "die" during the ball in both the film and the novel: in each he says good-bye to his youthful idealism, his sexuality, and above all his efforts to protect his class. Two couples chiastically switch during the dance, the betrothed Tancredi and Angelica, and the Leopard and his long-suffering wife—a woman, the Leopard remarked earlier, that had borne him seven children but never allowed him to see her bare navel. The waltz begins when, with a tight grin, Tancredi hands Angelica off to the "affascinante e bello" ("charming and handsome" [Tancredi's words]) Leopard, whom Angelica thanks for all his efforts on her behalf (figure 27). The Leopard tells Angelica that nobody could "resistere alla tua bellezza" ("resist your beauty"), at which point the camera cuts to a countershot close-up of an unsettled and shrinking Tancredi, a mirror image of the grimacing Concetta, who accepts the baton of marital disappointment and bitterness

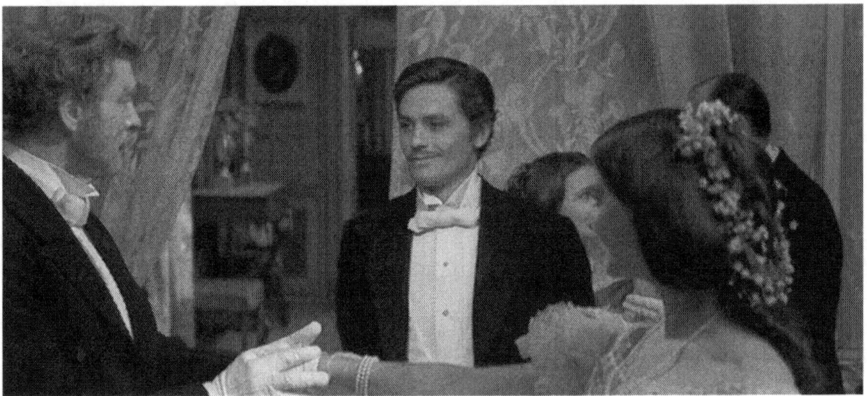

Figure 27 Visconti's Tancredi hands off his fiancée to the Leopard, setting off a chiastic dance of great historical symbolism *(The Leopard)*.

handed to her by her mother, also shown in a look of disappointment. The latter three are forced to the sidelines to watch the Leopard as he dances in suspended time with Angelica in a choreographed paean to his former glory and lost youth.

The Leopard sacrifices the two most important women in his life, his wife and daughter, to "couple" figuratively with Angelica, thereby establishing a crossover from noble to common bloodlines in the name of Angelica's extraordinary family wealth and the political power it will purchase Tancredi. In the waltz the flirtatious Angelica substitutes Tancredi with his much older uncle to acknowledge the forces set in inexorable motion by the Leopard's realpolitik—and not Tancredi's passionate love. Overall, the juxtaposition of the dancing partners and their bitter onlookers reveals the cynical political allegory that Lampedusa's novel and Visconti's film proclaim at every juncture. Manipulating the patterns of chiasmus, Lampedusa and Visconti use rhetorical and visual "crossings" to show how in art as in politics, the more things change, the more they can remain the same.

Chiastic Desire in Moravia and Bertolucci

Few commentators were more attuned to the psychological complexities of the Italian postwar than the prolific author Alberto Moravia. In a series of novels including *La ciociara* (*Two Women* [1958]), *Il disprezzo* (*Contempt* [1954]), and *La noia* (*Boredom* [1960])—all of which were adapted for the screen—he analyzed the relations between the inner worlds of his characters and the political backdrop that shaped them (and vice versa). His ability to project issues of sexuality onto the external world made his work appealing for filmmakers, who seized on his Freudian understanding of human nature by giving visual form to the neuroses, fantasies, and forbidden thoughts of his complicated protagonists.

One of his most troubled creations, Marcello Clerici in *Il conformista* (1951), exhibits a psychotic tendency for substitution that makes him, as early as childhood, "predestinato a compiere atti di crudeltà e di morte" ("predestined to create acts of cruelty and violence") (*Conformista* 24; *Conformist* 17). Moravia conflates Clerici's troubled childhood sexuality with the substitution complex that would define his adult life and its erotic chaos. When asked by his friend Roberto why he had killed some lizards, Marcello "stava sul punto di dire, 'perché mi faceva piacere,' poi non sapeva neppur lui perché . . . rispose, 'perché sono dannose'" ("was about to say, 'Because I enjoyed it,' but then, without even knowing why, he . . . answered, 'Because they're harmful'") (*Conformista* 14; *Conformist* 9). Following the exchange, Marcello assaults Roberto when he refuses to join him on his killing sprees. When he goes to confess his transgressions to his distracted mother, he finds her scantily dressed in her bedroom, where she asks him to help clasp a necklace over her naked shoulders. To capture her attention and activate her maternal instincts, he tells her that he killed a cat instead of the lizards—a lie that proves prophetic the next day, when he fires his slingshot into the bushes and fatally wounds the cat that he thought was Roberto.

This pattern of sadomasochistic violence and misdirected libidinal energy assumes chiastic patterns during Clerici's adult life as a functionary of the Fascist Party. In Paris to assassinate his former professor, the anti-Fascist Luca Quadri, Clerici falls in love with Quadri's much younger wife, Lina. Their dinner together late one evening sets in motion a visual chiasmus that, once again, conflates Clerici's sexuality with his murderous proclivities:

> Adesso il piede di Lina continuava a premere il suo, ed egli provava, a questo contatto, quasi un senso di sdoppiamento come se dai rapporti d'amore l'ambiguità si fosse trasferita in tutta la sua vita e invece di una situazione ce ne fossero due: la prima in cui egli indicava Quadri a Orlando e tornava in Italia con Giulia, la seconda in cui salvava Quadri, abbandonava Giulia, restava a Parigi con Lina. Le due situazioni, come due fotografie sovrapposte, si instersecavano e si confondevano coi varii colori dei suoi sentimenti di rimpianto e di orrore, di speranza e di malinconia, di rassegnazione e di rivolta. (*Conformista* 302–3)

[At the restaurant] Lina's foot continued to press against his own, and at the contact he almost felt like he was splitting in two, as if the ambiguity of his love relationships had invaded his whole life, and instead of one scenario, there were two: the first, in which he pointed Quadri out to [the Fascist thug] Orlando and returned to Italy with Giulia; and the second, in which he saved Quadri, abandoned Giulia, and stayed on in Paris with Lina. The two scenarios intersected and merged like two superimposed photographs, colored visually by his feelings of regret and horror, hope and sorrow, resignation and revolt. (*Conformist* 247–48)

This vertiginous crossing of elements from one scenario to the next points to Clerici's convoluted logic and confused morality, leaving him at the crossroads of conflicted emotions (regret and horror, hope and sorrow, resignation and revolt). The chiastic nature of the scene unfolds in the dancing that follows: Clerici takes Lina to the dance floor while Quadri accompanies Giulia. But this superficial crossing only masks the more threatening substitutions taking place in Clerici's psyche: Lina is the gendered namesake of Lino, the chauffeur who seduced the young Clerici, leading him to shoot and (he believed) kill the man. Symbol of both Clerici's guilt and ambiguous sexual orientation, Lino becomes the source of an original sin that leads the protagonist down the path of state-sanctioned political violence.

Later, on his way to Quadri's assassination in the woods of Savoy, Clerici reflects: "Buon marito, buon padre, buon cittadino, grazie anche alla morte di Quadri . . . avrebbe visto la sua vita acquistare lentamente ma solidamente quell'assolutezza che sinora le era mancata. Così, la morte di Lino, che era stata la causa prima della sua oscura tragedia, sarebbe stata risolta e annullata da quella di Quadri, proprio come, un tempo, l'offerta espiatoria di una vittima umana innocente, risolveva e annulava l'empietà di un precedente misfatto" ("He would be a good husband, a good father, a good citizen . . . thanks to Quadri's death . . . and he would watch his life slowly but surely acquire the certainty and solidity that up until now it had lacked. In this way, Lino's death, which had been the chief cause of his obscure tragedy, would be resolved and annulled by Quadri's, just as in the past the expiatory sacrifice of an innocent human being had served to resolve and annul the impiety of a previous crime") (*Conformista* 331–32; *Conformist* 272). Clerici is able to make this startling justification of his innocence because of the Fascist political structure that he inhabits and the ideology it espouses. As Clerici explains, the murder of Quadri and the chiastic substitutions that it entailed were related to "una trasmutazione completa dei valori" ("a complete trans-mutation of values"): "l'ingiusto doveva diventare giusto; il tradimento, eroi-smo; la morte, vita" ("injustice must become justice; betrayal, heroism; death, life") (*Conformista* 332; *Conformist* 272). If Lampedusa/Visconti's slogan for the revolutionary stasis sought by elites was that things must change in order for them to stay the same, the perverse moral logic of Moravia's *Conformista* is summed up in Bertolucci's film adaptation of the novel, when Clerici asks his confessor to absolve him today for the sins he will commit tomorrow.

Though he departs from Moravia's novel in fundamental ways (especially in his removal of the author's trademark emphasis on fate), Bertolucci contin-ues the piercing psychological inquiry into the link between eros and politics as he gives his substitutions a Freudian inflection. The filmmaker's engage-ment with the works of Sigmund Freud was a constant in his early career. "Stai attento" ("Be careful"), Pier Paolo Pasolini warned Bertolucci when he learned that his protégé was undergoing psychoanalysis, which Pasolini be-lieved "rovina la creatività" ("ruins creativity").[5] Not that Pasolini was averse to Freud per se, for he claimed to have had "letto tutto Freud" ("read all Freud").[6] But he imagined that psychoanalysis, because it rationalized the unconscious and penetrated the mystery of the self, could produce an explic-itness fatal to art (to repeat the Conradian maxim) and thus could prevent Bertolucci from attaining that *cinema di poesia* derived from the inchoate yet aesthetically productive psyche. So Pasolini exhorted Bertolucci to follow his lead and infuse "un Freud letterario" ("a literary Freud") into his works, while avoiding psychoanalytic praxis.[7] Diverging from his early *maître à penser,* Bertolucci drew on his experience of psychoanalysis to express Freudian no-tions in the unlikeliest of forms: the figure of chiasmus, whose discursive crossings he manipulated to meditate on the nature of political discourse, the rhetoric of sexual desire, and the syntax of crime and punishment.

In his discussion of the grammar of the schizophrenic unconscious, Freud underscores the "predominance of the word-relation over that of the thing" (*Major Works* 442). The speech of the mentally imbalanced, Freud writes, often depends on verbal "substitute-formation," where the subconscious will establish ad hoc relations between objects and concepts that lack genuine con-nections. In line with this Freudian notion of verbal substitution-formation, in *Il conformista* Bertolucci uses chiastic structures to reveal the faulty moral logic of his protagonist, Clerici, and the rhetorical sleights of hand in Fascist aesthetics.[8] Early in the film, chiasmus deconstructs the poetics of power articulated by Marcello's best friend, Italo Montanari. A spokesperson for

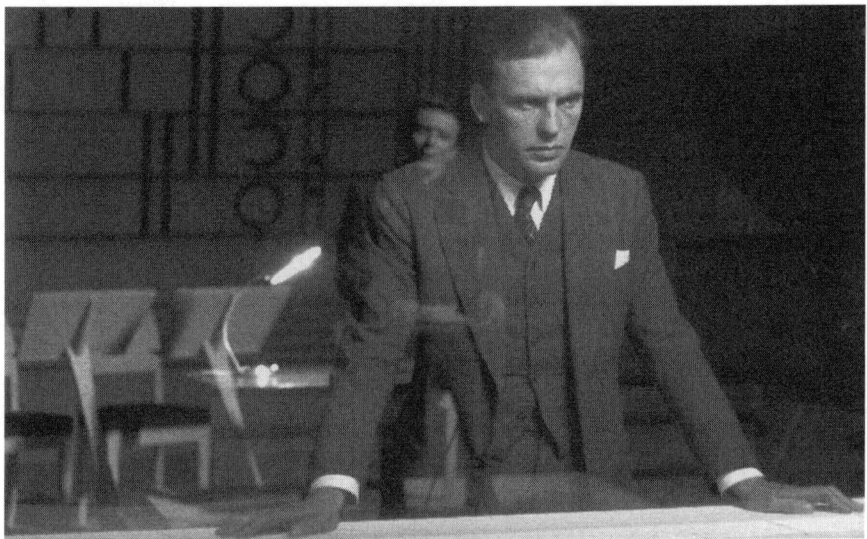

Figure 28 A hologram of the Fascist Montanari appears on Clerici after his chiastic radio speech *(The Conformist)*.

the Fascist Party, Montanari is an anti-Homer: a blind bard of false poetry whose language consists of forced inversions and empty rhetoric. Montanari's radio program, "Mistica di un'alleanza" ("Mystique of an Alliance"), speaks of Fascist Italy and Nazi Germany as "caposaldi di due civiltà" ("the capstones of two civilizations"), whose historical encounters have always represented a "svolta nel corso della storia del mondo" ("turning point in the history of the world"). This ancient kinship, he continues, now finds in 1930s Fascist Italy its modern expression, as the two nations rediscover their common virtues. Bertolucci ironizes the Italo-Germanic national friendship through a chiasmus: Montanari alludes to Joseph Goebbels's description of "l'aspetto prussiano di Benito Mussolini e l'aspetto latino di Hitler" ("the Prussian aspect of Benito Mussolini and the Latin aspect of Hitler"). The propagandistic nature of the statement needs no further comment, for Goebbels was of course the treacherous Nazi wordsmith. Just as Montanari's words come to him from this outside source, his body is filmed not directly but as a floating image on the glass partition of the studio, reducing him to a holograph swallowed by Clerici's form (figure 28). The verbal refraction of Montanari's words from Goebbels thus parallels the visual reflection of his disembodied person.

Clerici can barely stand to watch Montanari spin his deceits: he turns away and buries his head in his hands. But Marcello's retreat from the lies of Fascism is brief: a voice from a party official calls him to attention, and he falls in line as the faint drone of Montanari's sound bites lingers. By making Montanari the ape of Goebbels, Bertolucci suggests that there could be no union of equals between the German and Italian elements of this supposedly mystical alliance, for the real power rested on the German side. Though Hitler privately worshipped Mussolini, he believed that the Duce and his southern race were inferior to the Nordic Germans and the more Aryan British and Scandinavians. Logical enough in formal terms, Montanari's chiasmus breaks down once it is subjected to historical reality. The scene represents the first of many instances where Bertolucci deconstructs the tidy logic of Fascist rhetoric through the temporal irony of a look back at the political movement some thirty years after its defeat.[9]

With its sexual innuendo of trading favors and swapping identities, the badinage between Clerici and Montanari during the radio show offers an eroticized version of the political and moral inversions that will follow. When Clerici informs Montanari of his impending marriage to Giulia, Montanari remarks that Clerici is now gaining a wife, while he, Montanari, is losing a best friend. This language of sexual exchange value intensifies when Clerici exclaims to Montanari that yes, the voluptuous maid comes as part of his ménage with Giulia. Clerici believes that sexual substitutions will render him more normal in the eyes of the world. Politically, his conformism entails offering his services to a murderous Fascist regime; sexually, it requires him to channel his ambiguous and homoerotic desires into the institutions of marriage and mistress. This kind of "healthy" sex, Clerici believes, will cure him of his dreaded strangeness.[10] When his future mother-in-law, after learning of his father's syphilis, asks Clerici if he too suffers from such diseases, he answers no, that his own maladies were "profondamente morali" ("profoundly moral").

Like Visconti's *Il Gattopardo,* Bertolucci's *Il conformista* explores the chiastic possibilities of dance for political and sexual commentary. Clerici's exclusion from the public dancing in a Parisian *bal populaire* (local dance) suggests his estrangement from all forms of human solidarity. As in Moravia, the restaurant scene preceding the dance anticipates his isolation both visually and thematically. The object of his desire, Quadri's alluring wife, Anna (Lina in Moravia), is herself a human refraction who appears in two previous scenes: as the lover of a Fascist Party official early in the film and then as a sick prostitute during Clerici's brief stop for orders in Ventimiglia. These physical aliases (all played by Dominique Sanda) compel the audience

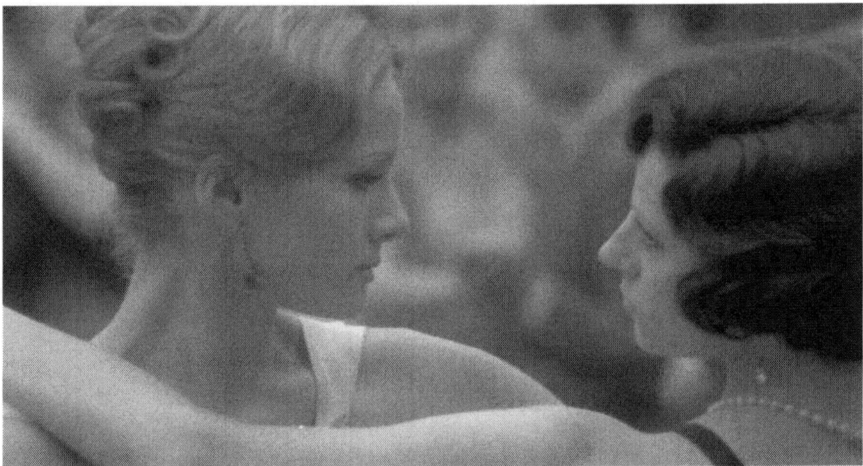

Figure 29 Giulia and Anna perform an erotic tango as part of the sexual substitutions permeating Bertolucci's representation of Fascism's perverse morality *(The Conformist)*.

to wonder whether Anna is real or a projection of Clerici's unconscious—indeed, whether Anna may be his doppelgänger, for the two share much: implicit to explicit bisexuality, desire for Giulia, and admiration for Quadri. Deepening the mysterious nature of Anna-Sanda's identity, Bertolucci's cinematographer Vittorio Storaro films her in a glycerin blue that lends her a melancholy, moonlit aura reminiscent of early screen divas like Marlene Dietrich and Greta Garbo.[11] During dinner, the chiastic mise-en-scène reveals the intrigues surrounding the desires of the two couples, Clerici-Giulia and Quadri-Anna. Marcello and Giulia are seated side by side, as are Anna and Quadri on the opposite side of the table. The women's talk of shopping and the men's political discussion form a sonic *x* over the plates of food. Clerici tries to break the same-sex chiasmus by playing footsie with Anna beneath the table. But Anna thwarts him with a crossing of her own: she switches seats with her husband so that she can face the tipsy Giulia and help her through a laughing fit.

This same-sex chiasmus Anna-Giulia / Quadri-Clerici continues as the scene moves from the restaurant to the *bal populaire*. While the men continue to talk politics on the side of the dance floor, Giulia and Anna perform an erotic tango (figure 29). Anna leads, verbally ("vieni" ["come"], she commands) and physically as she dips, twirls, and stares down Giulia. The incensed Clerici calls for them to stop; Quadri defends them, commenting on their loveliness. The bourgeois intellectual Quadri is capable of aesthetic experience while the neurotic Clerici is not. As Quadri had mentioned earlier, Clerici even as a student was "troppo serio" ("too serious"), and Giulia admits to Anna's prodding that her husband never laughs. Quadri follows Giulia's words with the admonition that genuine seriousness always shows a light touch, making him an adherent to the eminently Italian trait of sprezzatura. In the play world of dance, Quadri's words ring true, for the serious Clerici can never partake of the graceful movement and delicious choreography before him. He is forever on the outside grimly looking in on the pleasure of others, his chiaroscuro melancholy a visual blot in the film's otherwise vibrant chromatic world.

Clerici's isolation culminates in the farandole sequence of the *bal populaire,* when the entire dance hall joins hands and moves in sync. Shot from above, he emerges as the lonely center of a group that encircles him in ever-tightening arcs. His narcissism and solipsism thus find their visual analogue in a human wheel that pits him as its anxious and besieged nodal point. By dance's end, Marcello finally seems to get his desired chiasmus: the slow-dance partnerships Clerici-Anna and Quadri-Giulia. Quadri and Giulia, two aesthetes at heart, flirt and enjoy their impromptu union. When Giulia says that she feels like a student about to be examined by the professor, Quadri coyly remarks that as long as she is well prepared, he will pass her. Clerici and Anna, meanwhile, are strangers in each other's arms, each jealous of Giulia's relation with the other. Indeed, only when Clerici convinces Anna that Giulia admires her does Anna agree to remain with the newlyweds in Paris. The camera's subsequent shift from tense close-up to aerial panorama reveals the chiasmus that Marcello has long wanted: dreaming of Giulia, Anna clenches Clerici while his wife lingers in the arms of the man he is to assassinate. The lengthy dance sequence ends with a shot of Marcello in deep shadow, alone again in the backseat of the car that will convey him to Quadri and Anna's murder site. In the dim light obscuring his body, he appears to be hugging himself to compensate for the absence of Anna, that palindromic signifier whose meaning he can never control, even as he watches her bloody annihilation by Fascist henchmen in the woods of Savoy. He witnesses her death as a reflection on his car window, experiencing her shooting as a cinematic substitute for the real thing.

The Oedipal dramas of the film are well known.[12] Clerici's assassination of Quadri parallels Bertolucci's symbolic "murder" of his former mentor, Jean-Luc Godard: Quadri lives at Godard's Parisian address and shares his name (Luca/Luc) and phone number.[13] Just as Clerici abandons the youthful idealism he learned under Quadri's tutelage, so does Bertolucci eschew the avant-garde and intellectual filmmaking learned under masters like Godard and Pasolini in order to make *Il conformista,* a large-budget film released in the United States by the commercial behemoth Paramount. As the assassins surround Quadri, the drawn-out spectacle and operatic choreography represent the film's most overt inversion of Godard's rarefied film aesthetics, especially the final scene of his *Le petit soldat* (*The Little Soldier* [1963]), which also features a political assassination, though much more naturalist and subdued than the one at the conclusion of *Il conformista.* One might say that the traitorous knives thrust into Quadri, a visual allusion to the conspiratorial tyrannicide in Shakespeare's *Julius Caesar,* are symbolically buried in the heart of Godardian aesthetics. In acknowledging cinema as spectacle and entertainment, Bertolucci distances himself from his avant-garde masters and his earlier films like *La commare secca* (*The Grim Reaper* [1962]) and *Prima della rivoluzione,* two challenging and intellectual works made in thrall to Pasolinian aesthetics.[14]

In his study of the dialectic between capitalist structures and cinematic form during Italy's Economic Miracle, Angelo Restivo indicates that a defining characteristic of auteur films of the 1960s and 1970s was the "*reinsertion into history* of the Italian art cinema," with a concurrent "conceptualization of what is traditionally called 'history' or 'historiography'" (9, 11; Restivo's italics).[15] This writing of *italianità* onscreen took many forms. That the chiasmus became a privileged rhetorical mode for representing the national self makes sense when one considers the bitter legacies of power substitutions and switching alliances during the Risorgimento *(Il Gattopardo)* and Fascism *(Il conformista).* With their doublings, displacements, and crossovers, the chiastic imagery and themes in these novels/films distill the *scioltezza* impeding authentic and transparent political discourse. The brilliance of both Visconti and Bertolucci, and before them Lampedusa and Moravia, rests in their ability to translate an irresolvable dilemma—the quest for understanding historical phenomena as complicated as the Risorgimento and Fascism—into one of the most *sciolto* and elusive rhetorical forms, the chiasmus, the perfectly ambiguous shape for Italian political power and its protean economies of desire.

CHAPTER SEVEN

Verbal Montage and Visual Apostrophe

Zanzotto's "Filò" and Fellini's *Voice of the Moon*

Il discorso visivo di Fellini ha risvegliato per me un insieme di risonanze entro una certa aura linguistica. (Fellini's visual discourse alerted me to a set of resonances with a certain linguistic aura.)

—Andrea Zanzotto

It has become a commonplace to follow Federico Fellini's own words on the question of film's relationship to the sister arts and view him—like the man he called his cinematic father, Roberto Rossellini—as an antiliterary director. After all, Fellini insisted that any attempt to link literature and film represented a "lazy sentimentality" that failed to recognize the unique nature of each respective medium:

Io credo che il cinema non abbia bisogno di letteratura, ma bisogno soltanto di autori cinematografici, cioè di gente che si esprima attraverso i ritmi, le cadenze, che sono particolari del cinema. Il cinema è un'arte autonoma che non ha bisogno di trasposizioni su un piano che, nel migliore dei casi, sarà sempre e soltanto illustrativo. Ogni opera d'arte vive nella dimensione in cui è stata concepita e nella quale si è espressa. Che cosa si prende da un libro? Delle situazioni. Ma le situazioni, di per sé, non hanno alcun significato. . . . L'interpretazione letteraria di quei fatti non ha nulla a che fare con l'interpretazione cinematografica di quegli stessi fatti. Sono due modi da esprimersi completamente diversi. ("Interview with Tassone" 23–24)

I think that cinema does not need literature, but needs only cinematic authors, that is, people who express themselves in the rhythms and cadences particular to film. Film is an autonomous art that does not have any need for transpositions to a mode that, even in the best of cases, will always and only be illustrative. Each work of art lives in the dimension in which it was conceived and in which it is expressed. What does one take from a book? Some situations. But these situations, in themselves, have no significance. . . . Literary interpretation of these facts has nothing to do with the cinematic interpretation of these same facts. They are two completely different modes of expression. (Bondanella, *Fellini* 180–81)

The supposed antiliterary animus in Fellini becomes even more pronounced considering his stated contempt for the literary source of his longest and perhaps most-maligned adaptation, *Il Casanova di Fellini* (1976), based on Gian Giacomo Casanova's multivolume memoirs, *Histoire de ma vie* (*Story of My Life* [posthumous edition, 1826–37]).[1]

A closer look, however, at Fellini's career reveals a contradiction between his words and actions. In addition to *Casanova* he based at least three other films on literary sources—*La voce della luna* (*The Voice of the Moon* [1990]), *Satyricon* (1969), and *Toby Dammit* (1968)—and his range of authors, from Petronius and Casanova to Edgar Allan Poe and Ermanno Cavazzoni, was vast.[2] Moreover, in Fellini's frequent discourses on literary sources, the eloquence of the observations suggests the opinions of an acute literary mind, despite his declarations to the contrary. Yet the contradictions remain. In the first place, Fellini initially denied (then later admitted to) reading Poe's "Never Bet the Devil Your Head" for *Toby Dammit,* a story that interested him only because of its gothic scenery.[3] Second, as Joseph Markulin notes, his adapted sources were hardly the sort of conventional realist narrative typical of the "costume epics" that often appear onscreen (71). In truth, Fellini was not against the cross-fertilization of literature and film per se but rather the reduction of film to the terms and interpretive norms of the more prestigious framework of Italian literary history. As with Rossellini, the words *text* and *pretext* were often interchangeable for Fellini, as his versions of literary sources usually efface the signature of the author with Fellini's own cinematic *écriture.* For example, in adopting Casanova's memoirs, Fellini sought three criteria: episodes in the text that were "cinematic," passages he could freely and opportunely distort, and textual lacunae that he could reinvent for his film.[4] Fellini actually used the word *pretesto* (pretext) to describe his working relationship to the novel by Cavazzoni that inspired *La voce della luna, Il poema dei lunatici* (*The Lunatics' Poem* [1987]). Rather than any concrete narrative or formal structure, he took from the book "vecchie atmosfere, spunti, velleità, intenzioni, personaggi, situazioni" ("old atmospheres, impulses, foolish ambition, intentions, characters, situations").[5] Overall, Fellini's words on the cinematic adaptation of literary sources reveal his belief in an a priori cinematic mode in literary works that directors should exploit. He also shows his awareness of the productive tension that could result from the dialogue between the distinct forms of film and literature. By pushing aesthetic boundaries in this unbridled manner, Fellini's celebrated adventures in adaptation demonstrate how figures of speech associated with one medium—for example, cinematic montage and literary apostrophe—can migrate to others.

With its capacity to create metaphor through the frame-by-frame juxtaposition of images, montage is viewed as a means by which film distinguishes itself from other media and discovers its unique expressive capacities. Yet a landmark essay on the subject, Sergei Eisenstein's "Word and Image" (originally published as "Montage in 1938"), introduces its theories on montage by focusing on poetry and not film, to suggest that montage existed as a fundamental element of artistic exposition prior to its cinematic apotheosis.[6] Invoking the figure of enjambment, Eisenstein writes that a poem like Alexander Pushkin's *Eugene Onegin* (1833) creates its montage effect through the noncoincidence between sound and sense.[7] According to Eisenstein the following six translated lines from Pushkin's description of Peter the Great in *Eugene Onegin* express five semantic units:

1. And then with highest exaltation
2. There sounded, ringing, Peter's voice:
3. "To arms, God with us!" From the tent,
4. By crowding favorites surrounded,
5. Peter surges. His eyes
6. Are flashing. His look is terrible. ("Word and Image" 49)

These five semantic units, Eisenstein continues, could be filmed in the following five visual frames by a camera following a traditional shooting script:

1. And then with the highest exaltation there sounded, ringing, Peter's voice, "To arms, to arms! God with us!"
2. From the tent, by crowding favorites surrounded,
3. Peter emerges.
4. His eyes are flashing.
5. His look is terrible. ("Word and Image" 49)

This blurring of the visual and verbal anticipates Eisenstein's subsequent claim that some of the more powerful poetic voices of the past were also precinematic practitioners of montage, including John Milton.[8] Thus, in Eisenstein montage is an artistic means of expressing art through temporal sequence and *durée.* Although montage hits its stride with the sequential and image-based medium of film, it has always existed as a way of exploiting the serial juxtaposition, articulated in and through time, of formal units.[9]

Eisenstein's view of the dialectical interplay between poetic and cinematic forms of montage provides a useful perspective for considering the collaborative use of the technique by Fellini and Zanzotto in *Casanova*. One of Europe's most important contemporary poets, Zanzotto is in many respects the last person one would expect to follow a discussion by Eisenstein on intermedial aesthetics. From the beginning of his career, in the 1930s, he consigned his person and worldview to the "provinces," forsaking the metropolitan centers of Italy and the markets of the global village and remaining in his native Veneto—enclosed, the eminent philologist Gianfranco Contini writes, as though in his own catacomb (qtd. in Robert Harrison, *Forests* 239).[10] The tag here is apt because Zanzotto's poetry obsessively revisits the funereal landscape of the Montello, a prehistoric forest that received the bodies of great numbers of fallen soldiers in World War I, now gathered into massive *ossari*, collective depositories for anonymous and unmarked remains. Giuseppe Ungaretti remarked that Zanzotto's poetry expresses a tragic Leopardian feel for the landscape in all its elemental force and alterity ("Piccolo discorso" 694), but the natural world of the Veneto provided Zanzotto with more than the means to critique a rootless modernity and its accompanying technologies (including cinema). For Zanzotto the prehistoric landscape of the Veneto becomes, in his poetry and Fellini's *Casanova,* the epistemological ground where human and mineral nature find a common logos in a dialect verse that renders cinema verbal and poetry visual. Exquisitely attuned to the rhythms of modern life, Zanzotto realized the increasing interdependence of poetry on other more popular art forms, especially photography and film.[11]

In 1976 Zanzotto published *Filò per il "Casanova" di Federico Fellini,* a work that grew out of his collaboration with Fellini for his film on Casanova. The volume contains his verses for Fellini's film, as well as a letter from the director and five of his drawings. As part of their collaboration Zanzotto provided Fellini with the lyrics for an early scene in *Casanova,* where the tutelary deity La Venessiana is raised by a throng of worshippers—a purely fabricated rite that reflects the general atmosphere of artifice in a controversial film that centers on the question of sensuality and its melancholic effects.[12] The sets in *Casanova* were feigned, some (like the water of the Venetian lagoons represented by rippling waves of plastic) obviously so, and the literary "source" of the film, Casanova's memoirs, is adapted in haphazard fashion. Fellini claimed to loathe the work—he said he wasted a year reading it and wanted to rip it up—and he fashioned many scenes for the film that did not exist in Casanova's text, including the ritual with La Venessiana, as well as London Lullaby and Peasants Wake. Fellini likely asked Zanzotto to write verse for these rituals because he believed that the authenticity of the dialect poetry could balance the artificial dimensions of *Casanova,* whose garish and contrived look stands out as an extreme version of Fellini's trademark visual hyperbole.[13]

After filming *Casanova,* Fellini wrote to Zanzotto the letter asking him to help him shatter the "opacità, la convenzione del dialetto veneto che, come tutti i dialetti, si è raggelato in una cifra disemozionata e stucchevole" ("opacity, the convention[ality] of the Veneto dialect that like all dialects is frozen in an emotionless and tiresome cipher") (Zanzotto, *Poesie* 465; Zanzotto, *Peasants Wake* 4).[14] Zanzotto, he hoped, could "restituirgli freschezza, renderlo più vivo, penetrante, mercuriale, accanito" ("restore freshness to [the dialect], render it more alive, penetrating, mercurial, keen") (Zanzotto, *Poesie* 465; Zanzotto, *Peasants Wake* 4). Better yet, he continues, Zanzotto should rediscover "forme arcaiche o addirittura [inventare] combinazioni fonetiche e linguistiche in modo che anche l'assunto verbale rifletta il riverbero della visionarietà stralunata che mi sembra di aver dato al film" ("archaic forms or indeed [invent] phonetic and linguistic combinations in such a way that the verbal endeavor [of "Filò"] also reflects the reverberation of the confused visionariness that I seem to have given to the film *[Casanova]*" (Zanzotto, *Poesie* 465; Zanzotto, *Peasants Wake* 4).[15] Fellini saw a parallel between his visual project of bringing to life Enlightenment Venice in Cinecittà and Zanzotto's verbal challenge in finding the ancient words to match the film's "confused visionariness." Later in the letter, Fellini gestures again toward the dialect's capacity to visualize his film's imagery: "Mi sembra che la sonorità liquida, l'affastellarsi gorgogliante, i suoni, le sillabe che si sciolgono in bocca, quel cantilenare dolce e rotto dei bambini in un miscuglio di latte e materia disciolta, uno sciabordio addormentante, riproponga e rappresenti con suggestiva efficacia quella sorta di iconografia subacquea del film, l'immagine placentaria, amniotica, di una Venezia decomposta e fluttuante di alghe, di muscosità, di buio muffito e umido" ("It seems to me that the liquid sonority, the confused gurgling, the sounds, the syllables that melt in the mouth, that sweet broken baby's singsong in a mixture of milk and dissolved solids, a sleep-inducing lapping sound reproposes and suggests efficaciously the kind of subaqueous iconography that characterizes the film, the placental, amniotic image of a decomposed and shifting Venice of algae, mossiness, and musty dank darkness") (Zanzotto, *Poesie* 467; Zanzotto, *Peasants Wake* 5).

The raw dialect of the Veneto countryside and the primordial Venice of Freudian dreams it evokes both move, in Fellini's view, in the direction of submerged icons and a Venice of algae, moss, and womb-like fluids. Consistent with the letter's Freudian rhetoric, Zanzotto speaks in an essay on dialects appended to "Filò" about his native vernacular as emerging from beneath every conscious intention (*Poesie* 541; *Peasants Wake* 88); in "Filò" he writes that he is connected to this "vecio parlar" ("vecchio parlare"; "ancient tongue") with the deepest of roots (*Poesie* 530–31; *Peasants Wake* 83).[16] Fernando Bandini describes this rooted quality of Zanzotto's verse as part of his ethical "rifiuto inquieto della storia" ("troubled refusal of history") (lv): in fixing his gaze on a landscape outside of human time, Zanzotto sought to protect in human memory those prehistorical and primeval spaces that commercialization, globalization, and modernity writ large had not yet spoiled—or, Robert Harrison suggests, subjected to deforestation, literal and metaphysical.[17]

The featured poem of *Filò per il "Casanova" di Federico Fellini*, "Filò" was written in the vernacular of Zanzotto's native Pieve di Soligo and, as John Welle writes, "stages a dialogue between poetry and film and registers an encounter between the spoken idiom of a small agricultural community and the brave new visual language of an increasingly global society" ("Zanzotto" 2:2038).[18] "No dighe gnént del cine" ("Non dico niente del cinema"; "I'm not going to talk about movies"), Zanzotto writes in the poem's opening lines, adopting the colloquial tone of the peasants in the *filò*, the gathering of farmers by bonfire in bad weather to tell stories and exact propitious auguries for the harvest ("Filò," *Poesie* 512–13; *Peasants Wake* 55). But he then does talk about movies by alluding to the incantatory power of film to enrapture and overcome its audience: "al me strassina 'l cine—/ . . . parché 'l ne slózha spes/i pra i bòsch de le nostre àneme debole" ("mi trascina via il cinema—/ . . . perché spesso ci lorda/i prati e i boschi delle nostre anime deboli"; "I get carried away by movies/[because they] scare [and] soil for us/the meadows and wood of our weak souls") (*Poesie* 512–13; *Peasants Wake* 55). As part of his monitory words, Zanzotto's narrator refers to the materiality of film, its artificial celluloid makeup, and claims—in contrast to Pier Paolo Pasolini's reality-revealing and dreamlike *cinema di poesia*—that films can "inpastrociarne i nostri insònii" ("impiastricciare i nostri sogni"; "muck up our dreams") (*Poesie* 512–13; *Peasants Wake* 55). In a world of cultural commodification, film or the cinema's multiplexes "sbusa fin fora pa' i camp," "ne ciùcia," and "ne fa a tòch" ("bucano perfino in piena campagna," "ci succhia," "ci fa a pezzi"; "riddle the countryside like sores" and "suck us in and tear us apart") (*Poesie* 514–15; *Peasants Wake* 57). No mention is made early in "Filò" of the aesthetic value of the film medium; instead, the cinema appears as a voracious soul-destroyer that "roba 'l so propio DNA" ("ruba il suo proprio DNA"; "steal[s] its DNA") from the "pi scondest" ("più nascosto"; "most secret") part of our being (*Poesie* 514–15; *Peasants Wake* 57). Just like certain Petrarchan and Leopardian coordinating conjunctions and adverbs that deflate a rhetorical crescendo by introducing a devastating counterargument or temporal rupture, the whole of "Filò" hangs on this slight "ma" ("but") in line 24.[19] Zanzotto adds that "qualche òlta 'l cine arzh brusa e fa ciaro" ("qualche volta il cinema arde brucia e illumina"; "sometimes movies blaze and give light") and make us "s'ciopar sbociar fora come i but a la vertà" ("scoppiare sbocciar fuori come germogli a primavera"; "burst open and bloom like buds in springtime") (*Poesie* 514–15; *Peasants Wake* 57). In short, movies "squasi—'l par la la poesia, / al ciapa-dentro tut in poesia—'n'altra" ("quasi—sembra lui una poesia / cattura tutto in poesia—un'altra"; "seem almost to be a poetry, they capture everything in poetry—an other") (*Poesie* 514–15; *Peasants Wake* 57). Although I believe it is perilous to invoke the overused tag *Fellinian* in accounting for this sudden thematic shift in "Filò," Zanzotto himself writes that it was the guiding eye of the filmmaker with his spectacles, masquerades, and "ingorghi onirici" ("oneiric traffic jams")—one thinks of the nightmarish opening of *8 1/2* (1967)—that began to shape his poetic compositions (*Poesie* 539; *Peasants Wake* 87). In fact, Zanzotto introduces Fellini in "Filò" as the one who "me à mostrà carneai e Venezhie / che déa s'ciantis e balá 'fa ale de pavéi") ("mi ha mostrato carnevali e Venezie / che davano lampi e ballavano come ali di farfalle"; "showed me Carnevale and Venezia / throwing off flashes like butterfly wings"), an homage to Fellini's visible signature and lush psychologism (*Poesie* 514–51; *Peasants Wake* 59).

After invoking Fellini's poetic cinema, "Filò" describes how the days of winter have shortened with cold, the rain pelts the crops along with those who planted them, the winds howl, and the waters and lightning surge. Then the Fellinian summer cedes to the Leopardian autumn:

> inte 'ste ore che 'l sol par un momento
> libera, e po 'l le mola
> a morir inte 'l mój, tra restèi
> negri drio i crép de le montagne.

in queste ore che il sole per un momento
libera, e poi le lascia andare
a morire nel madido, tra i cancelli
neri dietro i greppi delle montagne. (*Poesie* 520–21)

In these hours the sun frees for a moment
and then lets go
to die in the west, between the black
gates behind the mountain rocks. (*Peasants Wake* 65)

The rhetoric of darkness and despair—"e tut quel che se vet par trat inte 'na cort / anca siben che de ori l'é piena 'sta cort" ("e tutto quello che si vede sembra buttato in un letamaio / anche se di ori è pieno il letamaio"; "and everything you see looks as though it's been thrown on a dunghill, / even if the dunghill's full of gold") (*Poesie* 520–21; *Peasants Wake* 65)—recalls the biblical epigraph to one of Leopardi's bleakest compositions, the acknowledged and privileged poetic subtext of "Filò," "La ginestra o il fiore del deserto" ("The Broom or the Flower of the Desert" [1836]): "E gli uomini vollero le tenebre piuttosto che la luce" ("And men loved darkness rather than light") (John 3:19).[20] The reference to "La ginestra" anticipates Zanzotto's subsequent discussion of the murderous earthquake of Friuli in 1976, which claimed almost a thousand lives and left more than 150,000 homeless, just as Leopardi's poem begins with an overture to the mighty volcano that obliterated Pompeii in AD 76, "sterminator Vesevo" ("exterminator, Mount Vesuvius") (see Leopardi, "Ginestra" 3).[21]

Doubling the apostrophic stance of Leopardi himself, who in "La ginestra" engages in an impassioned "conversation" with a broom flower, Zanzotto queries the earth as a child would approach a violent parent.[22] Although in the past the earth's moods could swing from the joyous to the tempestuous, never did it erupt with the ferocity of the Friuli earthquake. The end of Zanzotto's passage signals a break between human and natural environs, because in the horror of the quake the narrator no longer feels the reciprocity that bound him to the land, and alienation has replaced the earlier familiarity: "Chi sétu ti? Chi? / Na fedeltà granda la se a sfantà" ("Chi sei tu? Chi? / Una fedeltà grande si è dissolta"; "Who are you? Who? / A great loyalty has ended") (*Poesie* 522–23; *Peasants Wake* 67). The sentiment here is pure Leopardi, whose "La ginestra" ends with a crushing overture to the indifference of nature to human needs. Zanzotto references the cosmic natural pessimism of Leopardi's poem:

. . . mare-mostro tu torna
a esser, come senpre, inte 'l momento che
la verità la sfondra, dia che massa
massa ne passa, o pur
che—cussita 'l dis al libro de la Ginestra—
no tu sa gnént
né de ti né de noi.

. . . madre-mostro tu torni
a essere, come sempre, nel momento che
la verità sfonda, dea che troppo
troppo ci sopravanza; oppure
che—così dice il libro della Ginestra—
non sai niente
né di te né di noi. (*Poesie* 524–25)

. . . you [nature] go back to being,
mother/monster, as always, in the moment
truth breaks through, goddess,
way way ahead of us, and yet,
—according to the book of the Ginestra—
you know nothing
of yourself or of us. (*Peasants Wake* 69, 71)

"Filò" recapitulates the brutal geological clock of "La ginestra." Vesuvius, Leopardi writes, can wait thousands of years before, "con lieve moto" ("with the slightest movement"), obliterating man's might and, he adds, "dell'umana gente / *Le magnifiche sorti e progressive* (*the magnificent, progressive destiny / of humankind*") ("Ginestra" 45, 51). The bitter tone permeates the entire poem, whose narrative voice, devoid of the usual human hopes and fears, seems to issue from the grave itself. Zanzotto's narrator assumes a similar prosopopoeial stance, when he describes nature as, "una—siguro—che pôch la ne bada" ("una—certo—che poco di noi si cura"; "someone—certainly—who cares little for us") (*Poesie* 524–25; *Peasants Wake* 71). But the tone in Zanzotto is imploring rather than resigned: "Ma fursi l'è che no te són stati drio / che no te 'ón volést bastanzha ben / che no te 'vón studià vena per vena" ("Ma forse, forse non ti abbiamo corteggiata / non ti abbiamo voluto bene abbastanza / non ti abbiamo studiata vena per vena"; "But maybe, maybe we haven't courted you enough / we haven't loved you enough / we haven't studied you vein by vein") (*Poesie* 524–25; *Peasants Wake* 71). The signal difference between the narrators of "Filò" and "La ginestra" is that the former speaks to nature as one of the peasants participating in the bonfire chats and not, as in Leopardi, an isolated lyric voice outside the narrative. Leopardi's voice is a palimpsestic trace in Zanzotto's poem, never directly named and only indirectly invoked through the periphrastic "book of the Ginestra." More important, the stately rhetoric of "La ginestra" is undercut by the roughshod diction in "Filò," which speaks of people carving out one another's eyes and other sorts of vile acts, like men reducing nature to an "intossegada, scassada, rosegada, / castrada" ("intossicata, sconquassata, rosicchiata, / castrata"; "poisoned, smashed, chewed up, / castrated") state (*Poesie* 526–27; *Peasants Wake* 73). Zanzotto balances this base rhetoric with a Latin quotation from Francis Bacon ("non nisi parendo, vincitur" [nature can be defeated only if one obeys her laws]), which reminds the reader of an authorial erudition otherwise hidden in a stylized cloak of orality.

The shift in "Filò" from an august Leopardian lexicon to an edgier idiom prepares the reader for a series of cinematic interludes that lend a Fellinian visual imprimatur to what on the surface may appear to be a high-cultural idiom.[23] After mentioning Leopardi, "Filò" begins to focus on the corporeality of the Eternal Feminine (Rèitia, feminine deity of the paleo-Veneto), whom Zanzotto borrows for a cameo appearance after her central role in the Venetian Recitative, the imaginary ritual he wrote for Fellini (who had invented this pseudorite in the first place). Zanzotto writes:

Pensón che quela testa santa
onipotente e misera—
boca che (no) parla, réce che (no) sente
mente che (no) pensa divinamente—
. . . i só oci de bissa
de basilissa
un póch in ne pare de vera
mama, no de marégna, no de bissa. (*Poesie* 528)

Pensiamo che quella testa santa
onnipotente e misera—
bocca che (non) parla, orecchi che (non) sentono
mente che (non) pensa divinamente—
. . . i suoi occhi di biscia
di sovrana

ci appaiono un poco di vera
mamma, non di matrigna, non di biscia. (*Poesie* 529)

Let's think that that sacred head
omnipotent and shabby—
mouth that does (does not) speak, ears that do (do not) hear
mind that does (does not) think divinely
. . . her eyes of a snake
of a sovereign
appear to us a little like
those of a true mama, not a stepmother, not a snake. (*Peasants Wake* 75, 77)

The vibrant corporeality of *Venezhia,* whom Fellini films in *Casanova* from a variety of angles and filters to accentuate her looming physical presence, anticipates the visual descriptions of the dialect language to follow. In his letter to Zanzotto, Fellini described the rising woman as a "nume" ("deity"), "la femmina misteriosa che abita in ciascuno di noi" ("mysterious female who lives in each of us") and produces intense "immagini psicanalitiche" ("psychoanalytic images") (*Poesie* 466; *Peasants Wake* 3–4). The Venetian Recitative, he continues, is "la metafora ideologica di tutto il film" ("the ideological metaphor for the entire film") (*Poesie* 466; *Peasants Wake* 3–4). Fellini likely sought out Zanzotto's collaboration in the scene because of the poet's capacity to fuse mythic and psychological—hence, ancient and modern—representative modes that serve Fellini's purposes in fashioning a pastiche-like ritual ex nihilo. Just as Zanzotto's use of dialect points to the vanishing traces of modern languages' pregrammatical history, Fellini's images in the Venetian Recitative imply the archaic sources of now-vanished gender roles once located in a remote and highly eroticized Venetian past.[24] Given this extreme objectification of the female subject, it is no wonder that so many critics have seen Fellini's reading of the Casanova he supposedly despised as a covert autobiography.[25]

The synesthesia-like effect of translating language's aural elements into a visual and tactile mise-en-scène suggests in Zanzotto's "Filò" the cross-fertilization between cinematic and poetic forms:

Vecio parlar che tu à inte 'l tó saór
un s'cip del lat de la Eva,
vecio parlar che non so pi,
che me se á descuní

dì par dì 'nte la boca (e no tu me basta);

che tu sé cambià co la me fazha

co la me pèl ano par an;

parlar porét, da póreti, ma s'cèt

ma fis, ma tóch cofà 'na branca

de fien 'pena segà dal faldin (parché no bàstetu?) (*Poesie* 530)

Vecchio dialetto che hai nel tuo sapore

un gocciolo del latte di Eva,

vecchio dialetto che non so più,

che mi ti sei estenuato

giorno per giorno nella bocca (e non mi basti);

che se cambiato con la mia faccia

con la mia pelle anno per anno;

parlare povero, da poveri, ma schietto

ma fitto, ma denso come una manciata

di fieno appena tagliato dalla falce (perché non ti basti?). (*Poesie* 531)

Ancient dialect, your favor still has

a drop of Eve's milk,

ancient dialect that I've forgotten,

you've worn yourself out

day by day in my mouth (and you're not enough for me);

you've changed with my face

with my hide year after year;

poor speech, of poor fellows, but you're pure

thick and dense as a handful

of hay freshly cut with a scythe (why aren't you enough?). (*Peasants Wake* 79)

By this point in "Filò" Zanzotto manages to fashion an aesthetic hybrid that combines Leopardian themes and rhetoric with the riotous imagery of a Fellini-inspired montage. In his meditations on the nature of poetic language in "Filò," Zanzotto continued to locate his literary inheritance from the romantic poet in a cinematographic idiom indebted to Fellini. He writes that poetry may be everything or nothing at all, either "in gnessuna lengua / in gnessun logo" ("in nessuna lingua / in nessun luogo"; "not in any language / in any place"), or indeed "'l busnar del fógo / che 'l fa screcolar tute le fonde" ("il rugghiare del fuoco / che fa scricchiolare tutte le fondamenta"; "the crackling of fire / that makes all the foundations creak") (*Poesie* 532–33; *Peasants*

Wake 81). Then, employing the valedictory trope of *congedo,* the narrator bids "Filò" farewell, while speaking of a dialect tongue that will endure, just as embers outlast the flicker of fire, and just as the song of Leopardi's fragrant broom flower abides the ravages of natural history in "La ginestra." The concluding image, fittingly, is of the *filò* itself, a ritual whose mix of storytelling and image-making emerges as the homespun correlative for Zanzotto's sophisticated fusion of Fellini's film and Leopardi's verse. Zanzotto writes:

> . . . i nostri mili parlar e pensar nóvi
>
> inte 'n parlar che sarà un par tuti,
>
> fondo come un basar,
>
> vèrt sul ciaro, sul scur,
>
> davanti la manèra inpiantada inte 'l scur
>
> col só taj caro, 'pena guà da senpre. (*Poesie* 534)

> . . . i nostri mille parlari e pensieri nuovi
>
> in un parlare che sarà uno per tutti,
>
> fondo come un baciare,
>
> aperto sulla luce, sul buio,
>
> davanti la mannaia piantata nel buio
>
> col suo taglio chiaro, appena
>
> affilato da sempre. (*Poesie* 535)

> . . . our thousand tongues and new thoughts will kindle
>
> in a dialect that will be one for everybody,
>
> deep as kissing,
>
> open into light, onto the dark,
>
> in front of the great axe fixed firmly in the darkness
>
> with its bright blade, newly sharpened forever. (*Peasants Wake* 83, 85)

The dialect of "one for all" represents that single idiom resulting from, on a metalevel, the fusion of poetry and film in the transformative Veneto dialect whose synesthetic capacities—theorized by Fellini and instantiated in verse by Zanzotto—can combine word and image. The phrase "fondo come un basar" ("deep as kissing") suggests the sensual, visceral nature of the unifying dialect, which fittingly opens out "sul ciaro, sul scur" ("open into light, onto the dark"), as do all images forged in the camera's lens. In addition to establishing an emblem for the dialogue between poetry and film that defines "Filò," the concluding image of the luminous discourse of the Veneto dialect reverses the pessimistic biblical epigraph from Leopardi mentioned above ("and men loved darkness rather than light"). The narrator of "Filò" speaks of and with a rhetoric of moving light—a cinematography of gushing stars, sunshine, shadows, and embers that leaves the reader with projections of metaphor that continue to burn in the minds of readers long after the fires of the peasants' *filò* are spent.

The poet in the background of Fellini's adaptation of Zanzotto, Leopardi, also serves Fellini in his visual appropriation of the literary device apostrophe in *La voce della luna*. The figure of apostrophe, to quote a recent critic, is an "embarrassment" (Culler 135): it would have the reader believe that poets converse with the likes of plant life (William Blake's "O Rose thou art sick" in "The Sick Rose" [1794]), ancient heroines (Charles Baudelaire's "Andromaque, je pense a Vous!" in "Le cygne" ["The Swan" (1859)]), and nocturnal constellations like Leopardi's beloved moon. Whether solemn or celebratory, interrogative or exclamatory, the putative "O" and subsequent poetic form of address associated with apostrophe has, at least since Quintilian, represented what Northrop Frye famously described as a radical of presentation, the emphatic invocation of an external presence, especially in lyric poems. Yet whomever the poet invokes, the poet is in reality speaking to himself—with back turned, as it were, to his readers. To understand the lyric poem's textual economy, the reader must accept the implausibility of the apostrophe, which generally offers insight into the poem's diction, tone, and metaphoric register. Thus, although certain apostrophes seem improbable, the raw material of lyric, indeed its essence, often lies at the core of these artificial conversations between poet and addressee.

In the tradition of his poetic *maître à penser* Petrarch, many of Leopardi's lyrics begin with an imaginary address whose proverbial ear provides a target for his lyric outpourings.[26] As a mode, the apostrophic rhetoric in Leopardi often trumps the apparent thematic horizon in his lyric. For example, in the celebrated "A Silvia" ("To Silvia" [1828]) the narrator tells of his early love for a young spinning girl in his family's estate. The love is (typically for Leopardi) unrequited, and the girl's tragic early death serves as a reminder to the poet of how a cruel destiny ("la sorte dell'umane genti"; "man's fate" ["Silvia" 59]) is always ready to stamp out innocent hope. But the energy of the poem moves in an altogether different direction from this sad impasse. The apostrophic opening—"Silvia, rimembri ancora" ("Silvia, do you remember still")—is of an extraordinarily delicate and intimate feel, the soft *m* sounds coalescing into a hum whose tranquility is furthered by the subsequent series of imperfect verbs and their equally soft *v*'s: (*salivi, sonavan, sedevi,* and *solevi menare*)

("Silvia" 5, 6, 11, 13–14).[27] The Italian imperfect tense implies repetition, as in the previously mentioned series she would rise up, sing, sit, and so forth. This second-person, informal apostrophe establishes a sense of a young girl who is very much alive and whose vibrancy will be all the more starkly contrasted by the fact that, just verses later, the "tenerella" ("gentle girl") will perish: "Tu, pria che l'erbe inaridisse il verno, / Da chiuso morbo combattuta e vinta / Perivi" ("You, before winter had withered the grass, / stricken then overcome by hidden sickness, / died") ("Silvia" 40–42).

The life of Silvia in and through apostrophe recalls the words of Walter Benjamin in "The Work of Art in the Age of Mechanical Reproduction" (1936) about those art forms that privilege presence. As with the apostrophic uttering of the lyric poet, an art that exists as a function of its articulation in space and time—and that is not reproducible through purely technological means—may come under siege in an era that looks to media like photography and cinema. Because of their capacities for mass production, they can tarnish the aura of their more fragile aesthetic counterparts and reduce artistic experience to consumer spectacle. As he notes in his celebrated chiasmus, for Benjamin aesthetics in an era of nonauratic mass production had better become politicized before politics—the spectacle-infused politics of Benito Mussolini and Adolf Hitler come to mind—are aestheticized. In similar fashion *La voce della luna* obsessively returns to the trope of apostrophe in its visual form as part of its commentary on the loss of aesthetic aura in a postmodern world.[28]

Recent work has shown that the film can be read as Fellini's attempt to resist the postmodern reduction of everything to ironic self-quotation and media exploitation.[29] He does this by promoting the endangered need for fantasy both on an individual and a societal level and by insistently contrasting postmodern simulacra—and the forms of mass media they are often expressed in—with the authenticity of certain human modes of expression, especially voice.[30] The film's protagonist, Ivo, is haunted by both the aural and the oral. At the beginning of the film he hears voices and exclaims, "Avete sentite voi? Mi hanno chiamato" ("Did you hear? They are calling me"). He cites Leopardi early in the film when, returning to a childhood memory, he revisits the time he attempted to break into the house of his beloved Aldina. Gazing in full thrall at her sleeping body, he invokes the Leopardi of the "Canto notturno di un pastor errante nell'Asia" ("Night Song of a Wandering Shepherd in Asia" [1829–30]) and its opening lines: "Che fai tu, luna in ciel? dimmi, che fai, / Silenziosa luna?" ("What are you doing, moon, up in the sky; what are you doing, tell me, / silent moon?") (1–2). Then, engaging in an act of literary contamination, he adds from Leopardi's "Alla luna": "travagliosa / Era mia vita . . . / O mia diletta luna" ("my life / was torment . . . / beloved moon of mine") ("Alla luna" 8–10). But this would-be *luna* Aldina awakens and shouts "aiuto!" ("help!") and then hurls her Cinderella's slipper at Ivo. She is afraid of the intrusion and deaf to the poet's apostrophic gesture. It is difficult not to read the scene as a demystification of the pseudodialogic gesture of the lyric apostrophe, which always pretends to speak to another but is in reality a voice speaking to itself (or to its readers). When the addressee is allowed to answer the poet, the case is likely to be disastrous, as occurs with the ruffled Aldina. Leopardi's poetry, especially in later lyrics like "La ginestra," often conveys the nagging fear that the invoked apostrophic presence may not be listening. In "La ginestra" the indifference of nature functions as a threat to the fragrance that the humble broom, symbol of Leopardi's poetic voice, strives to emit against all odds. More pessimistically, the above scene from Fellini in *La voce della luna* stages a disenchantment of poetic aura. This postmodern age, Fellini suggests, has no ear for apostrophe. It considers its aural worshippers like Ivo at best an eccentric, at worst crazy. Even Gonnella, a partner of Ivo's in the pleasures of the imagination, asks his friend why he cannot just go to sleep like everyone else, instead of troubling the moon with his apostrophic gestures.[31]

The voice of Leopardi haunts the film throughout.[32] After Ivo is saved from the rooftops by a fellow "lunatic," one of the Michelozzi brothers who later in the film actually captures the moon, he mentions Leopardi's name, a common signifier of shared sensibilities that inspires the two to embrace. The film traces the devolution of Italian life into provincial tackiness and crass consumerism: Ivo's friend Nestore is married in a Las Vegas–style hall, replete with life-size murals of the AC Milan soccer team; the town's annual *sagra* (feast), the *gnoccata* (gnocchi festival), is grotesquely commercial; and Ivo sees his beloved Aldina-Luna either dancing with the lecherous Dr. Brambilla or out window-shopping. Ivo's antidote to this degraded quotidian, in classic Leopardian style, is silence: "Tutto è cominciato con quel silenzio" ("Everything began with that silence"), he says, referring to the solitude of his beloved boyhood room, where a portrait of Leopardi hangs. The voices would visit him there, when his ears were open to such prosopopoeia, the voicing of and by the inanimate.

Fellini's satire of the cultural decline that makes such childhood silence impossible in the noisy adult world culminates in the scene of the moon's capture. The momentous event is announced on a large-screen video to a mass of mesmerized viewers by a slick-talking politico who reduces the poetic aura of apostrophe to the manipulation of political discourse. After the standard *captatio* of classical oratory, in which he praises his fellow citizens and the local authorities, the politician shackles the moon with commonplace labels like "il satellite della terra" ("satellite of the earth") and "l'astro degli innamorati" ("beacon for lovers"). Leopardi's *luna* dies, I believe, when it is reduced to the instrumental discourse of dead metaphors. The citizens have physically tethered the moon to the ground and the politician's empty rhetoric stymies the poetic valence and literary energies of the *luna.* Man had once traveled to the moon, the politician says, but now the moon has come to us—and he is correct, for in the dreamless commercialism of Fellini's dystopia, the moon's banality seems all too human.

Things go from bad to worse. Someone in the crowd fires a shot at the moon, and in the ensuing chaos she disappears. Fellini's message, it seems, is that only silence, that same silence that made it possible for the young Ivo to hear voices, can inspire genuine apostrophe.[33] When Ivo once again faces his beloved *luna,* she provides him with a heartless echo of Fellini's earlier film *La strada:* "Che faccia buffa c'hai" ("What a funny face you have"), she says, as the Fool said to Gelsomina, yet with none of his compassion. This new postmodern moon is too preoccupied to heed Ivo's apostrophe: she turns from him and yells a buzzword of her age, "pubblicità!" ("commercial break!"). For the Fool of *La strada*—"tutto quello che c'è a questo mondo serve a qualcosa" ("everything in this world is good for something")—all was symbolic fodder, from the smallest of pebbles to the most celestial of stars. Now in a disenchanted consumerist world even the once holy moon shines with no transcendental beam; its rays merely fall cold on the skin.

Fellini's answer to this predicament comes in the form of a whimper rather than his typical bang. "Guai a capire le voci" ("Woe to him who understands the voices"), the Moon-Aldina tells Ivo; "bisogna sentirle e sperare che non finiranno mai di chiamarti" ("you need to feel them and hope that they don't ever finish calling you"). "Che melanconia" ("What melancholy"), Ivo responds; "questo mio povero cuore non sa più cosa pensare" ("this poor heart of mine no longer knows what to think"), an allusion to Leopardi's "stanco mio cor" ("worn-out heart"), line 2 of "A se stesso" ("To Himself" [1835]). But the moon, and I would argue Fellini, have in fact given Ivo a powerful clue about how to think. By listening to these voices, letting them apostrophize him without troubling over their meaning, Ivo is responding to the aura of a threatened fantasy-based mode of expression. The so-called *effet de réel* of everyday social life, Gonnella suggests, is but a representation, a simulacrum that distracts people from a more finely distilled essence. Ivo's quest for the unalloyed aura of existence leads him once again to what one might call the negative space of lyric utterance and its necessary companion, silence. With more silence we could understand the world, Ivo laments, reminiscent of Leopardi's emphasis on the "sovrumani silenzi" ("superhuman silences") and "profondissima quiete" ("depthless calm") in his celebrated lyric "L'infinito" ("The Infinite" [1819]) ("Infinito" 5, 6).[34] One critic has described the need for apostrophe by poets as an antidote to the fear over loss of voice.[35] It seems, however, that in this privileging of apostrophic voice as an aura-laden antidote to postmodern dislocations, both Leopardi and Fellini embrace the necessary silence or loss of sound that allows poetic voice to emerge in all its force. Thus conceived, apostrophe is as much about the ear of the addressee (and reader) as it is the mouth of the poet.

In the spirit of *La voce della luna* recent Italian cinema has shown how a collective incapacity for silence has eroded the aura of art and mitigated the sanctity of aesthetic experience.[36] On the one hand, this is not entirely negative: with the emergence of modern consumer culture the reach of art now encompasses at often bargain prices the great many and not just the wealthy or elite with the requisite credentials. Moreover, in such films as Pasolini's *Decameron* the playful solidarity between Giotto's pupil and his workmen subverts the idea of the bourgeois artist working in isolation and promotes in its place art that is accessible to all. But, for many artists, the relaxing of aesthetic standards has come with a high price. In making the Leopardian moon such a talkative and insensitive interlocutor, Fellini situates his adaptation of Leopardian apostrophe at the interstices between satire and elegy: satirical, because the absurd moon serves as a witty embodiment of some of society's collective ills; elegiac, because the deaf ear of the moon to poets' voices may represent our own increasing difficulties in hearing the Leopardis of today, who, if continually ignored, "forse finiranno di chiamarci," may end up no longer calling us.

Epilogue: Art Film Redux

Cinepoetics in the New Millennium

By the turn of the millennium, a once-mighty Italian film industry had long been mired in crisis. In 2001 box-office numbers dropped by fifty percent from the previous year, and in 2005 the Berlusconi government slashed funding of the nation's principal arts program by forty percent.[1] The fate of Cinecittà reflected the decline. Faced with crippling budget cuts, the migration of directors to cheaper production sites in Eastern Europe, and waning public interest in the spectacles that made it famous, the forty-acre heart of the Italian film industry had struggled to remain solvent for decades (it was privatized in the 1990s after facing bankruptcy).[2] To resuscitate its finances, the studio planned to unveil the $800 million theme park Cinecittà World in 2014, with attractions to include rides based on the films of its much-mourned patron saint, Federico Fellini. Indeed, to many the death of the maestro Fellini in 1993 symbolized the demise of the nation's cinema as a whole.[3] One can understand the pessimism, since the golden age of the neorealist and auteur art film had become a distant memory by this time.[4]

While statistics point to a decreased public interest in Italian film and its loss of international prestige,[5] there has also been talk of a minor renaissance in the nation's cinema.[6] After a long draught at Cannes, Italian films took two of the top awards in 2008, the grand prix going to Matteo Garrone's *Gomorra* (*Gomorrah* [2008]), an unflinching exposé of Neapolitan organized crime, and the grand jury prize to Paolo Sorrentino's *Il divo* (2008), a hallucinatory portrait of seven-time prime minister Giulio Andreotti, tried for Mafia collusion and ordering the death of a rival journalist among other crimes. A range of other sources in Italy and abroad confirms the good news from Cannes.[7] A cause for this limited resurgence stems from a return to the mix of aesthetic exploration and sociopolitical inquiry that marked the art-film tradition, combining its auteurist "cinema of poetry" with a creative interpretation of neorealism's legacy. In contrast to Lino Micciché's notorious label of recent filmmakers as the "heirs of nothing,"[8] some directors are rather the heirs of the neorealist exhortation to "remake Italy" and the auteurist mandate of translating ethical engagement into a personal artistic vision.

Matteo Garrone's *Gomorrah* captured critical attention for its use of such trademark neorealist techniques as nonprofessional actors, on-location shooting, local dialect, and a focus on the poor and marginal. But when reminded of the connection, Garrone insisted that neorealism proper involved a specific cinematic response to the socioeconomic plight of postwar Italy. His remark reveals the idiosyncratic nature of his relationship with the legendary movement in a film that cannot be reduced to a simple recapitulation of neorealist formulas. His scenes of violence are more graphic than any ever dreamed of by the neorealists—even the Nazi torture of partisans in Rossellini's *Rome, Open City* pales in comparison to the bloodletting in *Gomorrah*. Moreover, Garrone alternates gritty reportage from the Neapolitan urban wastelands with more surreal sequences, including an eerie shot of two crazed teenage boys wearing only underwear and randomly firing their machine guns on a beach.

Paolo Sorrentino's *Il divo* also balances its inquiry into the facts with dreamlike passages, such as when the insomniac Andreotti walks through the predawn streets of Rome with his bodyguards in tow on his way to morning mass. The livid-colored Andreotti seems embalmed in his stiff gait, and the empty streets bear the same dim lighting as the interior of the church, part of the film's strategy of trumping the natural with the artificial. A later shot of Andreotti's coalition reveals a *commedia dell'arte*–like troupe of cronies often filmed from low angles to accentuate their menacing presence, especially the enormous parliamentarian Sbardella, alias *Lo squalo* (The Shark). *Il divo* derives its light from a chiaroscuro forebear, Francis Ford Coppola's *Godfather* films, which anticipate Sorrentino's handling of dramatic interior contrasts to suggest intrigue, secrecy, even foul play. Sorrentino also borrows from Coppola his grisly sense of montage: *Il divo* begins with a multiple murder scene that recalls the spliced murders and Christening at the conclusion of *The Godfather*, where Michael Corleone's henchmen eliminate his enemies while their boss renounces Satan and all his works. Isolated examples of artistic excellence in an otherwise diminished cinematic tradition, Garrone and Sorrentino join a cadre of filmmakers seeking to rehabilitate the powerful cinematic legacies of the past as they engage the crises besetting their nation.[9]

Chorality in Crialese

A film that recalls the legacies of neorealism and then refashions them with elements from auteur cinema and contemporary culture is Emanuele Crialese's *Respiro* (2003), the story of a poor fishing family in Lampedusa, Sicily, and the wife/mother whose emotional imbalance tears the family apart. The film revisits the element of chorality long associated with neorealist film; but in Crialese the choral unity comes at a high cost, with the loss of the principles of class solidarity that underwrote Luchino Visconti's politicized version of the Homeric chorus.[10] Crialese also differs from the neorealists by capturing an ancient aspect of the chorus that would have been out of place in the leftist milieu of postwar Italy: its conservatism.

The transports of the ancient Greek chorus reinforce a social fabric that the tragic hero had once challenged but, after his decisive downfall, no longer threatens. In a celebrated ode from Sophocles's *Antigone* (441 BC), the chorus first praises the capacities of man ("Marvels are many, and none more marvellous than humanity"), a creature that "crosses the grey sea," that "leads the tribes of wild beasts," and that "only from death can . . . devise no escape" (Sophocles 350, 352, 359, 370). Yet the paean concludes by acknowledging that these gifts may be used for good or ill and that all who fail to honor the gods and uphold the laws of the city must be struck down ("Never may such a person share my hearth, / Nor match his thoughts with mine") (386–87). The finale of *Oedipus the Tyrant* reflects a similar conservatism, as the chorus has the last word on Oedipus's self-blinding:

> Inhabitants of Thebes our fatherland, behold
> This Oedipus that solved the famous riddle,
> That was the man of greatest power
> Upon whom there was no citizen but stared
> In admiring envy of his great good fortune;
> See into what deadly wave of circumstances
> He has come. Therefore, fixing our gaze
> Upon life's final day, we shall call no mortal happy
> Until he cross the threshold of this life, free from pain. (1656–64)

The chorus establishes a bond with the audience based on a mutual and comparative inferiority to Oedipus. Then, by signaling a temporal break between the once mighty and now fallen hero, the chorus—and by extension the audience—rises above him. By asking the populace to wait till the story of a man's life ends before passing judgment, the chorus requests an interpretive postponement that in sociopolitical terms attests to its watchful distrust of anyone who threatens the ties binding citizens to city and humans to gods.

The forces of choral conservation shape the responses of the villagers in Crialese's film to the female lead, Grazia. The film was based on a local legend in which a mentally imbalanced young woman is ostracized by her fellow villagers, leading the woman to commit suicide. Regretting their cruelty, the villagers pray so fervently for the woman's return that she comes back to life and rejoins them. *Respiro* follows this story, except that Crialese's Grazia escapes from the village with the aid of her son and hides out along the coast before returning to the community during a ritual burning of rubbish at film's end. Concerned with why societies need to create enemies in order to define themselves, Crialese explained that humans have the "tendency . . . to look for the black sheep," the "ones who get all the blame" (Interview). Though there is no evidence to suggest that Crialese read René Girard, this quotation epitomizes the latter's landmark study *Le bouc émissaire* (*The Scapegoat* [1982]), as Grazia follows the characteristics of the Girardian scapegoat to a tee.[11]

Though politically part of Italy, her island of Lampedusa is geographically closer to Africa than Sicily. The traditions of Lampedusa and its antiquated gender roles struggle to endure in a globalized world. The children of the town want to wear the latest fashions and listen to the newest music. They meet openly in the evening for strolls on the Via Roma or clandestinely, as in the case of Grazia's daughter, Marinella, who falls in love with a policeman from the north against the wishes of her hyperprotective brothers. Although the forces of globalization are not a "violence" against Lampedusa in the Girardian sense, they represent a threat in the eyes of the villagers, as suggested by their treatment of Grazia, who like all scapegoats becomes associated with these outside pollutants. Her husband, Pietro, chastises her when she tries to socialize with his male friends, and later these friends criticize her for putting makeup on the male children and dressing them up as women. According to Crialese, Grazia troubles the notion of womanhood on the island, where a "woman has a role or existence only if she is a mother or a wife" (Interview). By subverting these roles with her gender-bending and topless swims, Grazia refuses to adhere to established female norms, so the townspeople—especially her mother-in-law—seek to protect their social identity by forcing Grazia back into her abandoned roles. Like the oracle of Delphi proclaiming that the Theban plague will only be purged by the sacrifice of the man who embodies its crisis (Oedipus), the female chorus of Lampedusa proclaims that Grazia must be expelled for medical help—to Milan, no less, eternal northern other of the Italian south. Grazia also exhibits the signs of the scapegoat through her ambiguous illness, which like Giuliana's in Antonioni's *Red Desert* is never defined and reflects the hostile tension between a character and her environment. Like Oedipus, whom Girard describes as a conglomeration of sacrificial signs, Grazia intensifies the worries of the citizenry, as her perceived threat lies less in the malady associated with her mood swings than in the eccentricity of her behavior. With the help of her son Pasquale she escapes before the Lampedusan female chorus can lay hands on her and fulfill the final aspect of Girard's schema: the expulsion of the scapegoat to heal the sick social body.

Whereas Crialese's creation of a Girard-like scapegoat is probably unwitting, his visual recapitulation of neorealist notions of the choral is self-conscious. His debt to neorealism is evident in his use of proletarian characters, folkloric themes, nonprofessional actors, natural lighting, and the local Sicilian dialect. Yet an auteurist slant manifests itself in what Crialese refers to as the film's "magical realism." As much as it references neorealism, the rugged visual terrain of *Respiro* recalls Antonioni's *L'avventura*, a film that also involves the quest for a disappeared woman. Moreover, Grazia's (Valeria Golino) vague yet overwhelming illness brings to mind the existential malaise of Giuliana (Monica Vitti) in *Red Desert*, another film that depends on the energies of an otherworldly, beautiful, and expressive female lead.

The most lasting visual debts of Crialese are to the scenes of chorality in Visconti's *La terra trema*. One of the most elaborate choral sequences in Visconti's film, the salting of the fish after the first triumphant outing of 'Ntoni and his family on their private ship, provides the visual backdrop to a key sequence in *Respiro*. Historically, epic narratives have employed scenes of labor to suggest communal identity, as we see as early as Virgil's famous description of the Carthaginians "as hard at their tasks as bees in early summer" (*Aeneid* 1.520). When the Valastro family salts 'Ntoni's catch, the dialectic between part and whole typical of such scenes appears first in the dialogue between medium- and long-range shots of the clan at work (figure 30), then in the series of intimate close-ups ranging from a melancholic portrait of the embarrassed Lia to reaction shots of the boisterous and jovial family members who tease her. Further emphasizing the choral nature of the labor at hand, Visconti charts a vast generational compass, with images progressing from childhood, to motherhood and infancy, then finally old age.

In *Respiro* the collective salting of the fish assumes what appears to be

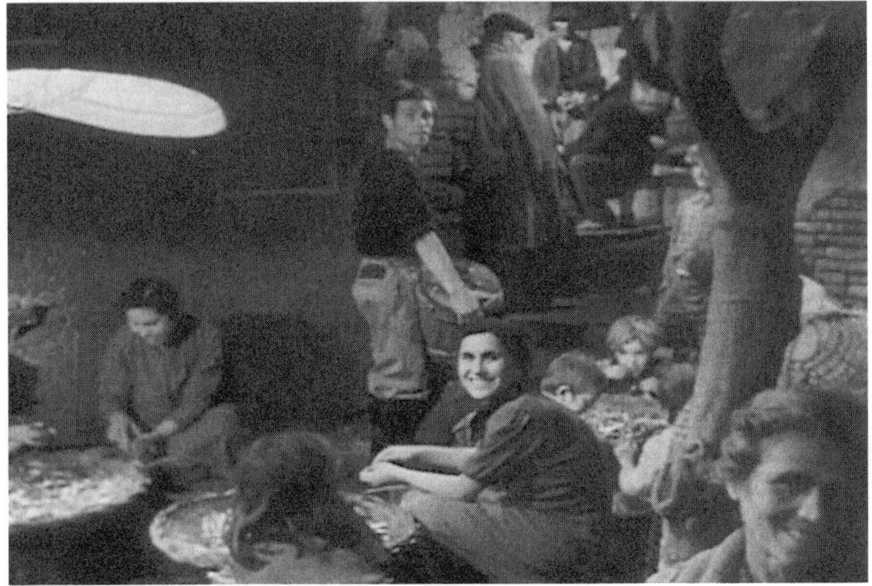

Figure 30 The choral nature of the Valastro family's salting of the fish is captured in this medium shot by Visconti *(La terra trema)*.

a similar intergenerational aspect, as both the young and old take part in the ancient manual process of preserving the daily catch. In Crialese, however, social and cultural antagonisms absent in Visconti permeate the scene. Women and children alone perform the work in *Respiro,* establishing a gender divide missing in the neorealist source. The social harmony of Visconti's choral mix and its visual analogue in the interplay between close-up and long-range shots are also absent in Crialese, who focuses on the claustrophobic atmosphere of Grazia's rebellion against the accusations of madness by her fellow townswomen. Unlike the Marxist Visconti, whose ideology led him to create imagery emphasizing class solidarity and the eclipse of bourgeois individuality, in Crialese there is no such cohesion. Thus, the choral unity of *La terra trema*'s exploited fishermen dissolves into the petty concerns and local feuds of *Respiro*'s housewives. Fittingly, many of the shots in the second half of Crialese's film after Grazia's ostracism by the villagers reveal her separateness—a quality that she shares with 'Ntoni, who is also rejected by his community because of his transgressions (figure 31).[12] This isolation is all the more resonant when one considers the usual Verghian density of life on the island, where most of the characters find it impossible to be alone—espe-

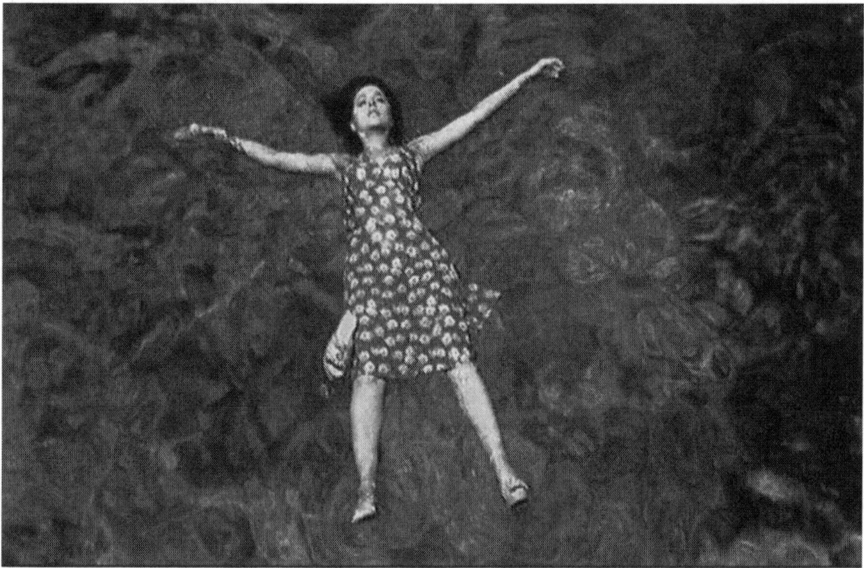

Figure 31 The breakdown of neorealist chorality à la Visconti is attested to by Crialese's solitary shot of the ostracized Grazia *(Respiro).*

cially Marinella, whose every move with her northern policeman paramour is tracked by her brothers.

The visual rhythms of Viscontian chorality reappear at film's end, when the village joins in a group swim after Grazia is discovered by her husband. The scene recalls the emphasis on communal life in Giovanni Verga's proverbs in *I Malavoglia,* Visconti's adapted source.[13] But Crialese departs from Visconti in the same motion that he gestures toward him. Earlier, when Pasquale walked on the beach where all mistakenly believe his mother, Grazia, had drowned, he fainted in the glaring heat against a white backdrop of the sand and villagers. On the surface the image recalls the villagers looking on, again in Verghian fashion, in scene after scene of *La terra trema.* On closer view, however, it is clear that Crialese differs from Visconti in allowing visual elements from pop culture and contemporary fashion to contaminate the film's otherwise monumental and epic visual subtext. Crialese's subversion of Visconti in his realistic portrayal of Pasquale's nonphotogenic onlookers cannot help but recall, in stark contrast, Orson Welles's criticism of Visconti as having made *Vogue* magazine models of his Sicilian fishermen. Crialese thus exposes a danger of an epic-minded work like Visconti's: its subject matter, no matter how cruel in content, can assume an appealing aesthetic dimension when abstracted from historical context and promoted to the status of myth. The absolute past, to tweak the Bakhtinian maxim, can often seem absolutely beautiful. Just as we marvel at ruins for their suggestion of a former and irretrievable grandeur, so might the epic genre pull us into an aesthetically appealing nostalgia for an irretrievable heroic past. By resisting Visconti's nexus between the epic and the choral, Crialese documents the sociocultural aspects of life on Lampedusa in all their unglamorous reality. In the process he locates his chorus more in global frameworks of contemporary consumer and popular culture than in the historic context—and, in the art-film tradition, eminently Viscontian domain—of Italy's embattled Southern Question.

Frammartino's Cinema of Poetry

That Crialese strays from certain elements of Visconti's film while incorporating others suggests the heterogeneous nature of neorealism and its ongoing capacity to stir debate. Another director who, like Crialese, takes on the movement's legacies and gives them his own signature is Michelangelo Frammartino. His *Le quattro volte* (2010) returns us to the neorealist notion of a regional cinema anchored in the everyday lives and customs of a local community, in this case a rural Calabrian village where a dying goatherd lives out his final days among his flock, as he tends to his terminal cough with the dust from a church floor. Evoking representations of peasant life like Ermanno Olmi's *L'albero degli zoccoli* (*The Tree of Wooden Clogs* [1978]), Frammartino crafts a cinematic poem based on the Pythagorean notion that life consists of four interlocking states: water, earth, air, and fire.

Crialese takes on the art-film tradition by setting his raw neorealist images into dialogue with more stylized cinematic techniques influenced by Antonioni and Pasolini. Frammartino's *Le quattro volte* opens with an Antonioni-like scene of otherwise silent images filled only with the diegetic sound of wind whistling through the leaves, as the smoke from carbonized timber releases vapors similar to the ones witnessed by Katherine Joyce during her visit to the ionized fields of Vesuvius in Rossellini's *Voyage to Italy*. Frammartino also offers visual echoes of Antonioni's approach to the landscape: lingering shots of the smoke from burning trees at the beginning and end of *Le quattro volte* recall the noxious smoke billowing from the factories of *Red Desert*. Like Antonioni, Frammartino uses a monochromatic filter for atmospheric effect, though his natural scenes are much more luminous than the degraded landscapes of *Red Desert.*

In addition to these aural and visual connections to Antonioni, Frammartino sets his work in intense dialogue with Pasolini. As we have seen, for Pasolini the key to cinematic poetry was the *stile indiretto libero* (free indirect style), which he argued was more powerful in film than in literature because in the former it was unmediated by language. The cinematic *im-segni* ("im-signs" or "image-signs") reveal the consciousness of human experience, unfiltered and highly metaphorical. This essential aspect of Pasolini's poetic cinema established touchstones for the art-film tradition in Italy. First, his influential essay offered a normative—if idiosyncratic—definition of a term, *poetic cinema,* that before him had generally been used only in a descriptive and suggestive sense. Second, in addition to poetic cinema Pasolini defined the most important term in Italian cinematic history: *reality* and its derivative *realism,* which from the neorealist movement on has been an endless source of debate for filmmakers and their critics. Thus, Pasolini's essay created a challenge—one could also say a burden—for directors in their subsequent attempts to create "poetic" cinema. After the appearance of "Il 'cinema di poesia'" in 1965, no discussion in Italy of what makes poetry translate to the screen can fail to mention Pasolini. Yet, as Frammartino shows, there is more than one way to create the *cinema di poesia.*

Frammartino rejects the Pasolinian view that human consciousness is the ultimate ground of reality and opts instead for a more objective camera work that locates the ground of existence in the rhythms of nature. Whereas Pasolini presented a theory of the unconscious with his essay on cinematic poetry, Frammartino provides a more cosmic, ecological vision: he replaces Pasolini's Freudian view, which holds that once something is formed in the unconscious it can never be destroyed, with the Lucretian notion that all the world is composed of swerving matter that migrates from one form to another in an infinite loop. Moreover, Frammartino substitutes Pasolini's indirect point-of-view shot with a more literal version of the cinematic poem: rhyming shots that structure the film into stanza-like sections. He does this in the series of establishing shots that denote a new day in the life of the village, often through the image of a small truck chugging up the village hill. None of these visual rhymes create "poetry" based on the free indirect point-of-view shot celebrated by Pasolini, in part because of the fundamental differences in worldview between the directors. In Pasolini the only rebirth possible is spiritual and hence personal, beholden to the unconscious realm that makes poetic cinema possible. Indeed, the body in Pasolini is often the site of physical degradation, from the sadomasochism of *Porcile* and *Salò* to the broken teeth and flowing excrement of *The Decameron*. For Frammartino the body is instead the site of renewal. The audience never gets inside the old goatherd's thoughts; he is opaque, of a piece with his natural environs. Frammartino follows the shot of his death with the birth of a kid goat. His continuity to the existence of his animals is expressed in a contiguous cinematic sequence, where his end flows into the animal's beginning through seamless editing.

Despite these differences in their understanding of cinematic poetry, Frammartino and Pasolini intersect in important ways. First, the two share a great affinity in their infusion of painterly motifs into their cinematography. When Frammartino's goatherd goes to collect his elixir from the local church, the lighting, composition, and atmosphere recall Caravaggio's use of chiaroscuro in such works as *St. John the Baptist* (1609) (figures 32 and 33). Similarly, when Pasolini's king of Thebes in *Edipo re* (*Oedipus Rex* [1967]) lies in bed after making love with his wife/mother, the camera bathes the tortured protagonist in light while the bedroom around him recedes into obscurity.[14] For both directors the chiaroscuro lighting underscores the sense of isolation of figures cut off from society and forced into searing existential predicaments. The effect is to project a physical entity, light, into an allegorical sphere: "Christian" would be too doctrinal a label for this sublimated realm, but the starkly contrastive lighting certainly points to a spiritual register beyond the homely and primitive physical coordinates that house the swathes of darkness.

Frammartino's film also recalls Pasolini's representations of the Italian south and reminds us how his notion of the free indirect point-of-view shot relied heavily on his myth of the Mezzogiorno. Famously, Pasolini believed the bourgeois world to be an irredeemably fallen one, as we see in the opening scene of *Teorema* (1966), when his interviewed factory workers claim that nothing a capitalist does is valid, not even when their boss donates his company to the proletariat. Pasolini clung to the myth of peasant, precapitalist society as the only one worth saving, and for this reason he set his adaptation of Boccaccio's *Decameron* in the southern Italian metropolis of Naples. He emphasized throughout his essay on cinematic poetry that once human experience lapses into language, it is subject to ideology and power biases—hence, his promotion of the image signs emanating from prelinguistic consciousness and, by extension, the unconscious perceptions of precapitalist cultures often located in the marginalized land- and cityscapes of the Mezzogiorno.

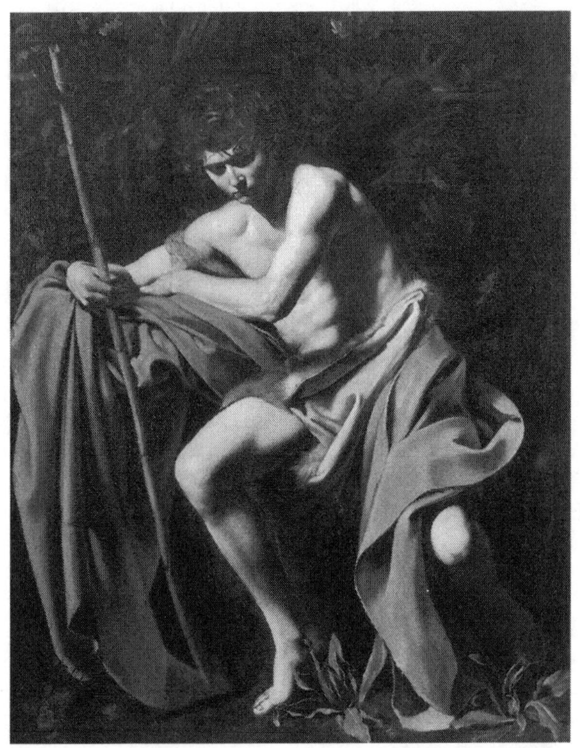

Figure 32 Caravaggio contrasts light and dark in a possible source for the chiaroscuro imagery in both Pasolini and Crialese *(St. John the Baptist)*.

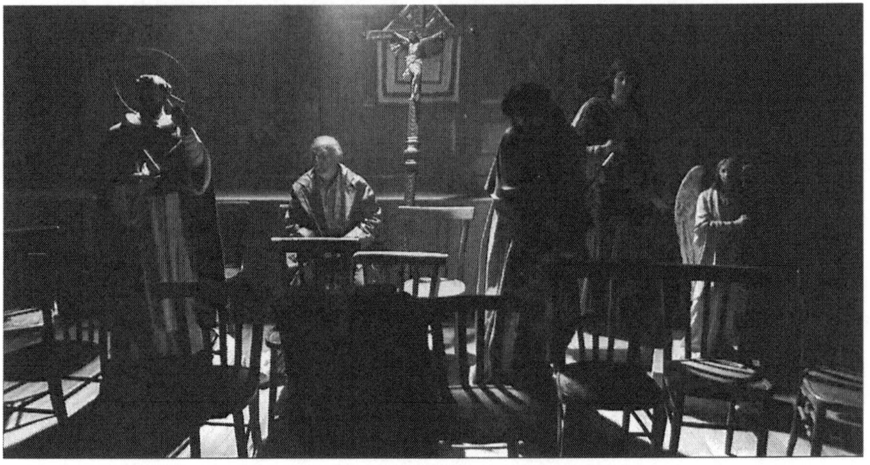

Figure 33 Frammartino's church scene exhibits the pictorial influence of the baroque chiaroscuro, one of many visual legacies he shares with Pasolini *(Le quattro volte)*.

Frammartino stands a world apart from Pasolini's militant ideologies, but he, too, favors cinematic sequences from the Italian south that underscore its distance from the nation's centers of official culture and power. The sentiment in *Le quattro volte* is similar to Giacomo Leopardi's "La ginestra," which anticipates Frammartino by showing how natural history dwarfs human history. Just as Pasolini sought to trump the sociopolitical notion of the real by replacing it with the class-free unconscious, Frammartino shifts the usual cinematic perspective from questions of society and human interaction to a natural framework indifferent to such machinations. The Calabrian setting is crucial because it, too, has often been at the margins of national history, a place celebrated for its natural beauty but rarely inscribed into the discourse of *italianità* that drove most of the engaged cinema of the 1940s and thereafter. For Frammartino and Pasolini—as it was for Leopardi—the Italian south becomes a laboratory for offering alternative views of history that disregard the usual criteria of human progress, cultural hegemony, and political power.

Although one finds little of the free indirect point-of-view shot in Frammartino's depiction of the goatherd, the opposite is true for the mineral world. When Frammartino films a goat trapped in a stream, we see his frightened, bleating perspective on what it is like to be separated from family and flock. Later, we even sense the suggested inner life of the massive pine that will be cut down as part of the village's Christmas festival, as Frammartino frames the tree in a lingering low-angle shot. He thus gives us the free indirect point-of-view shot of nature as it contemplates the human world on the periphery of the film, instead of vice versa. In so doing, Frammartino recalls what Stanley Cavell calls cinema's capacity to project a total world independent of the human subject, to create the comforting—and chilling—sense that nature will survive us. An original mix of neorealist and auteur elements, *Le quattro volte* blurs the lines between the human, animal, and mineral as it explores concerns and employs techniques that remind us of the etymology of *human* in *humus,* of or pertaining to the earth.

Epic and Ideology in Giordana

In line with the retrospective tendency in Crialese's *Respiro* and Frammartino's *Le quattro volte,* Marco Tullio Giordana's *La meglio gioventù* (*The Best of Youth* [2003]), a six-hour epic first released as a television miniseries, aims to be no less than a history of Italy from 1966 to 2003. Following the lives of two Roman brothers, Nicola and Matteo Carati, Giordana's narrative engages major literary and cinematic traditions, including the neorealist and auteur tendency to transform Homeric epic into cinematic form. In so doing, he offers both a reading of the Italian past and an interpretation of cinematic history that returns us to the tension between aesthetics and ideology in the neorealist and auteur periods.

Giambattista Vico argues in his *Scienza nuova* that the *Iliad* and the *Odyssey* could not have been written by the same person, for their worldviews are too different and their accompanying modes of expression too incompatible. Each epic poem represents for Vico a unique historical epoch, as he uses philological methods to posit that centuries must have separated the composition of the two works. The crucial distinction for Vico rests in the discrepancy between the protagonists: the impulsive athlete of war Achilles and the more introspective seafarer Odysseus. This "epic" difference, I believe, was very much on the mind of Giordana.

At one point Matteo's son, who never knew his father, asks Nicola what he was like. Nicola replies that he was "uno di quelli che non possono rimanere qui tra noi per lungo; sono [come Achille] chiamati presto dagli dèi" ("one of those who can't remain long with us; like Achilles, the gods call them back soon"). The allusion to the *Iliad* occurs during an *Odyssey*-like journey south by Nicola, as he sets out to find the woman who had taken an arresting photograph of his deceased brother, an image that he stumbled on by chance. In making the doomed and violent Matteo a modern Achilles, Giordana returns us to his earlier, more militant and politically engaged, cinema in films including *Pasolini: Un delitto italiano* (*Pasolini, an Italian Crime* [1995]) and *I cento passi.* In *Pasolini: Un delitto italiano* Giordana narrates the series of events that led to the brutal murder of Pier Paolo Pasolini by a young male prostitute in 1975. The film focuses on the ambiguities and intrigue surrounding the crime and leaves open the question of whether Pasolini's murder was a government conspiracy against one of its more severe and outspoken critics—an artist whose openly gay lifestyle and communist views had long made him the subject of intense public controversy. *I cento passi* is equally militant: focusing on the life of the Sicilian anti-Mafia crusader, Peppino Impastato, it sounds a furious critique of the damage wrought by organized crime in the Mezzogiorno.

The modern Achilles Matteo is a figure in the Pasolini-Impastato mode. Deeply ideological (though conservatively so, as opposed to the left-wing Pasolini and Impastato), he cannot accept the reality around him and seeks to impose his will on it. Early in the film Nicola is given an A on his medical exam because of his *simpatia* in the etymological sense, the ability to share the pain of others; Matteo is failed on his literature exam because of his inability to acquiesce to the tastes of his examiners. While Nicola goes on a journey through the 1960s counterculture of free love and protest, Matteo joins Italy's military police the Carabinieri and devotes himself to fighting protesters like his brother. Matteo is the mirror image of Nicola's wife, Giulia, who joins the terrorist Red Brigades and abandons her husband and child for her political causes. Nicola and Giulia represent that same ideologically driven worldview that stimulated many directors, including Giordana himself early on, to make movies that placed sociopolitical concerns above aesthetic ones. *La meglio gioventù* reflects on the strengths and limitations of this engaged film tradition through Matteo and Giulia, two characters who can barely stand to be in the same room with one another—in part because they are so alike in their unbendable principles.

The allusion to the *Iliad* draws on an earlier reference to another work on Italian political identity: Ugo Foscolo's poem "Dei sepolcri." When Matteo visits his paralyzed fellow Carabiniere Luigi—whose injury came as a result of fighting against protesters, including Nicola and Giulia, in Turin—he discovers that his southern friend has become a student of poetry under his mother's guidance. Proud of his studies, Luigi begins to recite a poem—only to have Matteo interrupt and finish it for him: the concluding lines of "Dei sepolcri":

> E tu onore di pianti, Ettore, avrai,
> ove fia santo e lagrimato il sangue
> per la patria versato, e finché il Sole
> risplenderà su le sciagure umane. (lines 292–95)

> And you, Hector, shall be honored by tears wherever men lament and hold
> sacred blood poured out for a fatherland, and as long as the sun shall shine
> on the calamities of man. ("On Sepulchers" 171)

In putting Foscolo's words in Matteo's mouth, Giordana has a modern-day Achilles speak of a latter-day Hector, two mortal enemies forever yoked in cultural memory. Foscolo's poem reflects on the value that the Florentine basilica Santa Croce holds in the Italian imagination as the pantheon that houses the remains of Galileo, Machiavelli, and Michelangelo, among others. As I have written elsewhere, the lines recall Ludwig Feuerbach's distinction between humans and animals in terms of the human capacity to think beyond our own individuality and contemplate the life—and, as Robert Harrison has shown in *Dominion of the Dead,* the death—of our species.[15] The final lines of "Dei sepolcri" signal this cosmic awareness of mortality and thus a relaxing of the instinct for survival on the individual level. It is clear by the time that Matteo quotes Foscolo that he is not long for this world, and he does indeed commit suicide soon after his allusion to "Dei sepolcri," terminating his agonized life. But, as with Foscolo's poem, in his end is his beginning: the woman he impregnates just before he dies will bear his child, and eventually she and Nicola will fall in love and begin a new life together (the same woman who took the photograph that led Nicola on an *Odyssey*-like quest to find her). Whereas Matteo is Achilles with an "Iliadic" view of Italian society and politics—and by extension, the representative of an ideological view of Italian cinematic history—his brother, Nicola, is the heir of Odysseus. Like the Greek hero, he sees a world of pain in the public arena and seeks his fulfillment in the domestic sphere. His patience, kindness, and resistance to dogma allow him to weather Italy's various historical crises with his integrity intact, and he emerges as the mouthpiece for Giordana's anti-ideological message.

Giordana's humanist message and its link to the healing power of art is on full display in the scenes of his film involving Florence. The city's Great Flood of 1966 reunites the divided brothers, bringing them together from their separate worlds to join in the relief effort (Nicola from his radical politics and Scandinavian sojourn, Matteo from his conservative militarism and soldier's barracks). Giulia and Nicola fall in love during this humanitarian effort; and two decades later, after her release from jail, Giulia will work as a librarian in the same Biblioteca nazionale she had helped save from the flood. A humanist version of art anchored in the city's Renaissance traditions of harmony, beauty, and grace permeates Giordana's representation of the flood, as Matteo and Nicola embrace in a physical union that parallels the surrounding architectural symmetry—just blocks away from the Florentine basilica of Santa Croce that inspired Foscolo's "On Sepulchers" (figure 34).[16]

As his allusions to Achilles and Hector show, Giordana inherited a question of Homer that had been a defining element of Italian cinema in neorealist and auteur film, from the mythic Sicily in Visconti's *La terra trema* to Rossellini's journey south to the villa of Uncle Homer in *Voyage to Italy* and Antonioni's claim that *L'avventura* was about people who still lived according to Homeric codes of morality. Echoing these directors, Giordana reminds us that his film is not just about history; it is a mode of historical writing in itself,

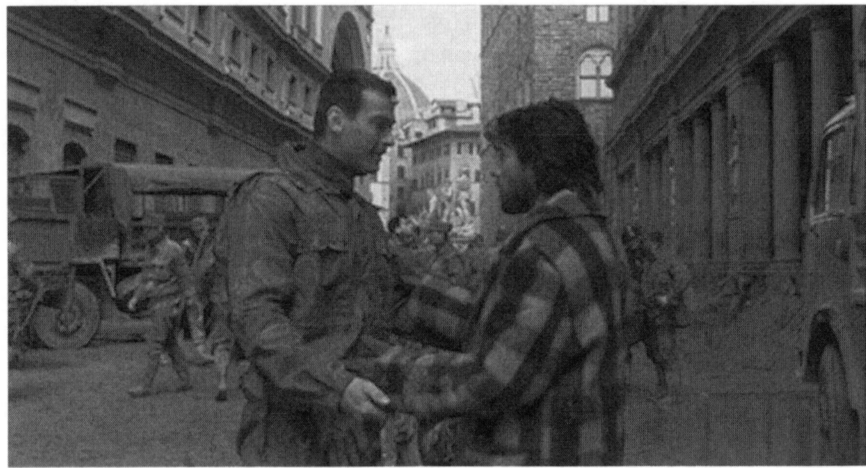

Figure 34 Giordana's Matteo (left) and Nicola (right) link arms in a fleeting gesture of solidarity occasioned by Florence's artistic heritage *(The Best of Youth)*.

as it inscribes the narrative arcs of Homeric epic while reflecting on Italy's political and cinematic past. He follows Foscolo in moving from a concern with the problems of the nation or party to the calamities of humankind, to signal his retreat from the militant viewpoint embodied in Matteo/Achilles and his move toward the more humane and open-ended narrative of the wandering Nicola/Odysseus.

Despite their differences, Crialese, Frammartino, and Giordana return us to aesthetic issues central to the art-film tradition and its sociopolitical concerns. But it would be a stretch to call their films "representative." As commentators from Brunetta to Vito Zagarrio have remarked, commercial interests far outweigh artistic ones in the current Italian film industry, and the forces of globalization have relegated the small number of complex films made each year to the margins of consumer culture—and the far reaches of the nation's cineplexes, which are dominated by Hollywood franchise films and homegrown forms of entertainment like the *cinepanettone* and other light fare.[17] But the memories of the nation's cinematic past, especially the legacies of intermedial exploration prevalent in neorealism and its auteur aftermath, endure. Even in the most unexpected of places.

In a film that elsewhere satirizes the remoteness of neorealist classics like Rossellini's *Stromboli*, Nanni Moretti's *Dear Diary* includes a sequence on the director-protagonist Moretti riding his Vespa along the shoreline of Ostia to the spot where Pasolini was murdered.[18] Filmed to the accompaniment of Keith Jarrett's musical score, the scene is devoid of Moretti's usual ironic commentary. This cinematic homage contains many of the elements that recent postmodern cinema lacks: silence, a deference to the authority of figures like Pasolini, and a sense of the transformative power of art. Tracking the hovels, shanties, and desolate beachfront with his mobile camera, Moretti achieves the gritty neorealist documentary feel that his film otherwise disavows. We have here an act of cinematic mourning, even more direct than Antonioni's meditation on the neorealist past in the tears of Claudia and Sandro at the conclusion of *L'avventura*. In bidding farewell to his *maître à penser* Pasolini, Moretti's polemical film pauses to acknowledge the source of its light—just as, in Bertolucci's words, the light from Antonioni's *L'avventura* first emanated from the lenses of Rossellini's *Voyage to Italy*.

Each of the films in this epilogue invokes aesthetic forms from the Italian art film that serve as the source for a cinematic rebirth. Likewise, this book has attempted to show that the advent of film introduced aesthetic modes that changed forever the way other art forms imagined their futures and interpreted their pasts. To return to the epigraph from Cocteau, for many cinema seemed capable of achieving an aesthetic immortality never before known. As with anything that endures, film's extension into the future was built on the remains of other, more mortal, art forms, whose themes and techniques the film medium transformed in unanticipated ways. In imagining what a cinema of poetry could be, filmmakers from the neorealist and auteur periods also dreamed of remaking their shattered nation. Along the way they resurrected a national film industry that would forever look back on this cinematic golden age—sometimes as a blessing, sometimes as a burden, and always as a challenge.

Introduction

The images in the introduction are digital frame grabs taken from *L'avventura,* directed by Michelangelo Antonioni (1960; Criterion, 2001), DVD.

1. Restivo offers critical analysis of the term *national cinema* (8–18).

2. Asor Rosa cites Alicata and De Santis's views and offers an accompanying analysis (*Il neorealismo* 85).

3. Andrew provides a genealogy of the term *art film*'s appearance in such classic studies as Rudolf Arnheim's *Film als Kunst* (*Film as Art* [1932]) (see Andrew, Foreword v).

4. See the discussion in Galt and Schoonover, Introduction 6.

5. This law stresses the need to "preservare il patrimonio culturale italiano" ("preserve Italian cultural patrimony") and designates "salle d'essai" ("art-film theaters"), which should devote at least seventy percent of their programming to suitably artistic films (fifty percent in cities with a population of fewer than forty thousand).

6. My definition of the art film as a mix of aesthetic innovation and sociopolitical engagement recalls Brunetta's words on Italian cinema as maintaining a "profondo nucleo unitario" ("deep unitary nucleus"), consisting of varied "processi inventivi ed espressivi" ("inventive and expressive processes") that coalesce into common "matrici, modi, forme, miti e luoghi comuni" ("matrices, modes, forms, myths, and commonplaces") (*Identikit* 19). See especially his observation regarding Italian cinema's strong spirit of sociopolitical intervention: "Non solo nei momenti critici della sua storia il cinema italiano ha agito da straordinario luogo di percezione e rappresentazione di ciò che unisce il paese nella sua molteplicità di luoghi e di comportamenti, ma ha anche agito da modificatore di comportamenti, da oracolo in grado di emettere profezie o più o meno catastrofiche sul futuro" ("Not only has Italian cinema in crucial periods of its history played a mighty role in perceiving and representing all that unites Italy in its multiplicity of sites and behaviors, but it has also served to modify these behaviors as a kind of oracle capable of issuing varying types of prophecies, more or less dire, about the future") (*Identikit* 19).

7. Zavattini glosses the word through a *via negativa*: "The term neorealism—in a very Latin sense—implies, too, elimination of technical-professional apparatus, screen-writer included. Handbooks, formulas, grammars, have no more application. There will be no more technical terms. Everybody has his personal shooting-script. Neorealism breaks all the rules, rejects all those canons which, in fact, exist only to

codify limitations. Reality breaks all the rules, as can be discovered if you walk out with a camera to meet it" ("Some Ideas" 225–26).

8. The first use of the term dates from Luigi Chiarini's mention of a "scuola neorealistica italiana" in the journal *Bianco e nero* in 1948 (see Parigi 92).

9. Sadoul lists the following unifying characteristics of the neorealist movement: well-delineated coordinates (Rome, 1945–52); the formation of disciples (Giuseppe De Santis, Pietro Germi, and Carlo Lizzani); the establishment of a vanguard (De Sica, Zavattini, Rossellini, and Visconti); and a set of guidelines, including dialect-based speech, long takes, natural lighting, time-space continuity, nonprofessional actors, and working-class protagonists (see Millicent Marcus, *Italian Film* 21–22). Ricciardi contrasts the emphasis on the unity of neorealism in such French critics as Bazin and Gilles Deleuze with the propensity of Italian critics to underscore the fragmentary and divided nature of the movement (483–84). The French journal *Films et documents* 5 (1952) announced ten common points of neorealism to designate the movement as a school (qtd. in Martin 34). See Rondi for a similar view. For an anthology of Bazin's influential views on neorealism see Cardullo. For further discussion of the term see Overbey, Introduction 1–33; and Pacifici.

10. See Bo 5; Millicent Marcus, *Italian Film* 27–28; and Miccichè, *Il neorealismo cinematografico* 27.

11. See their critique of "a 'certain tendency' that we believe inhibits and retards Italian film scholarship: the use of 'realism' as a value or prescriptive rather than a descriptive term in the writing of Italian cinema history and in the discussion of individual films" (107).

12. Casetti lists other important neorealist positions within the Zavattini-Aristarco polarity, including the drive to mediate between photographic representation and poetic recreation in Chiarini, the promotion of the director's imagination in Umberto Barbaro, and the emphasis on the symbiosis between linguistic and documentary elements in Fernaldo Di Giammatteo (*Theories* 30).

13. See Wagstaff, *Italian Neorealist Cinema* 37–40. Wagstaff lists fifty-five films he labels neorealist (435–39); he also gives statistics on the number of neorealist films released from 1942 to 1954 (417). Quaglietti charts the respective percentages of Italian and American films in Italy in 1945, the year typically considered the beginning of neorealism (245). Brunetta notes that during the early postwar period, Hollywood enjoyed a much greater presence in Italian movie theaters than any domestic movement or genre, including neorealism ("Long March" 145).

14. Forgacs analyzes the "process whereby, in the criticism of the Left, the concept Neorealism was first promoted and defended, then challenged and undermined" ("Making and Unmaking" 51).

15. Corrigan discusses the range of concerns associated with the term *auteur,* including commercial strategies and marketing aims (*Cinema without Walls* 103). Maule provides an overview of the emergence of the concept of the auteur in the light of key commercial, technical, and political developments in Europe in the second half of the twentieth century (31–59). See also Maule's words on the relation between "author film" and "art film" (14); and Polan's suggestive remarks on the critical "desire" to group films into auteurist categories and modes of interpretation.

16. Caughie's anthology includes important theoretical statements related to authorship/auteurism by Roland Barthes, Michel Foucault, Stephen Heath, Claude Levi-Strauss, and Geoffrey Nowell-Smith. See especially part 3, "Fiction of the Author / Author of the Fiction" (197–291).

17. See the landmark essays on auteur theory by Bazin, "Politique"; Sarris, "Toward a Theory"; Truffaut; and Woolen. Kael critiques Sarris's view and the notion of auteur ("Circles").

18. See, for example, Bondanella, *Italian Cinema*; and Brunetta, *Storia del cinema* and *Cent'anni*. The following studies emphasize the debt of Italian film to the novel and different narrative forms: Attolini; Bragaglia; and Millicent Marcus, *Filmmaking*.

19. See Brakhage; Cocteau; and Eisenstein, *Film Form*. Corrigan discusses the difficulty of studying poetry and film together (*Film and Literature* 30). Welle explores the links between poetry and film in Italy during the 1960s and 1970s ("Cinema of History"). For work on the poetry-film nexus outside of Italy see Dillon; McCabe; and Wall-Romana.

20. For a meditation on film's relation to the "rival arts" see Peucker. The journal devoted to the film-literature relationship is *Adaptation* (2007–), and the textbook is Corrigan, *Film and Literature*. Recent theoretical meditations include those by leading scholars of both film (e.g., Stam, *Literature through Film*) and literature (e.g., Hutcheon, *A Theory*). See also Cartmell and Wheldon, eds., *Cambridge Companion*. MacCabe analyzes the relation between film and literature within the context of academic institutions. Casetti reviews key issues in the study of film's relationship to literature and literary criticism (*Theories* 263–67).

21. Rhodes examines the discourse of postwar Roman urban and architectural planning in Pasolini's cinema *(Miserable City)*. Steimatsky analyzes cinematic responses to the political, physical, and symbolic elements of reconstruction in postwar Italy *(Italian Locations)*. For consideration of Italian neorealism's influence abroad see Ruberto and Wilson.

22. See Bondanella, *Italian Cinema* 1.

23. See Sitney, *Vital Crises* passim.

24. For studies of Italian film's relationship with the visual arts see Costa; and Dalle Vacche, *Cinema and Painting*. Pirandello discusses film's relation to theater and music ("Film parlante" 1032–35). See also Papini's words from 1907 on the relationship between film, theater, and the printed word:

> Rispetto al teatro—che in parte esso intende sostituire—il cinematografo ha il vantaggio di essere uno spettacolo più breve, meno faticoso e meno costoso. . . . Il cinematografo ha poi il vantaggio sul teatro di offrirci lo spettacolo di grandi avvenimenti reali pochissimi giorni dopo che essi sono accaduti. . . . In questo caso il cinematografo riunisce la proprietà dei giornali quotidiani e delle riviste illustrate: i giornali descrivono i fatti nel tempo, ma senza darcene le immagini; le riviste ci danno le immagini ma immote e fisse nello spazio, mentre il cinematografo ci dà le figure visibili e svolgentisi nel tempo. (2)

> In relation to theater—which in part it wishes to replace—film has the advantage of being a shorter show, less taxing and costly. . . . Film also has the

advantage over theater of offering us a show of great actual events, just days after they occur. . . . In this regard, film unites the property of the newspapers and illustrated magazines: newspapers describe facts in time but without giving us their images; magazines give us images, but they are static and fixed in space, whereas film gives us these images in visible form and unfolding in time.

25. See Millicent Marcus, *Filmmaking* 2; and Welle, "Dante" 392. The skeptical Pirandello believed that "l'errore fondamentale della cinematografia è stato quello di mettersi, fin dal primo principio, su una falsa strada, su una strada a lei impropria, quella della letteratura (narrazione o dramma)" ("cinema's fundamental mistake from the beginning was to set off on the wrong and inappropriate road of literature, whether fiction or drama") ("Film parlante" 1032; "Talkies" 218). In contrast, Canudo wrote in his influential "Reflections on the Seventh Art" (1923) that cinema was "renewing literature" by returning it to its original dependence on images (296). Laura Marcus discusses Canudo's remark and examines two moments in the relation between the nascent film medium and literary traditions: early film form and the responses it elicited from writers (18–98); and the aesthetics of the initial stage of film criticism, especially in the United States (179–233). Trotter reviews the "parallel histories" of early cinema and the literature of the period, as part of his study of the relation between film technology and modernist aesthetics (1–16). See also Pirandello's contrast between literary and cinematic modes of representation in the montage-like sequences of his novel *Shoot!* (4).

26. For general studies on the film-literature nexus, see Andrew, "Adaptation"; Bluestone; Boyum; Cohen; Leitch; and Naremore, *Film Adaptation*.

27. Rhodes connects Pasolini's theories on cinematic poetry to the Italian art-film tradition ("Exquisite Flowers").

28. See Restivo 8.

29. Benci discusses Antonioni's encounters with Visconti and other major neorealist figures from the 1940s, including De Santis ("Antonioni and Rome" 27–31).

Chapter 1 · The Chorus of Neorealism

The images in this chapter are digital frame grabs drawn from *Open City*, directed by Roberto Rossellini (1945; Image Entertainment, 1997), DVD; and *La terra trema*, directed by Luchino Visconti (1948; Image Entertainment, 2003), DVD.

1. See the discussions of Rossellinian chorality in Bondanella, *Rossellini* 37–38; Brunette, *Rossellini* 50, 280; Restivo 26–27; Rogin 149; and Sitney, *Vital Crises* 30–31. For analysis of Viscontian chorality see Millicent Marcus, *Filmmaking* 39; Re 147; and Steimatsky, *Italian Locations* 79–116. Gordon discusses the "choral" filmmaking techniques of another proponent of neorealist *coralità*, Carlo Lizzani (*Holocaust* 103).

2. Forgacs examines the economic, political, and social elements of the Italian culture industry in the neorealist era (*Italian Culture* 103–29).

3. *Oxford English Dictionary*, s.v. "chorus."

4. Padel discusses the public dimension of the chorus, which was generally composed of "a group of citizens, trained at the expense of a rich citizen [the *chorêgos*] who wanted to be seen as public-spirited. Many spectators had sung in the chorus themselves. They knew the people singing. They entered the theater by the same

route, the *eisodoi*, used by the actors and by the chorus on their entrance" (338). Wiles notes that the primary function of the chorus was "to offer an alternative, transformative mode of seeing," by oscillating between the perspectives of the audience and the actors (123). Arnott emphasizes this dual perspective of the chorus as an "intermediary" between the actors and the public, which "universalizes" the story onstage by "relating the tragic action to the audience's present" (34).

5. See Nehamas 546.

6. For Nietzsche the chorus embodied this metaphysical consolation because of its capacity to remain an immutable presence in the midst of the suffering and strife in "the terrifying destructive instincts of so-called world history" and "the cruelty of nature" (*Tragedy* 59).

7. Schnapp considers the nature of crowds and the masses under Fascism (14–31).

8. See Bertellini 44–45.

9. See Dalle Vacche, *Body* 39.

10. For reflections on the link between Christianity and *testimonianza* (testimony) in an important precursor to Rossellini, see Manzoni 314.

11. See Rossellini, "Ten Years" 63. Bertolucci discusses Rossellini's "profoundly moral style" (Bragin 44).

12. Rossellini describes *l'attesa* (expectation) as the most essential element of film narrative (*Il mio metodo* 91–92).

13. See Gottlieb 14.

14. Craig connects the pietà composition of *Roma, città aperta* to the iconography of "cradling wounded or dead bodies" in Rossellini's Fascist war films (25).

15. Craig analyzes the ideological and historical implications of Rossellini's use of spectatorship in his neorealist films as part of his desire to create a "new ethics and a new aesthetics" after Fascism (19).

16. Rossellini discusses the negative chorality of *Stromboli* ("Why I Directed" 30).

17. Ben-Ghiat examines the defense of chorality by De Santis and his colleagues at the journal *Cinema* as part of their desire to combat the alienation and repression of Fascism by promoting a link between the *ambiente* (environment) and *paesaggio* (landscape).

18. Vitti offers an overview of De Santis's filmmaking in the postwar years.

19. Farassino considers the relation between De Santis and his narrator (56).

20. See Cary 25–26.

21. Caesar lists three "pressure-points" compelling Italian authors of the postwar years: "the primacy of political and social themes, the politicisation of the writer, and the claims of the present" (41).

22. Anticipating Quasimodo, Giuseppe Ungaretti explored the nature of chorality in Italy during World War I—though, ironically, Quasimodo accused him of an evasive, Mallarméan lyricism. Ungaretti was mentioned by a pioneer of neorealist film, Lizzani, as an influence on the cinematic movement (104), contradicting his stereotype as the socially removed hermetic poet. Ungaretti's war poetry squares with the choral intentions in much Italian art of the neorealist generation. See his words on the feeling of human solidarity engendered by the suffering and terror of World War I in "Indefinibile aspirazione" 742; and his emphasis on the sense of brotherhood generated by the horrors of combat in the poems "Dannazione," "Fratelli," and "Veglia" (*Selected Poems* 18–19, 24–25).

23. Raya anthologizes Verga's views on film in his correspondence.

24. Steimatsky observes that *La terra trema*'s "cinematographic grasp of the location as an enframed chorale suggests a conception of nature as a contained, determinant, humanized stage" in the manner of the classical open-air theater (*Italian Locations* 113–14, 115). See her consideration of "Visconti's adaptation of . . . Verga's linguistic chorale" (*Italian Locations* 89); see also Sitney, *Vital Crises* 72–77. Moneti discusses Visconti's theatrical activities in the late 1940s (131–34).

25. See, for example, Verga, *Malavoglia* 182–83; *Medlar Tree* 9.

26. I examine the link between language and identity, especially in the many proverbs of *I Malavoglia,* in "Verga *Economicus*" 46–48; and "Work of Genre" 929–30.

27. For a description of Italy's linguistic crises in relation to the concept of cultural hegemony see Gramsci, "Sources of Diffusion." Gramsci censures the historical dichotomies and stereotypes invoked in distinguishing the Italian north and south ("Southern Question" 443).

28. See the discussion and statistics in De Mauro 61–62; Duggan 108; Lepschy 35; and Riva xi–xii.

29. De Sica writes similarly that his film *Ladri di biciclette* was dedicated "alla sofferenza degli umili" ("to the suffering of the poor") ("Perché *Ladri*") (596).

30. Steimatsky reads the opening scene of *La terra trema* in terms of Visconti's "choral spatiality," where the deep-focus representation of the fishermen preparing for a day at sea "suggests [Visconti's] conception of nature as a contained, determinant, humanized stage—and a conception of reality itself as such a set" (*Italian Locations* 111–16, 115). Invoking the precedent of Hellenic cities designed as great open-air theaters, she notes that Visconti's representation of "the landscape's unfolding in *[La terra trema]* in reciprocity with persons and actions [embodies] the place of a chorus" (*Italian Locations* 113).

31. See, respectively, Millicent Marcus, *Filmmaking* 27; and Nowell-Smith, "Pasolini's Originality" 61. Millicent Marcus also notes that Visconti's debt to the collective ethos of *I Malavoglia* entailed rejecting forms of Eisensteinian montage in favor of mise-en-scène and the use of deep-focus shots, which allow the audience to take in a panoramic view of village life and reveal the "thickness of Verga's descriptive technique, its density" and "narrative layerings" (*Filmmaking* 38).

32. Moneti remarks that *La terra trema* restructures *I Malavoglia* by making its characters into "diverse articolazioni dell'ordine socio-economico di cui sono rappresentanti" ("different articulations of the socioeconomic order that they represent") (136).

33. I provide only English translations for Visconti's film because the original Sicilian dialect was itself translated into Italian subtitles upon the film's release.

34. Bacon discusses the scene as representing the "peak of 'Ntoni's relations with the community" (46).

35. See my analysis of how Bakhtinian notions of epic relate to issues of genre and labor in Verga's *Malavoglia* ("Work of Genre" 929).

36. For Antonioni's and Rossellini's remarks see Bondanella, *Italian Cinema* 108 and 105, respectively.

37. Bazin confers the designation on both Fellini and Rossellini ("*La strada*" 57).

Chapter 2 · Beyond Beauty

The images in this chapter are digital frame grabs drawn from *Red Desert*, directed by Michelangelo Antonioni (1964; Image Entertainment, 1999), DVD; *La strada*, directed by Federico Fellini (1954; Criterion, 2003), DVD; *Rome, Open City*, directed by Roberto Rossellini (1945; Image Entertainment, 1997), DVD; and *La terra trema*, directed by Luchino Visconti (1948; Image Entertainment, 2003), DVD.

1. Benjamin considers the question of aura and its relation to the fine arts ("Work of Art"). Chow writes on the "inhumanism" of film (1387).

2. Lanham describes allegorical strategies of reading in the Greek commentaries on Homer (4). Curtius indicates that the ancient Greeks sought to resolve Plato's quarrel with poetry by allegorizing Homer in line with accepted philosophical traditions (204–6). Krieger discusses Plato's attack on poetry in light of his "demythifying" bias against the human imagination—a philosophical stance that resurfaced in the poststructuralist critique of the romantic preference for symbol over allegory (1–6). Fletcher locates an allegorical mode of expression in texts ranging from encyclopedic epic and chivalric romance to modern westerns and detective stories (3). Harrington analyzes the symbol and other rhetorical figures in cinema (149–50).

3. See Lanham 4; J. Hillis Miller 356; and *Oxford English Dictionary*, s.v. "allegory."

4. See Quintilian 3:8.6.44.

5. *Oxford English Dictionary*, s.v. "symbol." Morier discusses the polyvalence of the symbol and its historical attraction for poets (1161). Todorov (198–99) and Wellek (2:2–3) show how the distinction suggested by the terms' etymologies became a powerful element in the transition from Enlightenment and neoclassical literary models to those of romanticism.

6. See the influential definition of the symbol in Coleridge's *Statesman's Manual*, qtd. in Adams 73. For treatment of the symbol-allegory debate in the romantic period see Adams 46–98.

7. *Princeton Poetics*, s.v. "allegory" (14). Drawing on Walter Benjamin's seminal critique of the idealist symbol and his promotion of disjointed allegorical discourse (see *German Tragic Drama* 159–235), critics including Jonathan Culler, J. Hillis Miller, Maureen Quilligan, and Gayatri Spivak elaborated on the deconstructionist tendencies of allegorical discourse in relation to the metaphysical assumptions associated with the symbol. See especially de Man's influential attack on the aesthetic principles motivating many romantic writers to believe that a rhetorical construct like the symbol could achieve natural unity with its real-world referent (187–208). Krieger offers an opposing perspective (15–19). Jameson defends allegory from the perspective of Marxist dialectical historicism (33).

8. See Lyttelton, "National Question" 72; and Welle, "Dante" 383–84.

9. Based on a conversation with the neorealist director Carlo Lizzani, Millicent Marcus notes that Rossellini's "*Open City* had become for the director [Lizzani] a primary datum, an 'extramural' fact on the order of a workers' strike, a military campaign, or a parliamentary election. As cultural icon, the film, by synecdoche, had come to stand for its historical moment: it functioned as the part for the whole, the detail whose mere invocation was enough to conjure up an entire era" ("Palimpsest" 60).

10. Mussolini inaugurated Cinecittà on the anniversary of Rome's mythical founding, 21 April, to emphasize the importance his regime attributed to film (Bondanella, *Italian Cinema* 13). Lyttelton analyzes the iconography and patriotic imagery of visual media, especially historical painting, during the Risorgimento ("National Past"). Raimondi considers the contributions of Leopardi and Manzoni to Italian national discourses (*Letteratura* 30–66, 67–123).

11. Bondanella points out that, although only a small percentage of the more than seven hundred films produced during Mussolini's regime can be considered propaganda or explicitly pro-Fascist, it is impossible to gauge how critical filmmakers might have been of Italian institutions in a more open context (*Italian Cinema* 18). See his discussion of the films produced in support of Mussolini's policies and imperial campaigns: for example, Goffredo Alessandrini, *Luciano Serra pilota* (*Luciano Serra, Pilot* [1938]), scripted in part by Rossellini; Alessandro Blasetti, *Vecchia guardia* (*The Old Guard* [1935]); Carmine Gallone, *Scipione l'africano* (*Scipio Africanus* [1937]); and Augusto Genina, *Lo squadrone bianco* (*The White Squadron* [1936]), and *L'assedio dell'Alcazar* (*The Siege of the Alcazar* [1940]) (*Italian Cinema* 18–19). Patriotic films not necessarily linked to Fascist ideology include Blasetti's *Ettore Fieramosca* (1939) and his acclaimed *1860* (1934).

12. Restivo maintains that "history itself is a subject obsessively revisited by Italian cinema: the story of the Risorgimento and the unification . . . was told countless times in the cinema of the fifties and sixties" in such films as Visconti's *Senso* (1954), Rossellini's *Vanina Vanini* (1961), and Visconti's *Il Gattopardo* (*The Leopard* [1963]) (10). Dalle Vacche offers a broad consideration of the matter (*Body* passim).

13. Lizzani challenges the myth of the supposed antiliterary bias of neorealism by pointing out the interests of its filmmakers in a range of authors: Giuseppe Gioachino Belli, Ernest Hemingway, Franz Kafka, Karl Marx, Eugenio Montale, Carlo Porta, Marcel Proust, Giuseppe Ungaretti, and Giovanni Verga (104).

14. For a discussion of Verga's relationship to two poles of his literary formation—the romantic mysticism of Manzoni's *I promessi sposi* and the scientific naturalism of Émile Zola's *Rougon-Macquart* cycle—see the selection from "Per l'arte" (1883) by Verga's contemporary and a fellow pioneer of verismo, Luigi Capuana (Caretti 34–35).

15. Croce defines Verga's verismo (3:14–15). Asor Rosa explores Verga's understanding of the term ("Il primo" 11–20).

16. Musumeci examines Verga's ascription and eventual withdrawal of human affective qualities to the *Provvidenza* (61).

17. Luca was subjected to military service because 'Ntoni had requested a premature discharge from the navy; see Master 'Ntoni's identification of Luca as "un Malavoglia nato sputato!" and "tutto suo padre Bastianazzo" ("a real Malavoglia, born and bread"; "the spitting image of his father Bastianazzo") (*Malavoglia* 225–26; *Medlar Tree* 57).

18. See Dombroski 24: "The wholeness of social existence for Verga is not governed by a transcendental norm. . . . In contrast to Manzoni, the literary text for Verga was a controlled fiction of a difference to be interpreted; not a specific identity and unity that, once purged of its impurities, could be transmitted as an uplifting accounting of human experience. Verga's work thus contains no deep, symbolic levels

of meaning. . . . Its meaning is of a more comparative and abstract nature, allegorical rather than symbolical or representational."

19. Visconti's adaptation of Verga's novel was connected to his memories of the cultural legacies inspired by a fellow Lombard, Manzoni: "To me [Visconti], a Lombard reader, habituated through traditional custom to the clear rigor of Manzonian fantasy, the primitive and gigantic world of the Aci Trezza fishermen . . . always appeared aroused in an imaginative and violent epic tone. . . . Verga's Sicily truly appeared as Ulysses' island, an island of adventures and fervent passions, situated immobile and proud against the billows of the Ionian Sea. So I thought about a film on *I Malavoglia*" (qtd. in Korte 6).

20. See Bondanella, *Italian Cinema* 39–40; Ferrara, "Neo-realism" 202; and Millicent Marcus, *Italian Film* 44.

21. Agee critiques Rossellini's conflation of Christian and leftist discourses (194).

22. Bazin considers Rossellini's rejection of analysis in his representation of events and facts ("Defense" 97–98).

23. Benjamin offers an influential definition of allegory's temporal structure and tendency to call attention to its relationship to an anterior sign, just as the ruin recalls an earlier and once-complete architectural form (*German Tragic Drama* 178, 235).

24. Bondanella discusses the moral polarities of the Fool (*Cinema of Fellini* 105).

25. See Millicent Marcus, *Italian Film* 157. Bondanella and Gieri examine the lyrical elements of *La strada* in relation to neorealism ("Fellini's *La strada*").

26. For Antonioni's view on neorealism see "Talk with Antonioni" 65 (qtd. in Millicent Marcus, *Italian Film* 189): "I began as one of the first exponents of neorealism, and now by concentrating on the internals of character and psychology I do not think I have deserted the movement, but rather have painted a path towards extending its boundaries. Unlike early neorealist filmmakers, I am not trying to show reality, I am attempting to recreate realism." Tinazzi discusses Antonioni's *neorealismo interiore* (interior neorealism) and its relationship with the nonhuman cinematic world of things, the environment, and empty time (*Antonioni* 34–35).

27. See Montale's poem "Non chiederci la parola" (*Cuttlefish Bones* 40–41). Sitney analyzes Antonioni's engaged cinema during Italy's so-called economic miracle (*Vital Crises* 144). He also remarks on an "allegorical" Italian cinema from the 1940s to the 1960s (*Vital Crises* 13). Brunette explores the sociopolitical element in Antonioni's films and critiques the existentialist reading of Antonioni prevalent in the 1960s in critics including Leprohon (*Antonioni* 1–27).

28. For the use of color in *Deserto rosso* see Arrowsmith 96–100; Chatman, *Surface* 59; Dalle Vacche, *Cinema and Painting* 43–81; and Rohdie, *Antonioni* 155–60. Antonioni offers his own words on his predilection for painting ("Talk with Michelangelo" 44). Rascaroli distinguishes between two painterly styles in Antonioni's cinema of the 1960s: the modernism of the tetralogy films shot in Italy and the pop-art elements of those made abroad, beginning with *Blow-Up* (1966) ("Modernity" 65–66).

29. Critics of two Antonioni films prior to *Deserto rosso*, *La notte* and *L'eclisse*, took issue with what they deemed to be their overly explicit allegorical messages. In a special issue dedicated to *L'eclisse* by the left-wing journal *Il contemporaneo*, the editor Carlo Salinari writes that, because *L'eclisse* openly indicts the impersonality, lack of

communication, and emotional maladies of an advanced capitalist society—a large part of the film takes place in the Roman stock exchange—it represents Antonioni's "continual recourse to allegory (not to symbols) to express himself; that is to say, he had to superimpose from outside a purely intellectualistic ideological meaning, in place of the ideological clarity that he fails to attain through his poetic language as such" (17–18; qtd. in and trans. Sitney, *Vital Crises* 156). An opposite view is taken by Chatman, who calls into question the idea of a symbolic and metaphoric mode in Antonioni and argues instead for a metonymic reading of his images, which he claims should be considered in relation to one another on a primarily visual level rather than as codes for some external allegory, ideology, or theme (*Surface* 66–73).

Chapter 3 · Rossellini's Cinema of Poetry

The images in this chapter from Roberto Rossellini's *Voyage to Italy* (Sveva/Junior/ Italia Films [Italy] and SCG/Ariane/Francinex [France], 1954) are digital frame grabs drawn from *My Voyage to Italy,* directed by Martin Scorsese (1999; Miramax, 2004), DVD.

1. See the description of the lack of scripted dialogue and shots during the filming of *Europa '51* (Rossellini, "Discussion of Neorealism" 33). In this same interview Rossellini disavows script and scenario (39).

2. See Zavattini, "Some Ideas" 217; and the synthesis of the attendant critical debates in Millicent Marcus, *Filmmaking* 5–13.

3. Truffaut repudiates the literary strategies of adaptation in the cinema of quality tradition, whose scriptwriters "behave, *vis-à-vis* the scenario, as if they thought to educate a delinquent by finding him a job" ("Certain Tendency" 229). The term *cinepoema* is Bernardi's ("Prefigurazioni" 388).

4. Of some four thousand feature-length films made between 1940 and 1980, nearly half were adapted from literary sources (Andrew, "Adaptation" 98), most from novels. Bluestone notes that between 1935 and 1945, seventeen percent of films were adapted from novels and that about the time of his study, in 1957, some thirty percent of films derived from novels, while roughly eighty percent of bestsellers were made into films (3). In 1985, one in fifty American novels was optioned by Hollywood; in 1997, nearly one-fifth of the films came from novels (Naremore, *Adaptation* 10).

5. Asor Rosa lists the cascade of narrative works that neorealist filmmakers drew on, adding "sarebbe stato più semplice elencare [quei libri] che *non* erano stati tradotti in sceneggiature cinematografiche che non il contrario" ("it would have been easier to list those books that had *not* been translated into cinematic scripts instead of vice versa") ("Neorealismo" 81). Novels adapted by the neorealists include the texts of canonical authors (for example, Alessandro Manzoni, Alberto Moravia, Vasco Pratolini, Leonardo Sciascia, and Giovanni Verga), as well as lesser-known works refashioned in such classic films as De Sica's *Ladri di biciclette,* based on the eponymous novel by Luigi Bartolini (1948); and Visconti's *Ossessione* (*Obsession* [1943]), an important precursor to neorealism based on James Cain's noir *The Postman Always Rings Twice* (1938).

6. Deren, a pioneer of what Sitney calls the "lyrical" and "visionary" American cinematic avant-garde of the 1950s and 1960s (*Visionary Cinema* 3–46), described po-

etry as a transcendental category, a "vertical" investigation of a situation that "probes the ramifications of the moment, and is concerned with its qualities and its depth . . . not with what is occurring but with what it feels like or what it means" (Deren et al. 4). By contrast, she continued, the "horizontal" axis of a work of art connotes its more diachronic and sequential modes of articulation, especially plot and character development. In response to a question from the floor Arthur Miller eviscerated Deren's postulate ("To hell with that 'vertical' and 'horizontal'"), claiming instead that narrative must not be separated into constituent parts like the instrumental (Deren's term for plot) and the value-laden (her sites of poetic resonance) (16). For Miller's views on the dreamlike qualities of montage—similar to the later theories of Eisenstein and Pasolini—see 8; see also Deren's disquisition on the inherently "poetic" nature of film montage (9).

7. Corrigan notes that the presence of poetry in the history of film is at once the most elusive and least common of other adaptive strategies (*Film and Literature* 30). Though no systematic study of the relationship between film and poetry exists, recent criticism has begun to consider the matter from a range of methodological perspectives and national traditions. Dillon offers an overview of connection between film and poetry as a prelude to his discussion of Derek Jarman's "lyric" cinema (1–32). McCabe considers the role of modernist poetry in the emerging medium of film (1–17). Welle explores the confluence between cinematic and poetic modes of expression in Italian literature of the 1960s and 1970s ("Cinema of History"). Wall-Romana discusses the presence of Stéphane Mallarmé—and, more generally, French avant-garde poetry—in the early history of film. Richardson provides a rhetorical analysis of the common structures in poetry and film (91–103).

8. See, for example, Griffith's *Enoch Arden* (1911), based on Alfred Tennyson's eponymous work; as well as March's film versions of his narrative poems in "The Wild March" and "The Set-Up" (1928). Wall-Romana lists the following French poets as having written at least one poem-film scenario, filmic poem, or cinematic text between 1917 and 1928: Guillaume Apollinaire, Louis Aragon, Antonin Artaud, Blaise Cendrars, Jean Cocteau, Robert Desnos, Henry Michaux, Romain Rolland, Jules Romains, and Philippe Soupault (142). In Italy the most acclaimed early episode in the film-poetry relationship was when Gabriele D'Annunzio avidly accepted the exorbitant fee of fifty thousand lire for providing the intertitles to Giovanni Pastrone's blockbuster *Cabiria* (1914).

9. A pioneering work of this type was Marcel Duchamp's *Anémic cinéma* (*Anemic Cinema* [1923]), the fruit of his collaboration with the surrealist poet Desnos. The film consists of a series of images of concentric circles within spirals of graphic lines, followed by a verbal passage; for every two images, Duchamp inserts a title or selection of poetry. The words come from Desnos's pun-filled poem "Rrose Sélavy," whose title plays on the phrase "Eros, c'est la vie" ("Eros is life"), and one of whose lines, "Rrose Sélavy connaît bien le marchand du sel" ("Rrose Sélavy knows the salt seller well"), puns on the name *Marcel Duchamp,* an anagram of *marchand du sel.* See the discussion in Sitney, "Image and Title."

10. Corrigan discusses three traditional ways of considering the film-poetry nexus: how poets have been influenced by the movies or employed filmic structures and figures; how a poetic sensibility or vision is shared by creators of both literature and

film to create an imaginary or "poetic" quality; and how film and poetry construct metaphors, symbols, and other figurative idioms in different or similar ways (*Film and Literature* 30).

11. See, respectively, Pasolini, "Cinema di poesia" 179; Eisenstein, *Film Form* 58–62; and, for a discussion of Jarman's views, Dillon 2–6. In Brakhage the "lyrical film" entailed situating the filmmaker behind the camera as the protagonist of the film, in order to affirm "the actual flatness and the whiteness of the screen, rejecting . . . its traditional use as a window into illusion" (Sitney, *Visionary Cinema* 142).

12. Bondanella reviews the divided critical reactions to the film upon its immediate release (*Rossellini* 98–100). Forgacs analyzes the political and cultural contexts of the film's reception ("Rossellini and Critics" 4).

13. *Francesco, giullare di Dio* ostensibly derives from the thirteenth-century prose collections *I fioretti di San Francesco* (*The Flowers of Saint Francis*) and *La vita di frate Ginepro* (*The Life of Brother Juniper*), published after Francis's death. The film also incorporates arguably the first poem in the Italian vernacular, "Laudes creaturarum" ("Praises of the Creatures" [c. 1224]). In *Europa '51* Rossellini draws on Simone Weil's description of her difficult experience as a factory worker in *Attente de Dieu* (*Waiting for God* [1949]). Bernardi analyzes common themes in Rossellini's films from the early 1950s ("Prefigurazioni" 385–89).

14. In the first installment of Cocteau's trilogy on the question of poetry's relation to film, *Le sang d'un poète* (*The Blood of a Poet* [1930]), a principal concern is the struggle, figurative and actual, between the aesthetic vision of the artist and the recalcitrant energies of a work that has an actual mind and body of its own. In the second work, *La belle et la bête* (*Beauty and the Beast* [1946]), the focus switches to the capacity of childlike imagination to exist in an adult world and see beauty where others perceive deformity. Cocteau's third and best-known film of the trilogy, *Orphée* (*Orpheus* [1950]), considers mythic concerns in the history of poetry: the capacity of the poet's song to bring the inanimate to life, as well as his inability to conquer hubris and do as the gods bid him, even at the expense of his love and his life. Gallagher describes Cocteau's relationship with Rossellini (231–33, 236).

15. Katherine was to recite the following verses of Lewington:

Vita è la nostra unica parola.
Ma l'eco di questi luoghi
Risponde sommessamente: morte.
Gli uomini nascono
Già contagiati di vecchiezza
E la vita
È priva di fanciullezza.
Il silenzio si adagia
Su tutte le cose
Come la polvere.

Life is our only word.
But the echo of these places
responds meekly: [death].
People hide

already infected with old age
and life
is deprived of childhood.
Silence descends
on everything
like dust. (qtd. in Gallagher 747n10)

Gallagher examines the collaboration between Brancati and Rossellini (398–99).

16. Andrew describes the intersection between literary and cinematic sources as the most sophisticated form of adaptation because it includes a theoretical meditation on the transition from text to image while exposing the difficulties of translating from one medium to the other ("Adaptation" 99).

17. Naremore notes that Rossellini uses Joyce's tale "in much the same way that Joyce used Homer, Dante, and Shakespeare. Rossellini and his co-scenarist [Brancati] are cunning and strategically silent artists who acknowledge their sources through sly allusions, planting clues for the cognoscenti and then going on to fashion an 'autonomous' work expressive of the director's authorship" ("Return of the Dead" 198).

18. Brunette points out that *San Francesco, giullare di Dio* references its literary sources in an inchoate and arbitrary manner, as Rossellini creates "suggestive poetic anecdotes" that lead to narrative "dead ends," while implicating "a stylized world of symbolic values" (*Rossellini* 133).

19. See Bazin, "Defense" 99.

20. The director's daughter, Ingrid Rossellini, repeatedly referenced her father's distaste for the description of his work as "poetic" in her paper "Mio padre ha cent'anni!" ("My Father Is a Hundred Years Old!") at a symposium dedicated to Rossellini: "Italian Cinema for the New Millennium: Cinema as Witness," Yale University, 20 April 2007.

21. Siegel explores the journey to Italy as a literary pilgrimage by northern Europeans to a southern culture of artistic genius. Dainotto reflects on the place of Italy and its southern neighbors in the construction of European identity and its accompanying dichotomies (for example, the stereotypically rational, ordered, and productive north versus the creative, chaotic, and "backward" south).

22. See Brunette, *Rossellini* 162: "[Katherine's] encounter with the statues is turned into a series of profound, almost physical, confrontations with them, and the obviously foregrounded movements of the camera—all fast crane shots that whirl as they move closer, worthy of the most choreographed moments in Ophüls—bring her into a forced proximity with the statues that is clearly threatening."

23. Cavell discusses cinema's divergence from poetry and other art forms in its representation of human silence: "Movies, unlike performances in a theater, will contain long stretches without dialogue, in which the characters can be present without having to say anything (not: without having anything to say)" (151). Even when film does speak, Cavell writes, the most convincing moments of dialogue are the witty and the hard-nosed, which call as much attention to their surrounding silence as to their utterance (150). Kluge, Reinke, and Reitz argue that the emergence of sound corresponded to the descent of film into naturalism, resulting in a less imaginative and more realistic cinematic medium—which, they contend, lacks "the means to imitate

the internal movement of language" and is not "capable of antithetical discourse on . . . a level of [linguistic] abstraction" (85).

24. See Joyce 220: "'I suppose you were in love with this Michael Furey, Gretta,' [Gabriel] said. 'I was great with him at that time,' she said."

25. I disagree with Bohne's dismissal of Lewington's verses as the "bleating, whiny sounds" of the bourgeois artist (47). However idealized, Lewington's words represent a genuine attempt to communicate with Italian culture through an idiom of sublimation that writers on the order of François-Rene de Chateaubriand, Johann Wolfgang von Goethe, and Germaine de Staël had employed before him. I also take issue with Bohne's description of Alex Joyce as "full of sound, but very little Furey"; at the very least, Alex's impassioned sprint toward Katherine at film's end (when they are separated during the festival of San Gennaro) suggests that his feelings for his wife are of an intensity that his surface indifference and haughty demeanor try to hide.

26. Huston, Gibbons argues, achieves this effect through a mise-en-scène that associates the various characters' voices with their visual analogues (for example, filming the mementos of the spinster Julia Morkan's past as she recites "Arrayed for the Bridal," and cutting to the presumably sexually betrayed servant Lily as Mr. Grace recites "Broken Vows") (137).

27. The experimental filmmaker Amos Vogel critiques what he deemed to be the unnatural intrusion of narrative into cinema (see his comments in Bachman et al. 21).

28. Rossellini's hastily composed "script" of 340 words—scrawled on hotel stationary and written only because the production manager, Marcello D'Amico, insisted on it—merely listed the sites Katherine and Alex would visit during their Neapolitan sojourn (Gallagher 398–99). See the discussion in Mulvey 102.

29. See Rivette: "For there are films that begin and end . . . which conduct their story from an initial premise until everything has been restored to peace and order, and there have been deaths, a marriage or a revelation. . . . And there are films [like *Voyage to Italy*], which recede into time like rivers to the sea; and which offer us only the most banal of closing images" (194).

30. See Freud's notion of the memory trace and its urban analogy, Rome: "In mental life nothing which has once formed can perish," and "everything is somehow preserved." If the eternal city were not a physical but a "psychical entity," he continues, "the palaces of the Caesars would rise alongside those of the Renaissance and the fascists" (*Civilization* 17–18).

31. I share Gallagher's notion that Rossellini's changing attitude toward the film's "miraculous ending" resulted from his gradual acquiescence to the increasingly skeptical views of it (414).

32. I am indebted to Giuseppe Mazzotta's remarks on Rossellini's use of perspective in his paper "Archeology and Time in Rossellini's *Voyage to Italy*," at the symposium "Italian Cinema for the New Millennium."

33. The matter of Rossellini's transition out of neorealism remains a highly debated point. In a seminal early installment, the Marxist Aristarco condemned Rossellini's swerve from the "sincere, authentic, artistic," and politically engaged aesthetics of films like *Paisà* (*Paisan* [1946]) to what Aristarco termed the "moral deafness" of *Europa '51* (156–57). A few years later, in 1955, Bazin defended Rossellini from Aristarco's claims by arguing that the filmmaker remained true to neorealist principles in

such films as *Voyage to Italy,* by expanding the notion of the "real" into a welcomed realm of "abstraction" ("Defense" 101). Rossellini himself refused to admit any discontinuity between his war trilogy of the late 1940s—*Rome, Open City; Paisà;* and *Germany, Year Zero*—and the films of the early 1950s (see his "Interview with *Cahiers du cinéma*" 48). The consensus at present (pace Bazin) holds that the films Rossellini made in collaboration with Ingrid Bergman in the early 1950s exhibit a psychological focus, reliance on professional acting, and breakdown of *coralità* (chorality) that depart from his more documentary-like approach in the immediate postwar. Bondanella examines these differences (*Italian Cinema* 103–7; *Rossellini* 17–23).

34. See Bazin, "Defense" 101.

Chapter 4 · *Poesis* in Pasolini

The images in this chapter are digital frame grabs drawn from *The Decameron,* directed by Pier Paolo Pasolini (1971; MGM, 2002), DVD.

1. Fabbri reviews Pasolini's eccentric semiotic theories and the contentious debates they inspired in the 1960s and 1970s. Wagstaff surveys the major critical voices on Pasolini's "Il 'cinema di poesia'" ("Reality" 183–85, 224–25nn7–8).

2. The word *realism* has a volatile career in Pasolini, especially when considered in conjunction with his ideas on cinematic neorealism. Viano analyzes what Pasolini himself termed a "certain realism" (55–67).

3. Bazin writes on the "indexical" nature of film ("Ontology" 13–14). Pasolini emphasizes film's relationship with the world of memory and dreams ("Cinema di poesia" 168).

4. Eco offers a sharp critique of Pasolini's semiotics (154–55). See the discussion in Greene 98–99.

5. Casetti summarizes Pasolini's debate with Eco and the other semioticians who accused him of "naturalizing" language (*Theories* 136–38).

6. Pasolini's rebuttal to Eco continues: "Non vorrei arrestarmi sul ciglio dell'abisso su cui tu ti fermi. Non vorrei . . . che avesse nessun valore nessun dogma: mentre in te restano, inconsapevolmente, consacrati almeno due dogmi: il dogma della semiologia . . . e il dogma del laicismo" ("I do not want to stop on the edge of the abyss where you remain. I do not want . . . any dogma to hold any value, whereas you unconsciously cling to two sacred dogmas: the dogma of semiology . . . and the dogma of secularity") ("Codice dei codici" 279–80).

7. Recent interpretations of Pasolini's *cinema di poesia* emphasize that by "reality" Pasolini did not mean some "monolithic, unitary, ontological entity" but rather "a site that inhabits the dynamics of social negotiation, contradiction, and communication" (Bruno 92). See also Bruno 91: "There could have been nothing worse, in a moment when the semiotics of film was trying to gain a new status, than being labeled a partisan of reality [as Pasolini was]." De Lauretis claims that because "a *scientific* semiology of the cinema . . . is no longer a concern at all," there has been a rebirth of interest in Pasolini's unsystematic film theory (159). Greene considers Pasolini's notion of cinematic poetry in terms of its renewed relevance, especially as an influence on the French theorist Gilles Deleuze (107–10, 116–17, 123–24) and its link to the debates instituted by the Soviet formalist theory of the 1920s (110–15).

8. Wagstaff points out the influence of Benedetto Croce's thinking on Pasolini and his contemporaries in their drive to define "aesthetic value," which for Pasolini took the form of a distinction between poetic cinema and commercial film ("Reality" 223). Wagstaff also describes the Crocean inflection of Pasolini's understanding of *poesia* as both "the hypostatic union of an intuition and its expression" and the "immediate expression" that "stands between neo-capitalism and individual freedom" ("Reality" 223, 189).

9. In an interview from 1961 Pasolini said that although cinematic and literary experience were not "antithetical," he had decided to move from poetry to filmmaking to find a "new technique" for creative expression (Martini 136–37).

10. I am indebted to Tony Day for bringing to my attention Moretti's views on the free indirect style in the emergence of the modern novel.

11. Rohdie argues that Pasolini's desire to transcend linguistic mediation reflects his intent to follow the neorealist mandate of locating cinema outside of both language and a symbolic continuum in order to allow "images to speak directly" ("Neo-realism and Pasolini" 173–75). Such an attitude, Rohdie claims, set Pasolini against the proponents of a so-called critical realism, exemplified by Luchino Visconti's operatic and theatrical *Senso* (1954). Pasolini's complicated relationship to neorealism is the subject of Greene 23–51. See also Brunette, *Antonioni* 154; and Rohdie, "Neorealism and Pasolini" 167.

12. Rohdie discusses the importance of Pasolini's experience of post–World War II Resistance culture for his changing notion of the *discorso libero indiretto* ("Neorealism and Pasolini" 180).

13. Gordon speaks of Pasolini's cinematic practice as being founded on a poetics of the "gaze or look [that] drastically reduces dialogue and promotes . . . the visual and the static. The tendency of his camera [is] to remain fixed and/or distant" (*Pasolini* 209). Siciliano remarks on the "frontality" of Pasolini's filming style (227). Steimatsky traces this frontal aesthetic to Pasolini's university studies of Quattrocento painting under the influential art historian Roberto Longhi ("Pasolini" 248–50, 257n33).

14. See Pasolini, "Cinema di poesia" 178–79 (Pasolini's italics); "Cinema of Poetry" 178: "Quindi, se egli si immerge in un suo personaggio, e attraverso lui racconta la vicenda o rappresenta il mondo, non può valersi di quel formidabile strumento differenziante in natura che è la lingua. *La sua operazione non può essere lingusitica ma stilistica*" ("Thus, if he [the filmmaker] immerses himself in his character and tells the story or depicts the world through him, he cannot make use of that formidable natural instrument of differentiation that is language. *His activity cannot be linguistic; it must, instead, be stylistic*").

15. See Bevan 24.

16. See Pasolini, "Cinema di poesia" 169 (Pasolini's italics); "Cinema of Poetry" 168–69:

> Mentre la comunicazione strumentale che è alla base della comunicazione poetica e filosofica è già elaborata, è insomma un sistema reale e storicamente complesso e maturo—la comunicazione visiva che è alla base del linguaggio cinematografico è, al contrario, estremamente rozza, quasi animale. Tanto la mimica e la realtà bruta quanto i sogni e i meccanismi della memoria, sono fatti quasi pre-umani, o ai limiti dell'umano: comunque pre-grammaticali e

addiritura pre-morfologici (i sogni avvengono al livello dell'inconscio, e così i meccanismi mnemonici; la mimica è il segno di estrema elementarità civile ecc.). *Lo strumento linguistico su cui si impianta il cinema è dunque di tipo irrazionalistico:* e questo spiega la profonda qualità onirica del cinema, e anche la sua assoluta e imprescindibile concretezza, diciamo, oggettuale.

While the instrumental communication which lies at the basis of poetic or philosophical communication is already extremely elaborate—it is, in other words, a real, historically complex and mature system—the visual communication which is the basis of film language is, on the contrary, extremely crude, almost animal-like. As with gestures and brute reality, so dreams and the processes of our memory are almost prehuman events, or on the border of what is human. In any case, they are pregrammatical and even premorphological (dreams take place on the level of the unconscious, as do the mnemonic processes, gestures are an indication of an extremely elementary stage of civilization, etc.). The *linguistic instrument upon which film is predicated is, therefore, of an irrational type;* and this explains the deeply oneiric quality of the cinema, and also its concreteness as, let us say, object, which is both absolute and impossible to overlook.

17. Stewart defines the Greek word *poiesis* as a "historical process of anthropomorphization" that reaches its most powerful modern theorizing in Vico: "In Vico's thought, poetry serves human ends in the expression of the corporeal senses, in the imaginative reconfiguration of nature through such devices as onomatopoeia, personification, and other modes of projection, and as the coordination of various modes of temporal experience necessarily *preceding* any narrative forms. Following Vico, one could claim that poetry cannot be the *subject* of history, for poetry is necessarily *prior* to history" (14).

18. See Vico's formulation that "il vero è una cosa stessa col fatto" ("the truth and the made are one and the same") ("Sapienza italica" 248–50). See also his further elaboration of the *verum-factum* nexus in *Scienza nuova* par. 331. All references to *Scienza nuova* are to the internal paragraph divisions in both Nicolini's edition and Bergin and Fisch's translation.

19. Wagstaff indicates the possible influence on Pasolini of Mircea Eliade's *The Myth of the Eternal Return* (1949) ("Reality" 217).

20. Mazzotta discusses the Vichian link between philology and poetry as a privileged epistemological tool: "[For Vico] poetry is the key of access to the very foundation of humanity's time-bound existence, to the workings and culture of the mind. It reveals the mind not as a delimitable, discontinuous entity that stumbles into an impasse. Its mobile features, rather, are all refracted through (as) the very mobility of metaphoric language. In turn, poetry is the knot of threads that reaches out into all parts of Vico's intellectual and moral world. The insight into poetry makes possible his quest for the whole of knowledge (and for knowledge as a whole), which is his new discourse for the modern age" (10).

21. See the related discussion in *Scienza nuova* 460.

22. Millicent Marcus notes that Pasolini's use of "the great erotic storytelling tradition from England to the Middle East is thus recourse to the naked human body as

an irreducible medium of communication, to a semiosis of corporeality unobstructed by the civilizing veils of clothing and libidinal repression that culture has imposed upon it" (*Filmmaking* 137).

23. Rumble considers the question of adaptation in Pasolini's film (*Allegories* 104–8).

24. Pasolini considers the *questione della lingua* in relation to Italy's bourgeois-literary dialects ("Nuove questioni linguistiche" 6).

25. See the commentary on the scene in Bondanella, *Italian Cinema* 287; Lawton, "Theory" 400; and Millicent Marcus, who calls it an "allegory of adaptation" and an aesthetic "umbilical scene" (*Filmmaking* 140–41).

26. Naomi Greene considers Pasolini's transition from author to filmmaker (20).

27. Naomi Greene points out that the preoccupation with death in *Accattone* (1961), *Mamma Roma* (1962), and all of Pasolini's later films marks his swerve from the hopeful and militant messages of the neorealist era to a more Christian, fatalistic, and nihilistic worldview (25–29). Brunetta describes Pasolini's oeuvre as "una disperata ricerca e affermazione di vita e un'esibizione eccessiva di energia fatta in presenza della morte" ("a desperate quest and affirmation of life and an excessive display of energy made in the presence of death") (*Cent'anni* 151).

28. The journey back to the Middle Ages, according to Nowell-Smith, was hardly "historical" or "realistic"; it derived instead from Pasolini's stated despair over the negation of values, imagination included, that the present denied and that, Pasolini believed, only a make-believe past could revive ("Pasolini's Originality" 17). Nowell-Smith reads Pasolini's return to remote epochs such as the Middle Ages and prehistory as evidence of his quest for an "innocence" that, in the modern world, existed only among the subproletariat or the so-called Third World—that is, sites free from capitalism's reach (*Making Waves* 107, 209). Arecco discusses Pasolini's political despair during the filming of the trilogy (74–75). Lawton comments on Pasolini's turn to "culture" in the trilogy as the only hope for a society beyond political and spiritual redemption ("Evolving Rejection" 171). Viano critiques Pasolini's failure to communicate the joy of physicality in *The Decameron*'s hurried and brutish erotic encounters (except for the tender relationship of Isabetta and Lorenzo) (277–78).

29. Gordon examines Pasolini's role as Giotto's pupil and, more generally, his attitude toward acting (*Pasolini* 198).

30. Gerard considers Pasolini's choice of Naples for its prehistoric qualities (86). Viano criticizes what he calls the "Neapolitan fallacy": Pasolini's obsessive mythologizing of the city's supposed "innocent reality" and "prehistoric limbo" (273).

Chapter 5 · Threat of the Real

The images in this chapter are digital frame grabs drawn from *L'avventura*, directed by Michelangelo Antonioni (1960; Criterion, 2001), DVD; and *L'eclisse*, directed by Michelangelo Antonioni (1962; Criterion, 2005), DVD.

1. Antonioni describes the difficulties of adapting literary sources—and his preference for "inventing stories out of whole cloth"—in "Author and Theme" (1960) (Leprohon 87–88). He made only two adaptations in his career: *Le amiche* (*The Friends* [1955]), based on Cesare Pavese's short story "Tra donne sole" ("Among Women Only" [1949]); and *Blow-Up* (1966), derived from Julio Cortázar's short story "Las bablas del diablo" ("The Devil's Spittle" [1959]).

2. For Antonioni's discussion of the film-poetry relationship see Antonioni, "Colloquio" 89. In an interview with Jean-Luc Godard, Antonioni spoke of translating the "poetry" of the brutal industrial landscapes of Ravenna for *Red Desert* (Antonioni, *Architecture of Vision* 288–89). The many critics who have noted the "poetic" element in Antonioni's works include Aristarco, "Notes" 6; Arrowsmith; Kael, *I Lost It* 180; and Moravia, "New Feeling" 165.

3. Two works that probe the socioeconomic and political contexts for the Italian art cinema of the 1950s and 1960s are Restivo; and Sitney, *Vital Crises.*

4. Bondanella offers a history of the films that explored new aesthetic territories after the period of high neorealism in the 1940s (*Italian Cinema* 74–102 and 103–41).

5. Forgacs writes that "the photographer stands in as a sort of amoral alter-ego for the film-maker: arrogant, bullying, at once sensually drawn to his female characters and intolerant of their feelings" ("Antonioni and Actors" 176).

6. I designate the group of films a "trilogy" because of their broadly interrelated themes, common milieu (life in Italy during the so-called economic boom), and featuring of Monica Vitti (who plays the female lead in two of the films and an important supporting role in another). Kauffmann views the three films as a group because of their common inquiry into issues about love as a form of crisis similar to that of religion and social organization (*World* 307–8). Orban elaborates on the films' concern with emotional life in the modern world, as well as female loneliness (11–12). Unlike some, I do not add *Il deserto rosso* to the group to constitute a tetralogy because I believe that its self-conscious use of color (Antonioni's first such film) places it outside of the three earlier black-and-white films.

7. Perez distinguishes between Antonioni's "cinematic" notion of painting and the term's usual "static" sense (54).

8. Brunetta discusses Antonioni's relation to neorealism (*Storia* 2:740).

9. See Farinotti 262: "Il cinema—scrittura del sensibile—sfrutta la densità significante degli oggetti, la loro immediata evidenza; ne usa la carica simbolica e il ruolo di agente di scambio tra l'uomo e il mondo" ("Film—the writing of the palpable—exploits the dense meaning of objects and their immediate evidence; it draws from them their symbolic weight and role as an agent of exchange between humankind and the world"). She analyzes the object world in Antonioni's films (265–67).

10. "[Antonioni's] characters are often presented as sensitive to landscape, sometimes more to it than they are to each other. . . . Landscape and elements—mud, fog, rain, deserts—are powerful determinants of the action, but so are the smaller spaces, the emptiness or constriction of a room, the closeness of a blank wall" (Nowell-Smith, *Making Waves* 202). Brunetta examines the relationship between physical and mental space in Antonioni (*Cent'anni* 553–56).

11. See "Ontology" 13–14.

12. The locus classicus for discussion of Antonioni's *L'avventura* and *La notte* as "open" works is Eco 115–22 (the passage also mentions Robbe-Grillet).

13. See Celati 221:

If the essence of an era is revealed in the way in which it entrusts itself to time, we must say that our era's essence inheres in the dream of being another era: "more advanced," "future"—this is the continuous dream of the modern view of the world. Thus our era is an era which escapes itself. . . . In this kind of insight established by Antonioni, all places become observable; there is no longer a difference between beautiful and ugly places. They are all possible places in which to linger; and lingering is the trope of our inhabiting earth, inhabiting the realm of the indeterminate. When we cease to experience the landscape as the realm of the indeterminate, and home of the indescribable, it means that our understanding of the environment has been destroyed.

Nowell-Smith considers the centrality of time and duration in Antonioni's films (*Making Waves* 202).

14. Canby remarks cuttingly that the only appeal of Antonioni's "stunningly superficial" imagery in his much-maligned *Zabriskie Point* (1970) would be to "highway engineers" impressed with the "lovely aerial shots of macadam roads snaking into blue distances."

15. Rascaroli examines Antonioni's "discourse of objects" in *Il deserto rosso* as "suggestive of the direct association of things with the modern condition.... Objects are not only chosen, but also choose individuals and indissolubly tie them to their class and status" ("Modernity" 67).

16. Bonitzer analyzes the theme of disappearance in *L'avventura* (216).

17. Sitney notes that the absence of human presence in the final shot of *La notte*—a long view of the artificially manicured landscape with a mass of trees to the right and low hills to the left—contrasts the human-filled closing shot of *L'avventura* (*Vital Crises* 155). Thus, he writes, the "alfresco amours [of *La notte*] are only a grim parody of the revitalization Lidia sought" (*Vital Crises* 155).

18. See Perez 50: "Without Jeanne Moreau's character [Lidia], the sequence in *La Notte* wandering around the streets and outskirts of Milan would have yielded but a series of impressions, a vignette of everyday life.... Without the anticipation that the young lovers will turn up for a rendezvous they miss, with the resonance of their absence, the final sequence of *Eclipse* would likewise have been a little descriptive essay on an ordinary suburban corner where life winds down as usual at day's end, instead of the large, troubled, eerie reflection that it is."

19. See Affron 140–41; and Antonioni, *Screenplays* 356–61.

20. Both Antonioni and Vitti attended this seminar in Milan on 13 April 1962. Paci comments:

> In this film of Antonioni's, the environs are truly the *exteriorization* of the subjective relationship between the characters, just as the characters represent the *interiorization* of their environs. Any human rapport has disappeared: in the succession of gestures, in the streets of the city, in the Borsa [Roman stock exchange].... In my opinion, the film indirectly compels us to become aware of this process of objectification in order that we become different than we are today. It asks us to become human, and not descend to the level of object and thing. It teaches us to *return to the subject*. (trans. Joan Esposito in Sitney, *Vital Crises*; emphasis in original; see 155–57)

Chapter 6 · Chiasmus, Italian Style

The images in this chapter are digital frame grabs drawn from *The Conformist,* directed by Bernardo Bertolucci, ext. ed. (1970; Paramount, 2006), DVD; and *The Leopard,* directed by Luchino Visconti (1963; Criterion, 2003), DVD.

1. Silverman considers Andy Warhol's juxtapositions and repetitions for chiastic effect in some of his best-known paintings (74).

2. Lucente examines the tension between the narrative voice of the novel and the consciousness of its protagonist, the Leopard (204).

3. Italian publishers initially rejected Lampedusa's posthumous novel because of its apparent and controversial aristocratic sympathies. Largely on the recommendation of the author and editor Giorgio Bassani, *Il Gattopardo* eventually appeared with Feltrinelli and became an enormous best seller.

4. Visconti notes that the narrative of Lampedusa's novel boils down to "a marriage plot" (Interview 95). Mulholland considers the family structure in *Il Gattopardo* (57–58). Pache examines the theme of aristocracy in Visconti, especially in relation to his adherence to communist principles in the 1940s (72).

5. See Faldini and Gofi 142. Bertolucci described this period in the late 1960s as his "carrière psychiatrique" ("psychiatric career"), when his psychoanalytic sessions and reading of Freud informed his filmmaking, particularly when treating political issues (Gili, *Le cinéma italien* 57–58). Psychoanalysis, Bertolucci adds, was like an "objectif" ("lens") added to his camera (59). Gili describes Bertolucci's early relationship with Pasolini, whom Bertolucci credited with inventing a new cinematic language in the film *Accattone* (1961) (41). In this same interview from 1977 Bertolucci claimed that cinema "utilise des signes qui sont ceux de la vie réelle" ("utilizes signs that are those from real life"), a notion that recalls the theories articulated in Pasolini's seminal essay "Il 'cinema di poesia.'" In a similar Pasolinian vein Bertolucci notes: "Je trouve que le cinéma est beaucoup plus proche de la poésie que de la prose" ("I find that cinema is much closer to poetry than to prose") (Gili, *Le cinéma italien* 43).

6. Wagstaff discusses the Freudian elements in Pasolini's controversial essay "Il 'cinema di poesia'" ("Reality" 93). Greene analyzes the Freudian underpinnings of the desire by many Marxist critics (including Pasolini) to suppress their petit-bourgeois origins (30).

7. For the narrative emplotment of Pasolini's "literary Freud" see his film *Edipo re* (*Oedipus Rex* [1967]).

8. Dalle Vacche examines how Bertolucci reveals Freudian concepts of repression and sublimation through the contrasting acting styles of Jean-Louis Trintignant (Clerici) and Stefania Sandrelli (Anna) in *Il conformista* (*Body* 82).

9. *Il conformista* was part of a larger cinematic meditation on Fascism during the 1970s that included such films as Federico Fellini's *Amarcord* (1973) and Lina Wertmüller's *Film d'amore e d'anarchia* (*Love and Anarchy* [1972]).

10. Mellen comments on the link between Marcello's repressed homosexuality and his adherence to a brutal Fascism (3).

11. For Storaro's remarks on color theory and its pioneers, including Freud, Johann Wolfgang von Goethe, Carl Jung, and Isaac Newton, see Faldini and Gofi 550–51.

12. See Kline 82–105; Mellen 4; O'Healy 156–60; and Roud 63–64. Kolker considers the recurring theme of the Oedipal struggle in Bertolucci's films in the light of his Freudianism and Marxism. Bertolucci notes that in his films the "dialectic . . . has always been that of son/father" (Bachman 13). See Bertolucci's two poems on his well-known father, the poet Attilio Bertolucci: "La poetica vita" ("The Poetic Life") and "A mio padre" ("To My Father") (*In cerca del mistero* 83, 88). See also the gendered language in his poem "A Pasolini," where he speaks of coming to the famous director, "timida come una sposa" ("as timidly as a bride") (57). Santovetti analyzes the "triangolo [Bernardo] Bertolucci-Pasolini-[Attilio] Bertolucci," with a focus on the link between poetry and film in Bernardo Bertolucci's work (155).

13. Menand discusses Bertolucci's "killing" of his father-figure Godard, the embodiment of elite French cinematic culture (190).

14. Pasolini praises the "poetic" elements of Bertolucci's *Prima della rivoluzione* ("Cinema di poesia" 181–82).

15. Hay analyzes historical films in pre- and postwar Italy.

Chapter 7 · Verbal Montage and Visual Apostrophe

1. See "Interview with Tassone" 23. Fellini went so far as to call the memoirs a "telephone book of artistically non-existent and sometimes boring occurrences," and he labeled Casanova "proto-fascist" ("Interview with Tassone" 27, 30–31). See the discussion in Bondanella, *Fellini* 317; and Markulin 71. One wonders how closely Fellini read the enormously long text (4,545 pages in completed manuscript form), for its ironies seem to have escaped him. Casanova, for example, notes in the preface that "anyone who calls me a sensualist . . . will be wrong"; "far from my finding my history mere impudent boasting," he continues, the catalogue of his affairs has the "tone suited to a general confession," balanced between "repentance" and the desire to elicit "laughter" (1:27, 32).

2. Bondanella notes that because Fellini's "emphasis falls upon visual images rather than literary narrative," his approach to literary sources was always mediated by his use of sketches and drawings, which in turn shaped the *trattamento* (shooting scenario) and *sceneggiatura* (script) with their often dreamlike imagery ("Fellini and Petronius" 181–82). He adds: "In contrast to Hollywood practice . . . Fellini's script constitutes the only *literary* phase in a very complicated process," one in which any "literary source" quickly dissolves in "last-minute modifications, changes, and even radical departures from the script during the shooting of the sound track" (usually layered on after filming in Italy) (182). Pauluzzi discusses the lack of "standard literary convention" in Fellini's filming of *Casanova* (121).

3. See Bondanella, *Fellini* 28.

4. In *Casanova* and elsewhere Fellini's general approach was to "in-fill" the adapted literary source with his own aesthetic vision (Millicent Marcus, *Filmmaking* 206).

5. See Fellini on his adaptation of Cavazzoni's novel: "Lo sviluppo del film [*La voce della luna*] non ha avuto molto a che fare con la premessa iniziale" ("The development of the film did not have much to do with the initial premise") (*Voce* v–vi).

6. Trotter discusses the dialogue between literary and cinematic notions of montage during the modernist period, especially in relation to Eisenstein's theories (3).

7. Agamben offers a suggestive consideration of the tension between sound and sense in poetic discourse.

8. Milton, Eisenstein writes, was a supreme practitioner of montage, especially in his battle scenes, where "we [readers] become extraordinarily aware of the audio-visual distribution in his sound montage." The studied sequential linking of disparate images that Milton choreographs with cinematic intensity creates teeming visual tableaux in his readers' minds centuries before the camera was invented:

> Farr in th' Horizon to the North appeer'd
> From skirt to skirt a fierie Region, stretcht
> In battailous aspect, and neerer view
> Bristl'd with upright beams innumerable
> Of rigid Spears, and Helmets throng'd, and Shields
> Various, with boastful Argument portraid,
> The banded Powers of *Satan* hasting on
> With furious expedition. . . .

Commenting on the passage, Eisenstein writes: "Note the cinematographic instructions in the third full line to *change the camera set-up:* 'neerer view'!" ("Word and Image" 59).

9. See Eisenstein: "There is no measurable distinction between the method whereby the poet writes, the method whereby the actor forms creation within himself . . . and the method whereby his actions and whole performance . . . are made to flash in the hands of the directors through the agency of the montage exposition. . . . At the base of all these methods lie in equal measure the same vitalizing human qualities and determining factors that are inherent in every human being and in every vital human art" ("Word and Image" 64).

10. Bandini analyzes how Zanzotto's sense of isolation extends to his metrical forms and avoidance of other traditional techniques like enjambment: "Il verso di Zanzotto tend[e] a sottrarsi al predominio dell'endecasillabo che governa la poesia di tutta la generazione post-montaliana" ("Zanzotto's verse tends to absent itself from the hendecasyllable that dominates the poetry of the entire generation after Montale") (lxv–lxvi).

11. See Zanzotto et al., *Sulla poesia* 104: "Il riferimento alla fotografia ed al cinema rientra spesso nelle mie poesie, perché appartiene alla nostra esperienza quotidiana; tutti gli apparecchi della civiltà tecnologica hanno ormai condizionato la nostra quotidianità, ma possono anche fornirci delle chiavi di espressioni più complete" ("Reference to photography and film enters often into my poetry, because it is a part of our everyday experience. All the instruments of the technological world have by now conditioned our everyday life, but they can also provide us with a more complete set of expressive tools").

12. Reactions to Fellini's *Casanova* were especially harsh in the United States. See the negative reviews by Farber; Kauffmann; Porterfield; Sarris, "*Casanova*"; and especially Simon: "[*Casanova*] may well be the most ponderous specimen of imaginative vacuity ever devised" (57). More generous, Burke considers the undependable narrator-protagonist Casanova as a postmodern attempt to render narrative presence elusive and self-undermining ("Changing the Subject" 38). He also discusses Fellini's

self-conscious use of *Casanova* as a cinematic simulacrum ("Representation to Signification"). Fellini labels Casanova "*the* Italian" because of "the indefiniteness, the indifference, the commonplaces, the conventional ways, the façade, the attitude. . . . It is clear why he has become a myth, because he is really nothingness, universality without meaning" ("Interview with Tassone" 29–30). Fellini also describes the film as "anti-cinematic," one in which "there is no story" ("Interview with Tassone" 31).

13. Stubbs uses the term *Felliniesque* to signify visual excess, the grotesque, and overflowing form, texture, and color (55–62).

14. Gianfranco Contini remarks that Zanzotto's text is "one of the most singular contributions to the repertoire of Italian dialect literature" (qtd. in Welle, "Introduction" vii). Welle discusses the words of Gian Luigi Beccaria on the linguistic experimentalism of "Filò" (Welle, "Introduction" vii–viii). See also Zanzotto: "Oggi meno che mai si sa che cosa sono i dialetti nelle loro capillarizzazioni infinitesimali e le lingue, specie quelle a diffusione tendenzionalmente panterrestre, né come i loro destini s'intersechino" ("Today, less than ever, do we know what [dialects] are, in their infinitesimal capillary movements, and what languages are, especially those tending toward a paraterrestrial diffusion, nor do we know how their differences intersect") (*Poesie* 539; *Peasants Wake* 87).

15. Thomas Harrison considers the role that linguistic texture, connotation, origin, and metaphysical implication play in Zanzotto's poetry. Tyrus Miller reads Zanzotto's later poetry in the light of its "intense concentration on the material and the metaphysical aspects of language" (211).

16. Quotations of Zanzotto's poetry are given in the original dialect version followed by the Italian and English translations in, respectively, the editions by Dal Bianco and Villalta (Zanzotto, *Le poesie*); and Welle and Feldman (Zanzotto, *Peasants Wake*).

17. Robert Harrison analyzes Zanzotto's poetry in relation to the presence and gradual disappearance of the forest in the modern imagination (*Forests* 238–43). Elsewhere, he describes Zanzotto's poetry as "biopoetry [that] speaks the body, the biological, the earthly, the organic world-organism invaded by the alien psyche of technological enormities" ("Italian Silence" 98).

18. Welle indicates how Zanzotto and other recent poets including Pier Paolo Pasolini, Antonio Porta, Amelia Rosselli, Edoardo Sanguinetti, and Vittorio Sereni have alluded to films, adapted cinematic motifs and themes, and imported cinematic techniques and protocols ("Cinema of History").

19. See, for example, Petrarch's use of "or" ("even now") in line 7 of the madrigal "Non al suo amante più Diana piacque" ("Not so much did Diana please her lover") (*Rime sparse* 52); and Leopardi's use of "allor" ("then") in line 30 of "A Silvia."

20. For Zanzotto's reading of "La ginestra" see *Fantasie di avvicinamento* 127–30. He acknowledges his Leopardian debts in *Sulla poesia* 88.

21. References to Leopardi's poetry are to Galassi's edition; line numbers are the same for both the original and the translation. Welle reflects on how Zanzotto's "Filò" treats the decline of dialects in Italy and the phasing out of peasant culture after the Economic Miracle ("Cinema of History" 58)

22. Papa goes so far as to call "Filò" a "testo dichiaratamente leopardiano, una voluta ripresa di discorso dove Leopardi si era fermato" ("text that is explicitly Leo-

pardian, a self-conscious reprisal of the discourse that Leopardi left off") (496). He reads "Filò" in the light of its Leopardian formal and thematic elements, especially in relation to Zanzotto's use of dialect (500–504). Agosti discusses Zanzotto's debts to Leopardi's poetry, especially in translating interior sentiments into the illustrious idiom of Italian lyric history ("Introduzione" 10). See also Bandini lxvii–lxviii; and Moroni 83–84.

23. See Zanzotto, *Poesie* 526–27; *Peasants Wake* 75:

E anca se sarà
una busia de pi, un inbrójo de pi,
aver pensà de fàrghela
contro tut quel che ne sta schifoso dentro
e ne fa zhavariar.

E anche se sarà
ancora una menzogna, ancora un imbroglio,
aver pensato di farcela
contro tutto quello che di schifoso ci sta dentro
e ci fa delirare.

And even if it turns out to be another lie, another swindle,
to have thought of pulling it off
against everything lousy inside us,
everything making us crazy.

24. Agosti considers Zanzotto's capacity to mix ancient and modern linguistic forms ("Esperienza di linguaggio" xvii).

25. Bondanella discerns Fellini's own creative anxieties in those of Casanova's (*Fellini* 317–18). See the related viewpoint in Lederman 43; and Millicent Marcus, *Filmmaking* 219–20. Kroll connects Casanova to Fellini's autobiographical persona from *8 1/2* (1963), Guido Anselmi (60). Willis critiques the tendency by Kroll and others to identify Fellini with Casanova (25).

26. See the discussion of Leopardian apostrophe in Castronuovo; and Luzzi, *Romantic Europe* 186–87.

27. Elsewhere I have examined the use of the imperfect tense in "A Silvia" and its thematic functions (see Luzzi, "Unblurred Melody" 17).

28. I use the word *postmodern* in the sense defined by Hutcheon in her seminal study: "[*Postmodernism*] takes the form of self-conscious, self-contradictory, self-undermining statement. It is rather like saying something whilst at the same time putting inverted commas around what is being said. . . . Postmodernism's distinctive character lies in this kind of wholesale 'nudging' commitment to doubleness, or duplicity. . . . It seems reasonable to say that the postmodern's initial concern is to de-naturalize some of the dominant features of our way of life: to point out that those entities that we unthinkingly experience as 'natural' . . . are in fact 'cultural': made by us, not given to us. Even nature, postmodernism might point out, doesn't grow on trees" (*Postmodernism* 1–2).

29. Millicent Marcus comments on Fellini's "quarrel with postmodernism" (*Filmmaking* 238).

30. Casetti defines mass media ("the widest spreading of information that technology will allow") and its impact on the film medium (*Eye* 13).

31. Angelucci interprets the misfits Ivo and Gonnella as embodying Fellini's protest against an Italian present that "excludes" the two anachronistic figures because of their inability to fit in with an increasingly commercialized and dystopian nation (10), which Fellini himself labels "postmodern" (*Voce* viii). Bondanella similarly notes that Ivo and Gonnella are the only two characters in the film immune to the "static of mass media" and "open to any form of human communication"; as a consequence their fellow townspeople consider them "insane" (*Federico Fellini* 330). Roberto Benigni, the actor playing Ivo, seconds these views, noting that the innocence of his character contrasts with the vulgarity of the world he inhabits ("Maestro" 124) and that his character, Ivo, is a tragic figure sacrificed because of his naivety (Interview by Samueli 24). Fellini acknowledges his debt to the comic skills of Benigni and Paolo Villaggio (Gonnella) in bringing his vision of the film to life as they channeled *commedia dell'arte* figures including Harlequin, Brighella, and Lucignolo, as well as the film's oft-invoked Pinocchio (*Voce* viii).

32. Garofalo notes the Leopardian echoes of "L'infinito" in references by Ivo to "l'aria infinita" ("the infinite air"); "quel profondo infinito sereno" ("that profound infinite serenity"); and the query, "Che vuol dir questa immensa solitudine?" ("What does this immense solitude mean?") (47–48).

33. Degli-Esposti notes that Fellini "opposes the postmodern reaction to the notion of creative subjectivity" by staging a "recovery of voices—those of silence," in a film where the noisy hum of contemporary life is shown to be "inaudible" (42–43, 49–50).

34. The elegy of silence squares with the final chapter of Cavazzoni's *Poema dei lunatici:* "Per me se uno tace fa solo bene. . . . Io invece dico che uno deve stare tranquillo, e allora non c'è dubbio che non diventa un gran parlatore. . . . Quando sento che passa il tempo dappertutto e non c'è niente da fare, mi va via la voglia di aprire la bocca. . . . Il tempo si sente passare . . . quando non ci sono rumori" ("As far as I'm concerned, the best thing is for a person to keep quiet. . . . What I say is that a person must be at peace with himself, and then he won't feel the need to be a big talker. . . . When I have this feeling that time is passing, everywhere, and that there's nothing to be done about it, I find that my desire to open my mouth disappears. . . . You can actually hear time passing . . . only when there are no other noises around") (*Poema* 296–97; *Voice* 316–17).

35. See Kneale 22.

36. See, for example, the intrusion of soap opera gossip on Nanni Moretti and his friend Gerardo as they contemplate the iconic volcano Stromboli in Moretti's film *Caro Diario,* as well as the incessant channel surfing and obtrusive advertising spots in Maurizio Nichetti's *Ladri di saponette* (*Icicle Thief* [1987]).

Epilogue

The images used in the epilogue are digital frame grabs drawn from *Respiro,* directed by Emanuele Crialese (2002; Sony, 2003), DVD; *Le quattro volte,* directed by Michelangelo Frammartino (2010; Anamorphic, 2011), DVD; and *La terra trema,* directed by Luchino Visconti (1948; Image Entertainment, 2002), DVD.

1. See Brunetta, *History* 310.

2. Nochimson describes the modern feel of Cinecittà in the light of the transformations it has undergone.

3. See Millicent Marcus, *After Fellini* 3; and Singer 54.

4. By 2000 Italy produced only a third as many films as it did in 1960. Only one in five of these films found an American distributor, which in most cases meant that the films showed for a short run before being replaced by a blockbuster. Stanley connects the nation's commercial and aesthetic cinematic malaise to factors including the Italian industry's lack of savvy producers and the ever-increasing dominance of television.

5. Gili writes: "Sono rari i film italiani che, negli ultimi anni, hanno ottenuto un notevole successo in Francia" ("It is the rare Italian film that, in these recent years, has achieved success in France")—a poignant remark considering that it was in France where such movements as neorealism received important promotion ("Esiste in Francia" 280). Sklar's review of Italian cinema after 2000 in the United States distinguishes between the positive results of older directors and the problems faced by younger ones (276).

6. Zagarrio offers a balanced analysis of the virtues and defects of Italian cinema since 2000: on the plus side, a surge in political film, the creative energies of the digital revolution, the productive mixing of genres, the increased presence of women, and a rise in film festivals. Less optimistically, he points to the diluting of filmmakers' ideals, their unwillingness to disturb the status quo, and a lack of the experimental initiative typical of Hollywood ("Certi bambini" 13–19).

7. A 2002 *Economist* headline proclaimed that "Italian cinema is on its best form in more than 30 years," and a 2008 *New York Times* feature by Povoledo remarked, "Many critics and industry experts see the recent recognition at Cannes as a positive sign that after a protracted dark age, periodically brightened by hits that turned out to be flashes in the pan, Italian cinema is finally back on track." The Italian press employed a more flamboyant rhetoric: writing in *La repubblica*, Natalia Aspesi described the cinematic resurgence as "the Italian redemption" (qtd. in Povoledo).

8. Miccichè coined the term *orfano* ("orphan") to describe Italian cinema of the 1980s and 1990s, because of both the disappearance of the "grandi maestri" ("great masters") and the inexorable rise of "cineprogrammi televisivi" ("made-for-television movies"): "Non ci si sposta più per andare genericamente 'al cinema,' ma soltanto (un paio di volte l'anno, in media, con tendenza a diminuire) per vedere determinati film" ("One no longer goes in general terms 'to the cinema,' but only [a few times a year, usually, and always less so] to see certain movies") ("Eredi del nulla" 251–52). Zagarrio analyzes the limitations of Italian cinema in the 1990s in its screenwriting, preproduction, directing, promotion, and distribution (*Anni novanta* 115–18).

9. Millicent Marcus highlights a neorealist-inflected "memorialist" tradition in such films as Pasquale Scimeca's *Placido Rizzotto* (2000) and Marco Tullio Giordana's *I cento passi* (*The One Hundred Steps,* 2000), which recount the deaths of crusaders against organized crime in a manner that recalls Rossellini's staging of the execution of the partisan priest Don Pietro in *Open City.* In keeping with this reevaluation of painful moments in the nation's history, two works by Marco Bellocchio—*Buongiorno, notte* (*Good Morning, Night* [2002]), on the murder of former prime minister

Aldo Moro by the Red Brigades in 1978; and *Vincere* (2009), on Benito Mussolini's secret affair with Ida Dalser—incite Italians to confront unresolved political issues from their past.

10. Sklar comments on the absence of ideology in Crialese's "fable" (277).

11. Girard posits that collective acts of violence, rather than resulting from any cult of personality or contingent set of events, yield the following four immutable stereotypes. The acts of violence that inspire the community to sacrifice are real; real also is the crisis occasioning the call for sacrificial retribution; the victims or scapegoats are chosen not because of their crimes but because they bear certain signs associated with these crimes; and these victims are subsequently destroyed to purge the community of a crisis that, through their supposed infirmities and moral monstrosity, the sacrificial victims are believed to incarnate (24).

12. Small discusses Grazia's cinematic isolation (94).

13. See, for example, *I Malavoglia* 181; *Medlar Tree* 7: "Per menare il remo bisogna che le cinque dita s'aiutino l'un l'altro" ("To pull an oar the five fingers must work together").

14. Graham-Dixon discusses Caravaggio's influence on Pasolini (441).

15. See Luzzi, "Ends" 297–99; Feuerbach 1–2; and Robert Harrison, *Dominion* 127, 136.

16. D'Onofrio describes Nicola as a source of "unity" in the film (82).

17. O'Leary analyzes the phenomenon of the *cinepanettone*.

18. De Bernardis reads the sequence in terms of Moretti's adherence to Pasolini's notion of poetic cinema as the *lingua scritta dalla realtà* ("language written by reality") (125–26).

Adams, Hazard. *Philosophy of the Literary Symbolic.* Tallahassee: U Presses of Florida, 1983.

Affron, Mirella Joan. "Text and Memory in *Eclipse.*" *Literature/Film Quarterly* 9.3 (1981): 139–51.

Agamben, Giorgio. "The End of the Poem." *The End of the Poem: Studies in Poetics.* Trans. Daniel Heller-Roazen. Stanford: Stanford UP, 1999. 109–15.

Agee, James. *Agee on Film: Reviews and Comments.* New York: MacDowell, Oblensky, 1958.

Agosti, Stefano. "Introduzione alla poesie di Zanzotto." *Andrea Zanzotto, poesie (1938–1972).* By Andrea Zanzotto. Ed. Stefano Agosti. Milan: Mondadori, 1973. 7–25.

———. "L'esperienza di linguaggio di Andrea Zanzotto." Introduction to Zanzotto, *Le poesie* ix–xlix.

Alicata, Mario, and Giuseppe De Santis. "Verità e poesia: Verga e il cinema italiano." *Cinema* 6 (1941): 216–17.

Andrew, James Dudley. "Adaptation." *Concepts in Film Theory.* New York: Oxford UP, 1984. 96–106.

———. *Film in the Aura of Art.* Princeton, NJ: Princeton UP, 1984.

———. Foreword. Galt and Schoonover, *Global Art Cinema* v–xi.

Angelucci, Gianfranco. "Su *La voce della luna* e altre fellinità." *Cineteca* 6.2–3 (April–May 1990): 10–11.

Antonioni, Michelangelo. "Author and Theme." Leprohon 87–88.

———. "Cannes Statement." Chatman and Fink 177–79.

———. "Colloquio con Michelangelo Antonioni." 1958. Leprohon 88–89.

———. "Il 'fatto' e l'immagine." Di Carlo and Tinazzi, *Fare un film* 50–52; English translation: "The Event and the Image." Di Carlo, Tinazzi, and Cottino-Jones, *Architecture* 51–53.

———. *Screenplays: "Il grido," "L'avventura," "La notte," "L'eclisse."* New York: Orion, 1963.

———. "A Talk with Antonioni." Interview by Hollis Alpert. *Saturday Review of Literature* 27 Oct. 1962: 27, 45.

———. "A Talk with Michelangelo Antonioni on His Work." Di Carlo and Tinazzi, *Architecture* 21–47.

Arecco, Sergio. *Pier Paolo Pasolini.* Rome: Partisan, 1972.

Ariosto, Ludovico. *Orlando furioso*. Ed. Lanfranco Caretti. 2 vols. 2nd ed. Turin: Einaudi, 1992.

Aristarco, Guido. "Notes on Michelangelo Antonioni." Trans. Luciana Bohne. *Film Criticism* 9 (1984): 4–7.

———. "On *Europa '51*." Trans. Geoffrey Nowell-Smith. Forgacs, Lutton, and Nowell-Smith 156–57.

Arnott, Peter D. *Public and Performance in the Greek Theatre*. London: Routledge, 1989.

Arrowsmith, William. *Antonioni: The Poet of Images*. Ed. Ted Perry. New York: Oxford UP, 1995.

Asor Rosa, Alberto. "Il neorealismo o il trionfo del narrativo." *Cinema e letteratura del neorealismo*. Ed. Giorgio Tinazzi and Marina Zancan. 2nd ed. Venice: Marsilio, 1983. 79–102.

———. "Il primo e l'ultimo uomo del mondo." *Il caso Verga*. Ed. Alberto Asor Rosa. Palermo: Palumbo, 1987.

Attolini, Vito. *Dal romanzo al set*. Bari: Dedalo, 1988.

Aumont, Jacques. *Amnésies: Fictions du cinéma d'après Jean-Luc Godard*. Paris: POL, 1999.

Bachman, Gideon. "Films Are Animal Events: Bernardo Bertolucci Talks about His New Film *1900*." *Film Quarterly* 29.1 (1975): 11–19.

Bachman, Gideon, Parker Tyler, Amos Vogel, et al. "On the Nature and Function of the Experimental (Poetic) Film." *Poetry and Film*. New York: Gotham Book Mart, 1972. 17–26.

Bacon, Henry. *Visconti: Explorations of Beauty and Decay*. New York: Cambridge UP, 1998.

Bakhtin, Mikhail M. *The Dialogic Imagination*. Ed. Michael Holquist. Trans. Caryl Emerson and Michael Holquist. Austin: U of Texas P, 1981.

———. "Discourse in the Novel." Bakhtin, *Dialogic Imagination* 3–40.

———. "Epic and Novel." Bakhtin, *Dialogic Imagination* 259–422.

Bandini, Fernando. "Zanzotto dalla 'Heimat' al mondo." Zanzotto, *Le poesie* lii–xciv.

Bantcheva, Denitza, ed. *Visconti dans la lumière du temps*. Condé-sur-Noireau: Corlet, 2008.

Barański, Zygmunt G., ed. *Pasolini Old and New: Surveys and Studies*. Dublin: Free Court, 1999.

Bazin, André. "De la politique des auteurs." Trans. Peter Graham. *The New Wave*. Ed. Peter Graham. New York: Doubleday, 1968. 137–55.

———. "De Sica: *Metteur en scène*." Curle and Snyder 62–76.

———. "In Defense of Rossellini." Bazin, *What Is Cinema?* 2:93–101.

———. "*La strada*." Trans. Joseph E. Cunneen. *Federico Fellini: Essays in Criticism*. Ed. Peter Bondanella. New York: Oxford UP, 1978.

———. "The Ontology of the Photographic Image." Bazin, *What Is Cinema?* 1:9–16.

———. *What Is Cinema?* Ed. and trans. Hugh Gray. 2 vols. Berkeley: U of California P, 1967–71.

Bellour, Raymond. "The Film Stilled." Trans. Alison Rowe with Elizabeth Lyon. *Camera Obscura* 24 (1990): 99–123.

Benci, Jacopo. "Antonioni and Rome, 1940–62." Rascaroli and Rhodes 21–63.

Ben-Ghiat, Ruth. *Fascist Modernities: Italy, 1922–1945.* Berkeley: U of California P, 2004.

Benigni, Roberto. Interview by Anna Samueli. "*La voce della luna.*" Trans. Nathalie Sciardis. *Cahiers du cinéma* 431–32 (May 1990): 23–25.

———. "Roberto Benigni Is a True Maestro among Clowns, a Fool as Fine Artist." Interview by Robert Gerber. *Interview* 20 (1990).

Benjamin, Walter. *Illuminations.* Ed. Hannah Arendt. Trans. Harry Zohn. New York: Schocken, 1969.

———. *The Origin of German Tragic Drama.* Trans. John Osborne. New York: Verso, 2003.

———. "The Storyteller." Benjamin, *Illuminations* 83–109.

———. "The Work of Art in the Age of Mechanical Reproduction." Benjamin, *Illuminations* 217–51.

Bernardi, Sandro. "Prefigurazioni della modernità: Rossellini e Antonioni." De Giusti, *Storia del cinema italiano* 8:383–95.

———. "Rossellini's Landscapes: Nature, Myth, History." Forgacs, Lutton, and Nowell-Smith 50–63.

Bertellini, Giorgio. "Dubbing *l'Arte Muta:* Poetic Layerings around Italian Cinema's Transition to Sound." *Re-viewing Fascism: Italian Cinema, 1922–1943.* Ed. Jacqueline Reich and Piero Garofalo. Bloomington: Indiana UP, 2002. 30–82.

Bertolucci, Bernardo. "Bernardo Bertolucci Seminar." *American Film Institute Dialogue on Film* 3 (April 1974): 14–28.

———. *In cerca del mistero: Poesie.* Rome: Gremese, 1988.

Bevan, D. G. "Pasolini and Boccaccio." *Literature/Film Quarterly* 5 (1977): 23–29.

Blake, William. *Selected Poems.* London: St. Martin's, 1995.

Bluestone, George. *Novels into Films.* Baltimore: Johns Hopkins UP, 1957.

Bo, Carlo, ed. *Inchiesta sul neorealismo.* Turin: Radio Italiana, 1951.

Bohne, Lucia. "Rossellini's *Voyage to Italy:* A Variation on a Theme by Joyce." *Film Criticism* 3 (1979): 43–52.

Bondanella, Peter. *The Cinema of Federico Fellini.* Princeton, NJ: Princeton UP, 1992.

———. *The Films of Roberto Rossellini.* Cambridge: Cambridge UP, 1993.

———. *Italian Cinema: Neorealism to the Present.* 3rd ed. New York: Continuum, 2001.

———. "Literature as Therapy: Fellini and Petronius." *Annali d'Italianistica* 6 (1988): 179–98.

Bondanella, Peter, and Manuela Gieri. "Fellini's *La strada* and the Cinema of Poetry." Introduction to *La strada.* Ed. Peter Bondanella and Manuela Gieri. New Brunswick, NJ: Rutgers UP, 1987. 3–22.

Bonitzer, Pascal. "The Disappearance (On Antonioni)." Trans. Chris Breyer, Gavriel Moses, and Seymour Chatman. Chatman and Fink 215–18.

Bordwell, David. "Art Cinema as a Mode of Film Practice." *Film Criticism* 4.1 (1979): 56–64.

Boyum, Joy Gould. *Double Exposure: Fiction into Film.* New York, Universe, 1985.

Bragaglia, Cristina. *Il piacere del racconto: Narrativa italiana e cinema, 1895–1990.* Florence: La Nuova Italia, 1993.

Bragin, John. "A Conversation with Bernardo Bertolucci." *Film Quarterly* 20.1 (1966): 39–44.

Brakhage, Stan. *Metaphors on Vision*. New York: Film Culture, 1963.

Brooks, Peter. *Reading for the Plot: Design and Intention in Narrative*. Cambridge, MA: Harvard UP, 1992.

Brunetta, Gian Piero. *Cent'anni di cinema italiano*. Bari: Laterza, 1991.

———. *The History of Italian Cinema: A Guide to Italian Film from Its Origins to the Twenty-First Century*. Trans. Jeremy Parzen. Princeton, NJ: Princeton UP, 2009.

———. *Identikit del cinema italiano oggi: 453 storie*. Venice: Marsilio, 2000.

———. "Il cinema italiano oggi." *Annali d'Italianistica* 17 (1999): 17–30.

———. "The Long March of American Cinema in Italy: From Fascism to the Cold War." *Hollywood in Europe: Experiences of a Cultural Hegemony*. Ed. David W. Ellwood and Rob Kroes. Amsterdam: VU UP, 1994. 137–54.

———. *Storia del cinema italiano dal 1945 agli anni ottanta*. Rome: Riuniti, 1982.

———. "Temi della visione di Pier Paolo Pasolini." *Italian Quarterly* 21–22.82–83 (1980–81): 151–57.

Brunette, Peter. *The Films of Michelangelo Antonioni*. Cambridge: Cambridge UP, 1998.

———. *Roberto Rossellini*. New York: Oxford, 1987.

Bruno, Giuliana. "The Body of Pasolini's Semiotics: A Sequel Twenty Years Later." Rumble and Testa 88–105.

Burke, Frank. "Federico Fellini: From Representation to Signification." *Romance Language Annual* 1 (1989): 34–40.

———. "Fellini: Changing the Subject." *Film Quarterly* 43.1 (1989): 36–48.

Buzard, James. *The Beaten Track: European Tourism, Literature, and the Ways to "Culture," 1800–1918*. Oxford: Clarendon, 1993.

Caesar, Michael. "Writing and the Real World: Italian Narrative in the Period of Reconstruction." *The Culture of Reconstruction: European Literature, Thought and Film, 1945–50*. Ed. Nicholas Hewitt. New York: St. Martin's, 1989. 37–50.

Canby, Vincent. "Screen: Antonioni's 'Zabriskie Point.'" *New York Times* 10 Feb. 1970.

Canova, Gianni, ed. *Storia del cinema italiano*. Vol. 11, *1965–1969*. Venice: Marsilio, 2002.

Canudo, Ricciotto. "Reflections on the Seventh Art" (1923). Trans. Claudia Gorbman. *French Film Theory and Criticism: A History/Anthology, 1907–1939*. Ed. Richard Abel. 2 vols. Princeton, NJ: Princeton UP, 1988. 1:291–303.

Cardullo, Bert, ed. *André Bazin and Italian Neorealism*. New York: Continuum, 2011.

Caretti, Lanfranco, ed. *Manzoni e gli scrittori da Goethe a Calvino*. Bari: Laterza, 1995.

Cartmell, Deborah, and Imelda Wheldon, eds. *Cambridge Companion to Literature on Screen*. Cambridge: Cambridge UP, 2005.

Cary, Joseph. *Three Modern Italian Poets: Saba, Ungaretti, Montale*. Chicago: U of Chicago P, 1969.

Casanova, Giacomo. *History of My Life*. Trans. Willard Trask. 12 vols. Baltimore: Johns Hopkins UP, 1997.

Casetti, Francesco. *Eye of the Century: Film, Experience, Modernity*. Trans. Erin Larkin with Jennifer Pranolo. New York: Columbia UP, 2008.

———. *Theories of Cinema, 1945–1995*. Trans. Francesca Chiostra and Elizabeth Gard Bartolini-Salimbeni, with Thomas Kelso. Austin: U of Texas, P, 1999.

Castronuovo, David. "The Apostrophic Prayer: A Guiding Figure in Leopardi's Earliest Poetry." *Romance Languages Annual* 10 (1998): 216–24.

Caughie, John, ed. *Theories of Authorship: A Reader.* London: Routledge, 1988.

Cavazzoni, Ermanno. *Il poema dei lunatici.* Turin: Bollati Boringhieri, 1987. English translation: *The Voice of the Moon.* Trans. Ed Emery. London: Serpent's Tail, 1990.

Cavell, Stanley. *The World Viewed: Reflections on the Ontology of Film.* Enl. ed. Cambridge, MA: Harvard UP, 1979.

Celati, Gianni. "'L'avventura' and Waiting." Chatman and Fink 219–21.

Chatman, Seymour. *Antonioni, or, The Surface of the World.* Berkeley: U of California P, 1985.

———. *Michelangelo Antonioni: The Complete Films.* Ed. Paul Duncan. Cologne: Taschen, 2004.

Chatman, Seymour, and Guido Fink, eds. *"L'avventura": Michelangelo Antonioni, Director.* New Brunswick, NJ: Rutgers UP, 1989.

Chiaromonte, Nicola. "Italian Movies." *Partisan Review* 16.6 (1949): 621–30.

Chow, Rey. "A Phantom Discipline." *PMLA* 116.5 (2001): 1386–95.

Cocteau, Jean. *Cocteau on the Film.* London: Dobson, 1972.

Cohen, Keith. *Film and Fiction: The Dynamics of Exchange.* New Haven, CT: Yale UP, 1976.

Corrigan, Timothy. *A Cinema without Walls: Movies and Culture after Vietnam.* New Brunswick, NJ: Rutgers UP, 1991.

———. *Film and Literature: An Introduction and Reader.* Upper Saddle River, NJ: Prentice Hall, 1999.

Costa, Antonio. *Cinema e pittura.* Turin: UTET, 1991.

Cosulich, Callisto, ed. *Storia del cinema italiano.* Vol. 7, *1945–1948.* Venice: Marsilio, 2001.

Craig, Siobhan S. *The Shattered Screen: Cinema after Fascism.* London: Palgrave MacMillan, 2010.

Crialese. Emanuele. Interview by Jonathan Carter. 3 August 2008. www.bbc.co.uk/dna/collective/A1137232. Web. 27 July 2012.

Croce, Benedetto. *La letteratura della nuova Italia: Saggi critici.* 2nd ed. 3 vols. Bari: Laterza, 1921–22.

Culler, Jonathan. *The Pursuit of Signs.* Ithaca, NY: Cornell UP, 1983.

Curle, Howard, and Stephen Snyder, eds. *Vittorio De Sica: Contemporary Perspectives.* Toronto: U of Toronto P, 2000.

Curtius, Ernst Robert. *European Literature and the Latin Middle Ages.* Trans. Willard R. Trask. New York: Harper and Row, 1963.

Dainotto, Roberto M. *Europe (in Theory).* Durham, NC: Duke UP, 2007.

Dalle Vacche, Angela. *The Body in the Mirror: Shapes of History in Italian Cinema.* Princeton, NJ: Princeton UP, 1992.

———. *Cinema and Painting: How Art Is Used in Film.* Austin: U of Texas P, 1996.

Dante. *The Divine Comedy.* Trans. and commentary Charles S. Singleton. 6 vols. Princeton, NJ: Princeton UP, 1970–75.

De Bernardis, Flavio. *Nanni Moretti.* Milan: Il Castoro, 1993.

Decreto Legislativo 22 gennaio 2004, n. 28. www.camera.it/parlam/leggi/deleghe/testi/04028dl.htm. Web. 27 July 2012.

De Giusti, Luciano. "Disseminazione dell'esperienza neorealista." De Giusti, *Storia del cinema italiano* 8:3–32.

———, ed. *Storia del cinema italiano.* Vol. 8, *1949–1953.* Venice: Marsilio, 2003.

Degli-Esposti, Cristina. "Voicing the Silence in Federico Fellini's *La voce della luna.*" *Film Journal* 33.2 (1994): 42–55.

de Lauretis, Teresa. "Re-reading Pasolini's Essays on Cinema." *Italian Quarterly* 21–22.82–83 (1980): 159–66.

de Man, Paul. "The Rhetoric of Temporality." *Blindness and Insight: Essays in the Rhetoric of Contemporary Criticism.* 2nd ed. Minneapolis: U of Minnesota P, 1983. 187–208.

De Mauro, Tullio. "Lingua e dialetti." *Stato dell'Italia.* Ed. Paul Ginsborg. Milan: Saggiatore, 1994.

Deren, Maya, Arthur Miller, Dylan Thomas, Parker Tyler, et al. "Poetry and the Film: A Symposium." *Poetry and Film.* New York: Gotham Book Mart, 1972. 1–16.

De Sica, Vittorio. "De Sica on De Sica." Curle and Snyder 22–49.

———. "Perché *Ladri di biciclette.*" *La fiera letteraria.* 6 Feb. 1948. Cosulich, *Storia del cinema italiano* 7:596–97.

Di Carlo, Carlo, and Giorgio Tinazzi, eds. *Fare un film è per me vivere: Scritti sul cinema.* Venice: Marsilio, 1994. English translation: *The Architecture of Vision: Writings and Interviews on Cinema.* Ed. Carlo Di Carlo, Giorgio Tinazzi, and Marga Cottino-Jones. New York: Marsilio, 1996.

Dillon, Steven. *Derek Jarman and the Lyric Film: The Mirror and the Sea.* Austin: U of Texas P, 2004.

Dombroski, Robert S. *Properties of Writing: Ideological Discourse in Modern Italian Fiction.* Baltimore: Johns Hopkins UP, 1994.

D'Onofrio, Emanuele. "Identity and Ideology: Marco Tullio Giordana and *Impegno* in the Second Republic." Hope 75–88.

Duggan, Christopher. *The Force of Destiny: A History of Italy since 1796.* Boston: Houghton Mifflin, 2008.

Easterling, Patricia E. "Tragedy, Greek." *Oxford Classical Dictionary.* Ed. Simon Hornblower and Anthony Spawforth. 3rd ed. Oxford: Oxford UP, 1996. 1538–42.

Eco, Umberto. *La struttura assente.* Milan: Bompiani, 1968.

Eisenstein, Sergei. *Film Form: Essays in Film Theory.* Ed. and trans. Jay Leyda. New York: Harcourt Brace, 1949.

———. "Word and Image." *The Film Sense.* Trans. Jay Leyda. New York: Harcourt Brace. 1970. 3–68.

Elsaesser, Thomas. *New German Cinema: A History.* New Brunswick, NJ: Rutgers UP, 1989.

Esposito, Joan. "Dialectical Imagery in *Eclipse.*" *Film Criticism* 9.1 (1984): 25–37.

Fabbri, Paolo. "Free/Indirect/Discourse." Rumble and Testa 78–87.

Faldini, Franca, and Goffredo Gofi, eds. *Il cinema italiano d'oggi, 1970–1984: Raccontato dai suoi protagonisti.* Milan: Mondadori, 1984.

Farassino, Alberto. *Giuseppe De Santis.* Milan: Moizzi, 1978.

Farber, Stephen. "*Casanova:* Love's Labors Lost." *New West* 31 Jan. 1977: 74–75.

Farinotti, Luisella. "Il rovescio delle cose." Canova, *Storia del cinema italiano* 11: 262–71.

Fellini, Federico. "*Casanova:* An Interview with Aldo Tassone." *Federico Fellini: Essays in Criticism.* Ed. Peter Bondanella. New York: Oxford UP, 1978.

———. *La voce della luna.* Turin: Einaudi, 1990.

Ferrara, Giuseppe. "Neo-realism: Yesterday." Overbey, *Springtime in Italy* 199–205.

Feuerbach, Ludwig. *The Essence of Christianity.* Trans. George Eliot. New York: Harper and Row, 1957.

Fletcher, Angus. *Allegory: The Theory of a Symbolic Mode.* Ithaca, NY: Cornell UP, 1964.

Forgacs, David. "Antonioni and Actors." Rascaroli and Rhodes 167–82.

———. "Introduction: Rossellini and the Critics." Forgacs, Lutton, and Nowell-Smith 1–6.

———. *Italian Culture in the Industrial Era: Cultural Industries, Politics and the Public.* Manchester: Manchester UP, 1990.

———. "The Making and Unmaking of Neorealism in Postwar Italy." Hewitt, *Reconstruction* 51–66.

Forgacs, David, Sarah Lutton, and Geoffrey Nowell-Smith. *Roberto Rossellini: Magician of the Real.* London: British Film Institute, 2000.

Foscolo, Ugo. "Dei sepolcri." Ed. Franco Longoni. Vol. 1 of *Opere.* Ed. Franco Gavezzeni et al. 2 vols. Turin: Einaudi-Gallimard, 1994–95. 21–38. English translation: "On Sepulchers." *The Artifice of Reality: Poetic Style in Wordsworth, Foscolo, Keats, and Leopardi.* By Karl Kroeber. Madison: U of Wisconsin P, 1964. 167–71.

———. "Dissertation on an Ancient Hymn to the Graces." Ed. Franco Longoni. *Opere* 1:142–68.

Frammartino, Michelangelo. Interview by Jonathan Romney. *Sight and Sound* 21.6 (2011): 44.

Freud, Sigmund. *Civilization and Its Discontents.* Trans. James Strachey. New York: Norton, 1989.

———. *The Major Works of Sigmund Freud.* Chicago: Britannica, 1954.

Gallagher, Tag. *The Adventures of Roberto Rossellini.* New York: Da Capo, 1998.

Galt, Rosalind. "*L'avventura* and the Picturesque." Rascaroli and Rhodes 134–53.

Galt, Rosalind, and Karl Schoonover, eds. *Global Art Cinema: New Theories and Histories.* New York: Oxford UP, 2010.

———. Introduction. Galt and Schoonover, *Global Art Cinema* 3–27.

Garofalo, Marcello. "*La voce della luna.*" *Segnocinema* 10 (1990): 47–48.

Gerard, Fabien S. *Pasolini, ou le mythe de la barbarie.* Brussels: Éditions de l'Université de Bruxelles, 1981.

Gibbons, Luke. "'The Cracked Looking Glass' of Cinema: James Joyce, John Huston, and the Memory of 'The Dead.'" *Yale Journal of Criticism* 15.1 (2002): 127–48.

Gili, Jean. "Esiste in Francia il cinema italiano del duemila?" Zagarrio, *La meglio gioventù* 280–86.

———. *Le cinéma italien.* Paris: Veyrier, 1985.

Girard, René. *The Scapegoat.* Trans. Yvonne Freccero. Baltimore: Johns Hopkins UP, 1986.

Gordon, Robert S. C. *The Holocaust in Italian Literature, 1944–2010.* Stanford: Stanford UP, 2012.

———. *Pasolini: Forms of Subjectivity.* Oxford: Clarendon, 1996.

Gottlieb, Sidney. "Introduction: *Open City:* Reappropriating the Old, Making the New." Gottlieb, *Rossellini's "Rome, Open City"* 1–30.

———, ed. *Roberto Rossellini's "Rome Open City."* Cambridge: Cambridge UP, 2004.

Graham-Dixon, Andrew. *Caravaggio: A Life Sacred and Profane.* New York: Norton, 2012.

Gramsci, Antonio. "Some Aspects of the Southern Question." *Selections from Political Writings (1921–1926); with Additional Texts by Other Communist Leaders.* Ed. and trans. Quintin Hoare. Minneapolis: U of Minnesota P, 1978. 441–62.

———. "Sources of Diffusion of Linguistic Innovations in the Tradition of a National Linguistic Conformism in the Broad National Masses." *Selections from Cultural Writings.* Ed. David Forgacs and Geoffrey Nowell-Smith. Trans. William Boelhower. Cambridge, MA: Harvard UP, 1985. 183–84.

Greene, Naomi. *Pier Paolo Pasolini: Cinema as Heresy.* Princeton, NJ: Princeton UP, 1990.

Hainsworth, Peter. "The Poetry of Andrea Zanzotto." *Italian Studies* 37 (1982): 101–21.

Harrington, John. *The Rhetoric of Film.* New York: Holt, Rinehart and Winston, 1973.

Harrison, Robert Pogue. *Dominion of the Dead.* Chicago: U of Chicago P, 2003.

———. *Forests: The Shadows of Civilization.* Chicago: U of Chicago P, 1994.

———. "The Italian Silence." *Critical Inquiry* 13.1 (1986): 81–99.

Harrison, Thomas. "Andrea Zanzotto: From the Language of the World to the World of Language." *Poesis* 5.3 (1984): 68–85.

Hay, James. "Visconti's *Leopard:* Remaking a National Popular History." *Forum Italicum* 21 (1987): 36–48.

Heath, Stephen. "Film/Cinetext/Text." *Screen* 14.1–2 (1973): 102–27.

Holy Bible. International Bible Society. Grand Rapids, MI: Zondervan, 1984. New International Version.

Hope, William, ed. *Italian Film Directors in the New Millennium.* Newcastle-on-Tyne: Cambridge Scholars, 2010.

Hutcheon, Linda. *The Politics of Postmodernism.* 2nd ed. London: Routledge, 2002.

———. *A Theory of Adaptation.* New York, Routledge, 2005.

James, Clive. "Mondo Fellini." *New Yorker* 21 March 1994: 154–65.

Jameson, Fredric. *The Political Unconscious: Narrative as a Socially Symbolic Act.* Ithaca, NY: Cornell UP, 1981.

Joyce, James. "The Dead." *Dubliners.* Harmondsworth: Penguin, 1976. 175–225.

Kael, Pauline. "Circles and Squares." *Authors and Authorship: A Film Reader.* Ed. Barry Keith Grant. Malden, MA: Blackwell, 2008. 46–54.

———. *I Lost It at the Movies.* Boston: Atlantic Monthly, 1965.

Kauffmann, Stanley. "Fellini's *Casanova.*" *New Republic* 5 March 1977: 10.

———. *A World on Film: Criticism and Comment.* New York: Harper and Row, 1966.

Kline, T. Jefferson. *Bertolucci's Dream Loom: A Psychoanalytic Study.* Amherst: U of Massachusetts P, 1987.

Kluge, Alexander, Wilfried Reinke, and Edgar Reitz. "Word and Image." Trans. Miriam Hansen. *October* 46 (1988): 83–95.

Kneale, J. Douglas. *Romantic Aversions: Aftermaths of Classicism in Wordsworth and Coleridge.* Quebec City: McGill-Queen's UP, 1999.

Kolker, Robert Phillip. *Bernardo Bertolucci.* New York: Oxford UP, 1985.

Korte, Jr., Walter F. "Marxism and Formalism in the Films of Luchino Visconti." *Cinema Journal* 11 (1971): 2–12.

Krieger, Murray. "'A Waking Dream': The Symbolic Alternative to Allegory." *Allegory, Myth, and Symbol*. Ed. Morton W. Bloomfield. Cambridge, MA: Harvard UP, 1981.

Kroll, Jack. "A Sterile Casanova." *Newsweek* 24 Jan. 1977: 60–61.

Lampedusa, Giuseppe Tomasi di. *Il Gattopardo*. 48th ed. Milan: Feltrinelli, 1987. English translation: *The Leopard*. Trans. Archibald Colquhoun. New York: Pantheon, 1988.

Lanham, Richard A. *A Handlist of Rhetorical Terms*. 2nd ed. Berkeley: U of California P, 1991.

Lawton, Ben. "The Evolving Rejection of Homosexuality, the Sub-Proletariat, and the Third World in the Films of Pier Paolo Pasolini." *Italian Quarterly* 21–22.82–83 (1980–81): 167–73.

———. "Theory and Praxis in Pasolini's *Trilogia della vita*." *Quarterly Review of Italian Studies* 2.4 (1977): 395–415.

Lederman, Marie Jean. "Art, Artifacts, and Fellini's *Casanova*." *Film Criticism* 2.1 (1977): 43–45.

Leitch, Thomas. *Film Adaptation and Its Discontents: From "Gone with the Wind" to "The Passion of the Christ."* Baltimore: Johns Hopkins UP, 2007.

Leopardi, Giacomo. "Alla luna." Leopardi, *Canti* 112–13.

———. "A se stesso." Leopardi, *Canti* 234–35.

———. "A Silvia." Leopardi, *Canti* 172–77.

———. *Canti*. Trans. and annotated by Jonathan Galassi. New York: Farrar, Straus and Giroux, 2010.

———. "Canto notturno di un pastor errante nell'Asia." Leopardi, *Canti* 192–203.

———. "La ginestra." Leopardi, *Canti* 286–309.

Leprohon, Pierre. *Michelangelo Antonioni: An Introduction*. Trans. Scott Sullivan. New York: Simon and Schuster, 1963.

Lepschy, Giulio C. *Mother Tongues and Other Reflections on the Italian Language*. Toronto: U of Toronto P, 2002.

Liehm, Mira. *Passion and Defiance: Film in Italy from 1942 to the Present*. Berkeley: U of California P, 1984.

Lizzani, Carlo. "Eravamo eclettici." *Cinema e letteratura del neorealismo*. Ed. Giorgio Tinazzi and Marina Zancan. Vicenzo: Marsilio, 1990. 104–14.

Lucente, Gregory. *Beautiful Fables: Self-consciousness in Italian Narrative from Manzoni to Calvino*. Baltimore: Johns Hopkins UP, 1986.

Lukács, Georg. *The Historical Novel*. Trans. Hannah and Stanley Mitchell. Lincoln: U of Nebraska P, 1983.

Luzzi, Joseph. "The Ends of Poetry: Sense and Sound in Giorgio Agamben and Ugo Foscolo." *Annali d'Italianistica* 30 (2011): 291–99.

———. *Romantic Europe and the Ghost of Italy*. New Haven, CT: Yale UP, 2008.

———. "Unblurred Melody." Review of Giacomo Leopardi, *Canti*. Trans. Jonathan Galassi. *Bookforum* 17.4 (2010): 17–18.

———. "Verga *Economicus*: Language, Money, and Identity in *I Malavoglia* and *House by the Medlar Tree*." *The Printed Media in Fin-de-Siècle Italy; Publishers, Writers, and Readers*. Ed. Ann Hallamore Caesar, Gabriella Romani, and Jennifer Burns. Oxford: Legenda, 2011. 37–48.

———. "The Work of Genre: Labor, Identity, and Modern Capital in Wordsworth and Verga." *PMLA* 127.4 (2012): 925–31.

Lyttelton, Adrian. "Creating a National Past: History, Myth and Image in the Risorgimento." *Making and Remaking Italy: The Cultivation of National Identity around the Risorgimento.* Ed. Albert Russell Ascoli and Krystyna von Henneberg. Oxford: Berg, 2001. 27–74.

———. "The National Question in Italy." *The National Question in Europe and in Historical Context.* Ed. Mikulás Teich and Roy Porter. Cambridge: Cambridge UP, 1993. 63–105.

MacCabe, Colin. Foreword. Trotter ix–xi.

Manzoni, Alessandro. "Letter on Romanticism." Trans. Joseph Luzzi. *PMLA* 119.2 (2004): 299–316.

Marcus, Laura. *The Tenth Muse: Writing about Cinema in the Modernist Period.* Oxford: Oxford UP, 2007.

Marcus, Millicent. *After Fellini: Italian Cinema in a Postmodern Age.* Baltimore: Johns Hopkins UP, 2002.

———. *Filmmaking by the Book: Italian Cinema and Literary Adaptation.* Princeton, NJ: Princeton UP, 1993.

———. *Italian Film in the Light of Neorealism.* Princeton, NJ: Princeton UP, 1986.

———. "The Neorealist Memorialist Tradition." *Italian Neorealism and Global Cinema.* Ed. Laura E. Ruberto and Kristi M. Wilson. Detroit: Wayne State UP, 2007.

———. "Palimpsest versus Pastiche: Re-visiting Neorealism in the 1990s." *Annali d'Italianistica* 17 (1990): 56–68.

Markulin, Joseph. "Plot and Character in Fellini's *Casanova:* Beyond *Satyricon.*" *Italian Quarterly* 23.87 (1982): 65–74.

Martin, Marcel. "Le néoréalisme vu par la critique français." *Écran* 37 (1975): 28–36.

Martini, Daisy. "L'*Accattone* di Pier Paolo Pasolini." *Cinema nuovo* 10.150 (1961): 136–38.

Maule, Roseanna. *Beyond Auteurism: New Directions in Authorial Film Practices in France, Italy, and Spain since the 1980s.* Bristol: Intellect, 2008.

Mazzotta, Giuseppe. *The New Map of the World: The Poetic Philosophy of Giambattista Vico.* Princeton, NJ: Princeton UP, 1999.

McCabe, Susan. *Cinematic Modernism: Modernist Poetry and Film.* Cambridge: Cambridge UP, 2005.

Mellen, Joan. "Fascism in Contemporary Film." *Film Quarterly* 24.4 (1971): 2–19.

Menand, Louis. "After the Revolution: Bernardo Bertolucci Revisits Paris." *New Yorker* 10 Oct. 2003: 188–96.

Miccichè, Lino. "Gli eredi del nulla: Per una critica del giovane cinema italiano." *Una generazione in cinema: Esordi ed esordienti italiani, 1975–1988.* Ed. Franco Montini. Venice: Marsilio, 1988. 251–58.

———. "Il lungo decennio grigio." *Schermi opachi: Il cinema italiano degli anni '80.* Ed. Lino Miccichè. Venice: Marsilio. 3–16.

———, ed. *Il neorealismo cinematografico italiano.* Venice: Marsilio, 1975.

———. "Sul neorealismo, oggi." *Il neorealismo cinematografico italiano.* Ed. Lino Miccichè. Venice: Marsilio, 1999. ix–xxiii.

Miller, J. Hillis. "Two Allegories." Bloomfield, *Allegory* 355–70.

Miller, Tyrus. "In Darkness, in Snow: Figures beyond Language in the Poetry of Zanzotto." *Stanford Italian Review* 9 (1991): 211–29.

"The Moment Is Now: Italian Cinema Is on Its Best Form for More Than 30 Years." *Economist* 18 April 2002: www.economist.com/node/1087017. Web. 27 July 2012.

Monaco, James. *The New Wave: Truffaut, Godard, Chabrol, Rohmer, Rivette.* New York: Oxford UP, 1977.

Moneti, Guglielmo. "Visconti dalla Resistenza a *La terra trema:* Lo spettacolo della realtà." Cosulich, *Storia del cinema italiano* 7:128–42.

Montale, Eugenio. *Cuttlefish Bones (1920–1927).* Trans. and commentary William Arrowsmith. New York: Norton, 1992.

Moravia, Alberto. *Il conformista.* Milan: Bompiani, 1951. English translation: *The Conformist.* Trans. Tami Calliope. South Royalton, VT: Steerforth, 1999.

———. "A New Feeling for Reality." Leprohon 163–65.

Moretti, Franco. *Atlante del romanzo europeo: 1800–1900.* Turin: Einaudi, 1997.

———. *The Way of the World: The "Bildungsroman" in European Culture.* London: Verso, 2000.

Morier, Henri. *Dictionnaire de poétique et de rhétorique.* 5th ed. Paris: PUF, 1961.

Moroni, Mario. "Andrea Zanzotto: L''io' come unita minima di testimonianza critica." *Italica* 73 (1996): 83–102.

Mulholland, Rory. "Ambivalences de la famille." Trans. Denitza Bantcheva. Bantcheva 58–61.

Mulvey, Laura. "Vesuvian Topographies." Forgacs, Lutton, and Nowell-Smith 95–112.

Musumeci, Antonino. "Verga and the Changing Metaphor." *Modern Language Notes* 93.1 (1978): 52–63.

Naremore, James. *Film Adaptation.* New Brunswick, NJ: Rutgers UP, 2000.

———. "Return of the Dead." *Perspectives on John Huston.* Ed. Stephen Cooper. New York: G. K. Hall, 1994. 197–206.

Neale, Steve. "Art Cinema as Institution." *Screen* 22.1 (1981): 11–39.

Nehamas, Alexander. "Nietzsche, Friedrich." *The Johns Hopkins Guide to Literary Theory and Criticism.* Ed. Michael Groden and Martin Kreiswirth. Baltimore: Johns Hopkins UP, 1994. 546–48.

Nichols, Bill, ed. *Movies and Methods: An Anthology.* 2 vols. Berkeley: U of California P, 1976–85.

Nietzsche, Friedrich. *The Birth of Tragedy; and The Case of Wagner.* Trans. and commentary Walter Kaufmann. New York: Vintage, 1967.

Nochimson, Martha P. "The Cinecittà Pentimento Effect: A Firsthand Account. *Cineaste* 35.2 (2010): www.cineaste.com/articles/the-cinecitt-pentimento-effect-a-firsthand-account. Web. 8 May 2013.

Nowell-Smith, Geoffrey. *Making Waves: New Cinema of the 1960s.* New York: Continuum, 2008.

———. "Pasolini's Originality." *Pier Paolo Pasolini.* Ed. Paul Willemen. London: British Film Institute, 1977. 4–20.

O'Healy, Áine. "Re-envisioning Moravia." *Annali d'Italianistica* 6 (1988): 148–61.

O'Leary, Alan. "The Phenomenology of the *Cinepanettone.*" *Italian Studies* 66.3 (2011): 431–43.

O'Leary, Alan, and Catherine O'Rawe. "Against Realism: On a 'Certain Tendency' in Italian Film Criticism." *Journal of Modern Italian Studies* 16.1 (2011): 107–28.

Orban, Clara. "Antonioni's Women, Lost in the City." *Modern Language Studies* 31.2 (2001): 11–27.

Overbey, David. Introduction. Overbey, *Springtime in Italy* 1–33.

———, ed. and trans. *Springtime in Italy: A Reader on Neo-realism*. Hamden, CT: Archon, 1979.

Oxford English Dictionary. 2nd ed. Oxford: Oxford UP, 1989.

Pache, Raphaëlle. "L'univers de l'aristocratie." Bantcheva 72–81.

Pacifici, Sergio. "Notes Toward a Definition of Neorealism." *Yale French Studies* 17 (1956): 44–53.

Padel, Ruth. "Making Space Speak." *Nothing to Do with Dionysos? Athenian Drama in Its Social Context*. Ed. John J. Winkler and Froma Zeitlin. Princeton, NJ: Princeton UP, 1990. 336–65.

Papa, Marco. "Il dialetto e la ginestra: Leopardismo dell'ultimo Zanzotto." *La rassegna della letteratura italiana* 82 (1978): 496–504.

Papini, Giovanni. "La filosofia del cinematografico." *La stampa* 18 May 1907: 1–2.

Parigi, Stefano. "Neorealismo: Le avventure di una parola." Cosulich, *Storia del cinema italiano* 7:85–96.

Pasolini, Pier Paolo. "Il 'cinema di poesia.'" *Empirismo eretico*. 3rd ed. Milan: Garzanti, 2000. 167–87. English translation: "The 'Cinema of Poetry.'" *Heretical Empiricism*. Ed. Louise K. Barnett. Trans. Ben Lawton and Louise K. Barnett. Bloomington: Indiana UP, 1988. 167–86.

———. "Il codice dei codici." Pasolini, *Empirismo eretico* 277–84.

———. "Nuove questioni linguistiche." Pasolini, *Empirismo eretico* 5–24.

———. "Tabella." Pasolini, *Empirismo eretico* 293–97.

———. *Trilogia della vita*. Ed. Giorgio Gattei. Bologna: Cappelli, 1975.

Pauluzzi, Fausto. "Materials on Fellini's *Casanova:* An Update." *Italian Culture* 7 (1986–89): 119–35.

Perez, Gilberto. "A Man Pointing: Antonioni and the Film Image." *Yale Review* 82.3 (1994): 38–65.

Petraglia, Sandro. *Pier Paolo Pasolini*. Florence: La Nuova Italia, 1974.

Petrarch. *Petrarch's Lyric Poems: The "Rime Sparse" and Other Lyrics*. Trans. and ed. Robert M. Durling. Cambridge, MA: Harvard UP, 1976.

Peucker, Brigitte. *Incorporating Images: Film and the Rival Arts*. Princeton, NJ: Princeton UP, 1994.

Pirandello, Luigi. "Se il film parlante abolirà il teatro." *Saggi, poesie, scritti vari*. Ed. Manlio Lo Vecchio-Musti. 3rd ed. Milan: Mondadori, 1973. English translation: "Will Talkies Abolish the Theater?" Trans. Nina DaVinci Nichols. Pirandello, *Shoot!* 215–22.

———. *Shoot! The Notebooks of Serafino Gubbio, Cinematograph Operator*. Trans. C. K. Scott Moncrieff. Chicago: U of Chicago P, 2006.

Polan, Dana. "Auteur Desire." *Screening the Past* 12 (1 March 2001). Web. 8 Nov. 2012.

Porterfield, Christopher. "Waxwork Narcissus." *Time* 21 Feb. 1977: 70.

Povoledo, Elisabetta. "Cannes Success Gives Italian Cinema a Boost." *New York Times* 9 July 2008.

Princeton Encyclopedia of Poetry and Poetics. Ed. Alex Preminger, Frank J. Warnke, and O. B. Hardison. Enl. ed. Princeton, NJ: Princeton UP, 1974.

Quaglietti, Lorenzo. *Storia economico-politica del cinema italiano.* Rome: Riuniti, 1980.

Quasimodo, Salvatore. "Discorso sulla poesia." *Poesie e discorsi sulla poesia.* Ed. Gilberto Finzi. 9th ed. Milan: Mondadori, 1994. 281–91. English translation: "Discourse on Poetry." *The Selected Writings of Salvatore Quasimodo.* Ed. and trans. Allen Mandelbaum. New York: Farrar, Straus and Cudahy, 1960. 3–14.

Quintilian. *The Orator's Education.* Ed. and trans. Donald A. Russell. 5 vols. Cambridge, MA: Harvard UP, 2001.

Raimondi, Ezio. *Letteratura e identità nazionale.* Milan: Mondadori, 1998.

Rascaroli, Laura. "Modernity, Put into Form: *Blow-Up,* Objectuality, 1960s Antonioni." Rascaroli and Rhodes 64–81.

Rascaroli, Laura, and John David Rhodes, eds. *Antonioni: Centenary Essays.* London: Palgrave Macmillan, 2011.

Raya, Gino. *Verga e il cinema.* Rome: Herder, 1984.

Re, Lucia. *Calvino and the Age of Neorealism: Fables of Estrangement.* Stanford: Stanford UP, 1990.

Restivo, Angelo. *Cinema of Economic Miracles: Visuality and Modernization in the Italian Art Film.* Durham, NC: Duke UP, 2002.

Rhodes, John David. "Pasolini's Exquisite Flowers: The 'Cinema of Poetry' as a Theory of Art Cinema." Galt and Schoonover, *Global Art Cinema* 142–63.

———. *Stupendous, Miserable City: Pasolini's Rome.* Minneapolis: U of Minnesota P, 2007.

Ricciardi, Alessia. "The Italian Redemption of Cinema: Neorealism from Bazin to Godard." *Romanic Review* 97.3–4 (2006): 483–500.

Richardson, Robert D. *Literature and Film.* Bloomington: Indiana UP, 1969.

Rittaud-Hutinet, Chantal, and Jacques Rittaud-Hutinet. *Dictionnaire des cinématographes en France (1896–1897).* Paris: Champion, 1999.

Riva, Massimo. Introduction. *Italian Tales: An Anthology of Contemporary Italian Fiction.* Ed. Massimo Riva. New Haven, CT: Yale UP, 2004. xi–xxxi.

Rivette, Jacques. "Letter on Rossellini." *The 1950s: Neo-realism, Hollywood, New Wave.* Ed. Jim Hiller. 1985. Vol. 1:192–202. *Cahiers du cinéma.* Ed. Jim Hiller. 4 vols. London: Routledge and Kegan Paul with British Film Institute, 1985– .

Rogin, Michael P. "Mourning, Melancholia, and the Popular Front: Roberto Rossellini's Beautiful Revolution." Gottlieb, *Rossellini's "Rome, Open City"* 131–60.

Rohdie, Sam. *Antonioni.* London: British Film Institute, 1992.

———. "Neorealism and Pasolini: The Desire for Reality." Barański 163–83.

Romney, Jonathan. "*Le quattro volte.*" *Independent* 29 May 2011.

Rondi, Brunello. *Il neorealismo italiano.* Parma: Guanda, 1956.

Rossellini, Roberto. "A Discussion of Neorealism, an Interview with Mario Verdone." Trans. Judith White. Rossellini, *My Method* 33–43; *Il mio metodo* 84–94.

———. "An Interview with *Cahiers du cinéma.*" Rossellini, *My Method* 47–57.

———. "An Interview with Roberto Rossellini." By Adriano Aprà and Maurizio Ponzi. Trans. Judith White. Rossellini, *My Method* 153–71.

———. *My Method: Writings and Interviews.* Ed. Adriano Aprà. Trans. Annapaola Cancogni. New York: Marsilio, 1992. Italian edition: *Il mio metodo: Scritti e interviste.* Ed. Adriano Aprà. Venice: Marsilio, 1987.

———. "Ten Years of Cinema." Trans. David Overbey. Rossellini, *My Method* 58–78. Originally appeared as "Dix ans de cinéma." *Cahiers du cinéma* 50 (April/Sept. 1955): 3–9 (I), 52 (Nov. 1955): 3–9 (II), 55 (Jan. 1956): 9–15 (III).

———. "Why I Directed *Stromboli.*" Rossellini, *My Method* 29–30.

Roud, Richard. "Fathers and Sons." *Sight and Sound* 40.2 (1971): 61–64.

Ruberto, Laura E., and Kristi M. Wilson, eds. *Italian Neorealism and Global Cinema.* Detroit: Wayne State UP, 2007.

Rumble, Patrick. *Allegories of Contamination: Pier Paolo Pasolini's "Trilogy of Life."* Toronto: U of Toronto P, 1996.

Rumble, Patrick, and Bart Testa, eds. *Pier Paolo Pasolini: Contemporary Perspectives.* Toronto: U of Toronto P, 1996.

Russo, Luigi. *Giovanni Verga.* Bari: Laterza, 1919.

Santovetti, Francesca. "L'angoscia e la rivoluzione: Bernardo Bertolucci e il cinema di poesia." *Modern Language Notes* 108.1 (1993): 152–66.

Sarris, Andrew. "Fellini's *Casanova:* A Failure in Communication." *Village Voice* 28 Feb. 1977: 39.

———. "Toward a Theory of Film History." *The American Cinema.* 1969. Chicago: U of Chicago P, 1985. 19–37.

Schnapp, Jeffrey T. "Mob Porn." *Crowds.* Ed. Jeffrey T. Schnapp and Matthew Tiews. Stanford: Stanford UP, 2006. 1–46.

Shelley, Percy Bysshe. "A Defence of Poetry." *English Essays: Sidney to Macauley.* Vol. 27. Harvard Classics. New York: Collier and Son, 1909–14. Bartelby.com, 2001. www.bartelby.com/27/23.html. Web. 1 Oct. 2012.

Siciliano, Enzo. *Pasolini: A Biography.* Trans. John Shepley. New York: Random House, 1982.

Siegel, Jonah. *Haunted Museum: Longing, Travel, and the Art-Romance Tradition.* Princeton, NJ: Princeton UP, 2005.

Silverman, Hugh J. "Chiasmatic Visibility." *Impossible Presence: Surface and Screen in the Photographic Era.* Ed. Terry Smith. Chicago: U of Chicago P, 2001. 193–207.

Simon, John. "*Casanova:* Dead Film in a Dead Language." *New York* 21 Feb. 1977: 57–59.

Singer, Jerome. "GATT and the Shape of Our Dreams." *The Nation* 17 Jan. 1994: 54.

Sitney, P. Adams. "Image and Title in Avant-Garde Cinema." *October* 11 (1979): 97–112.

———. *Visionary Cinema: The American Avant-Garde.* 2nd ed. Oxford: Oxford UP, 1979.

———. *Vital Crises in Italian Cinema: Iconography, Stylistics, Politics.* Austin: U of Texas P, 1995.

Sklar, Robert. "Uno sguardo statunitense." Zagarrio, *La meglio gioventù* 275–79.

Small, Pauline. "Crossing Continents in the Cinema of Emanuele Crialese." Hope 89–102.

Sophocles. *Three Theban Plays.* Trans. Jamey Hecht. Ware, UK: Wordsworth, 2004.

Spiegel, Robert Alan. "Verga and the Realist Cinema." *Carte italiane* 2 (1980–81): 43–55.

Stam, Robert. *Literature through Film: Realism, Magic, and the Art of Adaptation.* London: Blackwell, 2004.

Stanley, Alessandra. "So Few Fellinis." *New York Times* 25 May 2000: B10.

Steimatsky, Noa. *Italian Locations: Reinhabiting the Past in Postwar Cinema.* Minneapolis: U of Minnesota P, 2008.

———. "Pasolini on *Terra Sancta:* Towards a Theology of Film." *Yale Journal of Criticism* 11.1 (1998): 239–58.

Stewart, Susan. *Poetry and the Fate of the Senses.* Chicago: U of Chicago P, 2005.

Stewart-Steinberg, Suzanne. *The Pinocchio Effect: On Making Italians, 1860–1920.* Chicago: U of Chicago P, 2007.

Stubbs, John C. "The Fellini Manner: Open Form and Visual Excess." *Cinema Journal* 32 (1993): 49–64.

Tinazzi, Giorgio. *Antonioni.* Florence: La Nuova Italia, 1974.

Todorov, Tzvetan. *Theories of the Symbol.* Trans. Catherine Porter. Ithaca, NY: Cornell UP, 1982.

Trotter, David. *Cinema and Modernism.* London: Wiley-Blackwell, 2007.

Truffaut, François. "A Certain Tendency of the French Cinema." Nichols 1:224–37.

Ungaretti, Giuseppe. "Indefinibile aspirazione." *Vita d'un uomo: Saggi e interventi.* Ed. Mario Diacono and Luciano Rebay. 5th ed. Milan: Mondadori, 1993. 741–46.

———. "Piccolo discorso sopra *Dietro il paesaggio* di Andrea Zanzotto." *Vita d'un uomo: Saggi e interventi.* Ed. Mario Diacono and Luciano Rebay. Milan: Mondadori, 1974. 694–695.

———. *Selected Poems.* Trans. Andrew Frisardi. New York: Farrar, Straus and Giroux, 2002.

Verga, Giovanni. *I Malavoglia. Opere.* Ed. Luigi Russo. Milan: Ricciardi, 1968. English translation: *The House by the Medlar Tree.* Trans. Raymond Rosenthal. Berkeley: U of California P, 1964.

Viano, Maurizio. *A Certain Realism: Making Use of Pasolini's Film Theory and Practice.* Berkeley: U of California P, 1993.

Vico, Giambattista. "Dell'antichissima sapienza italica." *Opere.* Ed. Fausto Nicolini. Milan: Ricciardi, 1953. 243–308.

———. *Principj di scienza nuova. Opere* 365–905. English translation: *The New Science of Giambattista Vico.* Trans. Thomas Goddard Bergin and Max Harold Fisch. Ithaca, NY: Cornell UP, 1968.

Virgil. *The Aeneid.* www.gutenberg.org/ebooks/228. Web. 27 July 2012.

Visconti, Luchino. "Anthropomorphic Cinema." Overbey, *Springtime in Italy* 83–85.

———. Interview by Alan Sanzio and Paul-Louis Thirard. *Luchino Visconti, cinéaste.* Paris: Persona, 1984.

Vitti, Antonio. *Giuseppe De Santis and Postwar Italian Cinema.* Toronto: U of Toronto P, 2002.

Wagstaff, Christopher. *Italian Neorealist Cinema: An Aesthetic Approach.* Toronto: U of Toronto P, 2007.

———. "Reality into Poetry: Pasolini's Film Theory." Barański 185–227.

Wall-Romana, Christophe. "Mallarmé's Cinepoetics: The Poem Uncoiled by the Cinématographe." *PMLA* 120 (2005): 128–47.

Welle, John. "The Cinema of History: Film in Poetry of the 1960s and 1970s." *From Eugenio Montale to Amelia Rosselli: Italian Poetry in the Sixties and Seventies.* Ed. John Butcher and Mario Moroni. Leicester: Troubadour, 2004. 50–62.

———. "Dante in the Cinematic Mode: An Historical Survey of Dante Movies." *Dante's "Inferno": The Indiana Critical Edition.* Ed. and trans. Mark Musa. Bloomington: Indiana UP, 1995. 381–94.

———. Introduction. Zanzotto, *Peasants Wake* vii–xiv.

———. "Zanzotto, Andrea." *Encyclopedia of Italian Literary Studies.* Ed. Gaetana Marrone. 2 vols. New York: Routledge, 2007. 2:2037–41.

Wellek, René. *A History of Modern Criticism: 1750–1950.* 8 vols. New Haven, CT: Yale UP, 1955–92.

Wiles, David. *Tragedy in Athens: Performance Space and Theatrical Meaning.* New York: Cambridge UP, 1987.

Wilinsky, Barbara. *Sure Seaters: The Emergence of Art House Cinema.* Minneapolis: U of Minnesota P, 2001.

Willis, Don, and Albert Johnson. "Two Views on Fellini's *Casanova.*" *Film Quarterly* 30.4 (1977): 24–31.

Woolen, Peter. "The Auteur Theory." Nichols 1:529–41.

Zagarrio, Vito. "Certi bambini . . . i nuovi cineasti italiani." Zagarrio, *La meglio gioventù* 11–22.

———. *Cinema italiano anni novanta.* Venice: Marsilio, 1998.

———, ed. *La meglio gioventù.* Venice: Marsilio, 2006.

Zanzotto, Andrea. *Fantasie di avvicinamento.* Milan: Mondadori, 1991.

———. *Le poesie e le prose scelte.* Ed. Stefano Dal Bianco and Gian Maria Villalta. Milan: Mondadori, 1999.

———. *Peasants Wake for Fellini's "Casanova" and Other Poems.* Trans. John Welle and Ruth Feldman. Urbana: U of Illinois P, 1997.

Zanzotto, Andrea, et al. *Sulla poesia: Conversazioni nelle scuole.* Ed. Giuliana Massini and Bruno Rivalta. Parma: Pratiche, 1981. 63–107.

Zavattini, Cesare. "Poesia, solo affare del cinema italiano." *Sul neorealismo: Testi e documenti (1939–1955).* Pesaro: 1974. Originally appeared in *Film d'oggi* (August 10 and 25, 1945).

———. "Some Ideas on the Cinema." Trans. Pier Luigi Lanza. *Film: A Montage of Theories.* Ed. Richard Dyer MacCann. New York: Dutton, 1966. 216–28.